I'm Married to Your Company!

ASIAN VOICES
A SUBSERIES OF ASIAN/PACIFIC/PERSPECTIVES
Series Editor: Mark Selden

I'm Married to Your Company!

Everyday Voices of Japanese Women

Masako Itoh

Translated, Edited, and Annotated by
Nobuko Adachi and James Stanlaw

ROWMAN & LITTLEFIELD PUBLISHERS, INC.
Lanham • Boulder • New York • Toronto • Plymouth, UK

ROWMAN & LITTLEFIELD PUBLISHERS, INC.

Published in the United States of America
by Rowman & Littlefield Publishers, Inc.
A wholly owned subsidary of The Rowman & Littlefield Publishing Group, Inc.
4501 Forbes Boulevard, Suite 200, Lanham, Maryland 20706
www.rowmanlittlefield.com

Estover Road, Plymouth PL6 7PY, United Kingdom

British Library Cataloguing in Publication Information Available

Library of Congress Cataloging-in-Publication Data

Itō, Masako, 1939–
    [Onna no serifu 120. English]
    I'm married to your company! : everyday voices of Japanese women / Masako Itoh ;
translated, edited, and annotated by Nobuko Adachi and James Stanlaw.
        p.   cm. — (Asian voices)
    Includes bibliographical references and index.
    ISBN-13: 978-0-7425-5463-4 (cloth : alk. paper)
    ISBN-10: 0-7425-5463-5 (cloth : alk. paper)
    ISBN-13: 978-0-7425-5464-1 (pbk. : alk. paper)
    ISBN-10: 0-7425-5464-3 (pbk. : alk. paper)
    1. Women—Japan. I. Adachi, Nobuko. II. Stanlaw, James. III. Title.
    HQ1762.I817 2008
    305.48'8956—dc22

                                                    2007024402

Printed in the United States of America

∞™ The paper used in this publication meets the minimum requirements of American
National Standard for Information Sciences—Permanence of Paper for Printed Library
Materials, ANSI/NISO Z39.48-1992.

Contents

Introduction

Nobuko Adachi and James Stanlaw

OH, NO, NOT *HER* AGAIN!

*I*s Madam Butterfly still alive and living in Japan? Recently, the titles of a number of films and books appearing in the United States—*Memoirs of a Geisha, Madame Sadayakko: The Geisha Who Bewitched the West, Geisha of Gion, Geisha: A Life*—might lead us to think so.[1] And at anthropology and linguistics conferences we still hear things like the following from Western academics: "Though the new millennium has begun, Japanese women still are stereotyped in the West as being submissive and patient."[2] Such comments can only give one pause.

The Madam Butterfly image was the result of "uncivilized," "exotic" Japan meeting the civilization (read, "power") of the West in the nineteenth century. To phrase it in the kind of twenty-first-century argot some academics are fond of, Asian women became pawns in the discourse of hegemony between the West and the East: "The material culture of Orientalism packaged the mixed interests Americans had about Asia—Asia as seductive, aesthetic, refined culture, and Asia as foreign, premodern, Other—and made them into unthreatening objects for collection and consumption" (Yoshihara 2003, 18). Popular culture was—and some would say continues to be—particularly enthusiastic in embracing this view of Japanese women. In 1888 Pierre Loti's *Madame Chrysanthème*—his fictionalized account of one of his various "marriages" to local "native" women—became an international best seller. The American manifestation came shortly thereafter in John Luther Long's *Madame Butterfly* (1903). His tragic heroine, Cho-Cho-san, was immortalized the next year by Giacomo Puccini in his opera of the same name.

1

Setting aside for the moment the kind of stereotypes Westerners might have about Japan and Japanese women, what are Japanese women *really* like? Do these claims of submissiveness and docility have any truth, particularly in capturing the multiplicity of Japanese women and their roles in a complex modern society? Consider the voices presented here in this book.[3]

While working with housewives at the Kunitachi Community Center in Tokyo, Itoh Masako, the author of these essays, noticed that women express their opinions quite openly, criticize society harshly, and often argue at length about social issues and philosophy. While hardly unusual, such findings are often ignored or unacknowledged, certainly in the English-language literature. To give another example, one of us (Adachi), who is Japanese and teaches in North America, has been told more than once by both North Americans and Japanese that she "likes to argue and criticize," "unlike other Japanese women." These commentators quickly add—in her defense, apparently—that this is no doubt due to her having been in the West too long. But she is perplexed by such comments, as her female friends in Japan perennially argue and express a range of critical views. In our view, many Japanese women are indeed independent, opinionated, vocal, and articulate. While Japanese husbands and other men may say otherwise—and idealize a traditional kind of woman as the ultimate in femininity—particularly among themselves Japanese women often pull no punches. Such blows are, however, rarely seen or heard outside of Japan.[4]

Itoh's book—whose title we translate here as *I'm Married to Your Company!*—is a series of 120 essays and vignettes about the everyday lives of women in Japan, in their own words. They were selected from pieces Itoh wrote in the women's magazine *Shufu no tomo* (she still writes her column every month). This book was a big success in Japan and was first published as *Onna no serifu 120* (120 Women's Words) by Mirai-sha in 1995, with a revised edition appearing in 2002 under the title *Kikizute ni dekinai onna no serifu* (Women's Words We Cannot Ignore) from Kōdansha+αBunko. One reason for the book's popularity was that it somehow struck a chord in the hearts and minds of women. Itoh received many letters in response to her first edition from Japanese women of all ages and all walks of life saying how these vignettes resonated with their own experiences.

These are stories "from the trenches," if you will, of what life is like for women in a rapidly changing industrial society with a highly developed consumer culture. Topics here range from problems with in-laws (no doubt a universal complaint, but with a Japanese twist) to very culturally specific issues such as the role of women in maintaining Japan's postwar pacifism.

Most important, however, is that these are tales—for the most part—of ordinary mothers and housewives, heard by a sympathetic listener. Itoh is not an academic or a professional journalist. Though involved in feminist causes, she is not an activist. Itoh (b. 1939) is a staff member at a local community center (*kōminkan*). Each town, ward, precinct, and village has a community center, and there are about twenty thousand of them in the country. They were established by the Ministry of Education after World War II in an attempt to promote democracy and community development. Local community centers offer adult education courses and workshops on technical and social topics, as well as information on health and safety. They are also places for recreational programs and artistic and cultural development. Each center has a paid professional staff. As a staff member, Itoh has met thousands of women in various capacities and roles over the years.

"OH NO, I'M MARRIED TO YOUR COMPANY!"

Some of the words and phrases uttered by Itoh's friends and associates in this book are well known to all Japanese, but many others are unique, created by the participants as issues came up in conversation. Itoh examines how these expressions are used to reflect upon the changing social roles, new dilemmas, and conflicting demands currently faced by Japanese women entering the new millennium.

For example, the phrase "*Watashi wa kaisha to kekkon shitanoni!*" ("Oh no, I'm married to your company!")—which we use in the title of this volume—verbalizes a common situation that many Japanese housewives find themselves in. They may be financially well off, with their children in good schools, but their "husbands" are actually one of the big Japanese conglomerates (their physical husbands literally having disappeared into the company world). Thus, if a woman's real husband decides one day to quit his job on the fast track—unwilling, perhaps, to accept the excessive personal commitment or overtime demanded by many large Japanese companies—the wife actually becomes a divorcée. Some women have a sense of disappointment or even betrayal and the unspoken, or at least often felt, next sentence would be, "*Naze kaisha o yameru no yo!*" ("How dare you want to quit [after I have made such a commitment]!"). Notice that this is subtly—but significantly—different from the lament of some Western women who complain that *their husband* is the one who is married to the company (and that they are at best the "other woman"). For these Japanese women the feelings are more complex. Some might believe they have made personal or career sacrifices to join their husbands in working toward the "Japanese dream." Others might simply decry the loss of status, economic security, and sense of place in society.

Phrases like "I'm married to his company!" may not be standard or universally used. Yet anyone in Japan would understand what is being expressed. However, phrases like "*Anna otoko demo oku-san niwa yoku mieru-no kashira?*" ("I wonder if even the wife of a guy like that thinks he's OK?") could be voiced by women anywhere in the world. And many of the incorrigibles described in the text—like the high-maintenance *boku-chan* (one who sulks if he is not constantly flattered) or the grandma's boy who was spoiled as a child—would be ridiculed by women in many cultures.

This book, then, invites readers to consider universal views held by women (some that are rarely discussed in gender studies programs), as well as perspectives specific to Japanese culture and society.

We find it worthwhile to see the phrases spoken by Japanese housewives as "conversation rituals" or "ceremonies of communication." Important—and public—information is expressed and reified in performance and ritual, but for the uninitiated, these activities remain clouded in mystery. These rituals make plain that Japanese women are hardly the meek and mild Madam Butterflies—linguistically cowering under the yoke of a male-dominated language—that they are often portrayed to be. Some may be as socially independent and linguistically unbound as the most ardent Western feminist, though their techniques in the realms of both linguistic and cultural choices might sometimes surprise non-Japanese.

Such preconceptions are to be expected considering that (1) others often speak *for* Japanese women (e.g., Japanese men or scholars working outside the country), and (2) some Japanese women may be reluctant to express themselves directly, especially in public. This book attempts to rectify these misconceptions by giving recognition to ordinary Japanese women, in their own words.

JAPANESE WOMEN'S LANGUAGE AND A CAVEAT

Before we go on, it might be worthwhile to mention a few things about Japanese women's language. As will soon become apparent, Japanese men's and women's speech differs in ways quite unlike that of English.

As a fun exercise, we often ask American students in our linguistic anthropology classes to "talk like a woman" for a few sentences. Interestingly, even the women in the class have trouble with this. Aside from adding a few "oh dears" and avoiding some of the more colorful street expressions, there are few structural linguistic differences between the genders in English.[5] Such an exercise is much easier in Japanese, however, because the language is often marked for gender in terms of phonology, morphology, and syntax (i.e., sounds, the structure of words, and grammar). There are also distinct differences in tone of voice and body language.

Three areas often cited to differentiate Japanese men's and women's speech are (1) honorifics and polite language, (2) sentence-final particles, and (3) pronouns. Itoh directly or indirectly illuminates each of these topics.

Honorifics and Polite Language

The Japanese language is noted for having an extremely complex system of honorifics to indicate degrees of politeness, formality, humility, distance, and hierarchy. In general, the most obvious way that Japanese differs from English is that in Japanese, politeness is encoded in the grammar while in English it is generally encoded in words or phrases. Consider the following Japanese sentences:

Are-ga	*toshokan*	*da-yo.*	informal
Are-ga	*toshokan*	*desu.*	polite
Are-ga	*toshokan*	*de gozaimasu.*	more polite
"there"	"library"	"is"	
pronoun	noun	copula verb	

All translate grammatically as "That's the library over there" but differ from top to bottom on formal levels of politeness. Notice that the level of politeness (underlined) is in the different *forms* of the verb *is*. That is, politeness in Japanese is largely incorporated into the grammar. In the English, politeness, if present, is indicated by words, not grammar; it is almost an afterthought. Some factors affecting levels of politeness and use of honorifics include (among others):

familiarity (e.g., stranger, family, friend)
age (older or younger than speaker)
professional relationship (e.g., boss, salesman, customer)
gender (same or different from speaker)
in-group/out-group (e.g., same family, school, department, company)
situation (e.g., a request, a command, a greeting)

In general, the major sociolinguistic rule in Japanese is, in most contexts, women should always use more polite speech forms than men (particularly when both genders are present). Probably all Japanese women are well aware of this rule, even if they don't follow it all the time.

Sentence-Final Particles

One of the most conspicuous features of the Japanese language is the use of sentence-final particles. These are little words that are added to the ends of sentences to show the speaker's emotion. They are similar to the so-called tag-question markers found in English: "This is the one you wanted, *right?*" There are literally dozens of them in Japanese, as well as many regional and dialectal variants. Probably the most frequent and famous one is -*ne*, roughly asking for the listener's confirmation (as in the above English example). The word -*ne* also carries with it an attempt to soften requests and generally solicit empathy and agreement from the listener. The sentence-final particle -*yo* is also very common and expresses intensity, assertion, or exclamation.

Japanese sentence-final particles are notorious for marking gender. While -*ne* and -*yo* can be used by both men and women, others are primarily used by one gender only. For example, the most common particles for men are -*ze*, -*zo*, and -*ka nā* (and various informal or vulgar forms like -*kai*). Both -*ze* and -*zo* mark strong assertion, while -*ka nā* expresses uncertainty. For women, the common equivalents might be -*wa*, -*no*, and -*kashira* (though there is some overlap; for example, -*ka nā* is often said by women as well as men).

Women can often connect several particles together; the forms -*wa ne* and -*wa yo* are the most frequent. However, it is hard to define what they exactly mean. Depending on the context they can solicit agreement, make a soft reprimand, or offer a suggestion. Women seem to be particularly creative in the use of these "compounded" sentence-final particles. Men do not combine

Examples of Japanese Pronouns

	First-Person Pronouns		Second-Person Pronoun	
	Men's Speech	*Women's Speech*	*Men's Speech*	*Women's Speech*
Formal	watakushi watashi	watakushi atakushi	anata	anata
Plain	boku	watashi; atashi	kimi	anata
Deprecatory	ore	—	omae/anta	anta

particles so frequently, if at all. Regardless, the use of sentence-final particles is ubiquitous—it is hard to even speak Japanese without them—and clearly indicates the gender of the person speaking.

Pronouns

The Japanese pronominal system is notoriously complex. The table on the previous page shows abbreviated examples of choices available to men and women regarding first-person pronouns (i.e., *I*) and second-person pronouns (i.e., *you*).[6] Note that choices also differ depending on level of formality as well as gender.

In general, while pronouns like *watakushi* can be used by both women and men, others—such as *boku*, *atashi*, or *kimi*—are supposedly restricted to one gender.

Caveats

The differences between women's and men's speech in Japanese is well documented and described. There are few Japanese linguistics or language textbooks that do not discuss gender differences. Feminists often use Japanese as one of the prime examples of institutionalized linguistic sexual discrimination. That said, however, we feel that a few comments are in order, as things may be a bit more subtle than what appears at first glance.

First, consider the use of the pronoun *kimi* above. In theory, this is a term available to men but denied women. The exemplary case is when a husband addresses his wife. In fact, women *do* use it—but under certain conditions. For example, a teacher may address her students—even male students—using *kimi*, as might a female supervisor to her subordinates. In other words, this word actually marks power or hierarchy, rather than gender per se. But because women in Japan are still somewhat marginalized economically and politically, it seems to be a word from the domain of men.

As another example, consider the following ways of saying "Do it quickly." The first three sentences (M1, M2, and M3) are said to be men's speech, and the last three (W1, W2, and W3), women's speech. Within each gender, sentences are ranked for politeness, from high to low. The first word in each sentence, *hayaku*, means "hurry up"; *kudasai* at the end of a sentence (if it is found) means "please"; and the middle words (which all begin with *s*) are variants of the verb *suru*, "to do."

M1. *Hayaku shite kudasai*	polite request
M2. *Hayaku shiro*	neutral command
M3. *Hayaku suru-na*	negative command
W1. *Hayaku shite kudasai*	polite request
W2. *Hayaku shinasai*	polite command
W3. *Hayaku shinaide (kudasai)*	negative polite request

The thing to notice here is that most of the sentences in the first group are imperatives, or "demands" in nonlinguistic terminology. Most of the sentences in the last group are requests. In actual fact, men can and do use sentences W1, W2, and W3, especially in public situations. And women can use the demand forms M1, M2, and M3 in certain circumstances. The difference is, in terms of the social nexus, in most cases women are not in a position to make demands. Once more, what might be called "women's speech" may mask power differentials rather than marking gender.

THE VOICES OF THE EVERYDAY JAPANESE HOUSEWIFE

Having discussed at length topics of submissiveness and docility—perhaps being co-opted by the Madam Butterfly mystique ourselves—these are *hardly* the only concerns of Japanese women, and *hardly* the only theme in Itoh's book. In any case our ultimate goal is not to dispel the Madam Butterfly myth, but just to use it as starting point for discussion. Itoh offers a whole range of perspectives and topics, from how the world is socially, cognitively, and aesthetically experienced by men and women (usually quite differently), to problems of child rearing and old age. Some contemporary problems have a long and colorful past, and Itoh and her friends often have a keen historical eye for nuance and detail.

In other words, for the most part, this book focuses on concerns of Japanese housewives, mothers, homemakers, older women, daughters-in-law, and a few single mothers. Certainly the world of Japanese women is changing rapidly, almost from moment to moment, and we do not mean to say that there are no radicals, politicians, feminists, or artists living in Japan. Perhaps these "ordinary" women—to use a very dangerous term!—are not even in the majority anymore, though they certainly are a large presence. What we want to do is to capture and present the voices of a certain woman,

Itoh Masako, and a certain group of women—not all Japanese women. No doubt career women, the growing numbers of unmarried working women in their twenties and thirties, teenagers, or Japanese women working overseas would find much to argue with here. And we agree that in some ways, these essays often paint in broad strokes, cast value judgments, and are certainly opinionated. Some might even argue that these pieces deal in stereotypes, repeating often-stated concerns of status-conscious housewives, complaining about spoiled and immature Japanese husbands, and lamenting an oppressive women's language. But, the fact that this book was so popular in Japan, and was read by so many people, means that it resonates with at least some significant readership (women *and* men).

Popular culture can teach a great deal about a society. Some of the most popular TV shows are still samurai dramas. Does everyone like samurai dramas in Japan? Hardly. Do these programs reflect Japan today? Not at all. But the fact that they are so watched is indicative of certain beliefs, traditions, cultural norms . . . and, yes, self-stereotypes . . . that Japanese people hold. Thus, even if these shows no longer reflect the values of the majority, they show how such values are being presented, which demonstrates that they have much to convey about the nature of public discourse and popular culture. At the very least, they can be vehicles for learning and for sparking discussion.

We think that the women in Itoh's book are saying things that many can empathize with. For the most part, these voices—while circulating widely in Japan—have not been clearly heard internationally. While neither representative of the experiences of all women in a diverse Japanese nation, and still less of some sort of cultural ideal, their words convey significant dimensions of women's experiences. Actually, an argument might be made that in Japan-specialist circles these days—in a well-intended effort to present the full dynamics of the changing roles of Japanese women and to avoid stereotyping—great emphasis is placed on marginalized populations. But just as not all Japanese women are housewives, not all Japanese women are bar hostesses, lesbians, yellow-cab sexual thrill seekers, political activists, Burakumin, Korean residents, Ainu, poets, or authors. (Of course, all these voices *should* be heard and have been in recent books, a few of which we have listed in the references.) Nevertheless, we would like to think that the individual stories and essays presented here are just that—individual stories as much as Japanese stories—and that cumulatively they convey a range of Japanese women's experiences that challenges dominant stereotypes.

We should mention, too, that we feel these stories also illuminate gender *relations*, and not just gender *roles*, in Japan. It is true that men often come off badly in some of Itoh's descriptions. But there is also an underlying discussion—sometimes implied, sometimes quite overt—about what it means to be a man or a woman, and about the interactions between men and women, in a postmodern, industrial, globalized, transnational society. Readers will see that Japan is economically diverse and socially heterogeneous—like America—and that both men and women are trying to negotiate achieving private happiness while satisfying family obligations and meeting social expectations. For example, Itoh's women may criticize men for their unquestioned devotion to their companies or their silly quests for trivial symbols of status—such as a set of professional golf clubs that are never used. But they realize that everyone is in some ways at the mercy of forces larger than themselves, and everyone is struggling to get by. As the women discuss in one story, can—or *should*—a mother raise a son to want something other than the "Japanese dream"? So there is optimism and empathy in these accounts, as well as criticism and complaint.

We believe, then, that these essays actually do a very good job of locating this group of ordinary women and housewives in Japanese society. In these stories we find their dreams, their sense of place, their thinking on various social and personal issues, their views of themselves and Japan, their hopes for the future.

Readers should be reminded, however, that it would be dangerous to think that these are the *only* views held by Japanese women (though we think they are at least anecdotally representative of many). Western feminists, and even knowledgeable scholars of Japan, might disagree with much that Itoh has to say. These disagreements we welcome. We would be delighted if this book could be used to spark discussion about the nature not only of Japanese women-cum-housewives, but of the feminist critique of both the discourse and values of such women. In other words, the book poses such questions as: What are the implications of these women's stories for the state of women, gender relations, and feminism in Japan? What are the implications of the stereotypes cultures can have of themselves? Such questions, we feel, can emerge effectively from the words of ordinary people, such as those presented here.

THE STRUCTURE OF THE BOOK

Itoh originally presented her essays in chronological order, as written in her magazine column. For Japanese readers, this was convenient, as they often followed her and her friends' reactions to events taking place on the national scene of Japan—for example, the marriage of the crown prince, the scandal of the latest pop star, or various disputes in the media over war guilt. While Japanese readers could easily follow the development of these stories, for outsiders not steeped in Japanese news or cultural background, this was difficult. Thus, we have chosen to group these stories thematically. We have divided Itoh's 120 essays—linguistic expressions of ideas, criticisms, or opinions—into three major parts.

Part 1, "Looking at . . . ," consists of four chapters: (1) "Marriage and Tradition," (2) "Men," (3) "Ourselves," and (4) "Other Women." The key element of each chapter is how Japanese women observe themselves, people they associate with, and their social environments. In part 2, "How to Deal with . . . ," we have placed thirteen essays in two chapters: (5) problems of human relationships in "Families, Parents, and Parents-in-Law" and (6) social problems of "Life and Society." Part 3, "Thinking about . . . ," consists of eight chapters: (7) "Women's Social Roles and Our Behavior in Men's Society," (8) "Social Attitudes toward Women," (9) "How We Are Seen," (10) "What I Want to Be," (11) "How Society Should Be," (12) "Married Life," (13) "Social Issues," and (14) "Nature and Beauty." This last part examines how Japanese women are constantly forced to take the outside social environment into account in their inside daily lives.

At the beginning of each essay we have added cultural notes and commentaries to clarify certain aspects of Japanese literature, history, or current affairs that are discussed in the piece and might not be known to Western readers. However, we have tried not to impose our views or judgments on any of the stories presented here, and we have tried to retain the conversational and emotional tone found in the stories.

As the reader will soon see, Japanese and English can a little tricky to translate. The reader should to be sensitive to some of these problems of translation from Japanese to English. Even simple words that seem like perfect synonyms can end up having subtle differences. As an example, when one of us (Stanlaw) was learning Japanese, he was certain the first week of class that he had at least mastered the Japanese equivalents of *eat* (*taberu*) and *drink* (*nomu*) and could therefore obtain sustenance if ever stranded in Tokyo. While both Americans and Japanese "eat" sushi and hamburgers, he soon found out, however, that Japanese "drink" chicken soup rather than "eat" it like they do in Illinois. In a similar way, Japanese "drink" aspirin and other medicines while Americans "take" them; an American dog, however, could "eat" an aspirin that fell on the floor. Still, Pepto-Bismol is something that Americans would "drink." For several years Stanlaw went into denial and just assumed these linguistic oddities were some of the weird things that one encounters here and there when learning another language. But it became clear to him several years later when he went to the Ueno Zoo that *drink* in Japanese did not necessarily mean "to ingest fluids." Children standing around the python on display wanted to know what did it "drink"? Not knowing much about snakes, he assumed water, of course. The answer—mice—surprised him. Pythons swallow mice whole—without chewing—and it is the motion of the mouth that makes the difference in Japanese. You only "eat" in Japanese if chewing is involved; otherwise it is "drinking." Because this is so obvious, his Japanese teachers never bothered to tell him (nor do most dictionaries, either).

We therefore include the original Japanese (in Roman letters) for some of the words and phrases in these essays. We think that students studying Japanese, or native speakers without access to the original, will find this helpful. More important, however, is the fact that sometimes there is no exact English-Japanese equivalent. Rather than try and translate a single Japanese word, for example, with a series of additions and caveats, we sometimes simply left it untranslated. The Japanese in the text is always in italics. Finally, we should mention that we used the Japanese name order in referring to persons—that is, with the last (or family) name first (this applies to Korean and Chinese names as well). However, Asian authors who write in English using their family names last follow the Western order.

FINAL THOUGHTS

We think that general readers as well as students of Japanese society will find much of interest here to illuminate the world of contemporary Japan and the multifaceted world of women. But this may happen after some laughs, a little anger and frustration, and perhaps a tear or two. Come with us now as we join Itoh Masako at the Kunitachi Community Center. Let's see who has just stopped by . . .

NOTES

1. See Golden, *Memoirs of a Geisha* (2005) (also a film directed by Rob Marshall); Downer, *Madame Sadayakko: The Geisha Who Bewitched the West* (2003); and Iwasaki, *Geisha of Gion* (2003a) and *Geisha: A Life* (2003b).

2. To give just one example, a popular mainstream magazine—*Hiragana Times*—intended for foreign students learning Japanese (and Japanese interested in foreign countries) published a collection of essays in book form a few years back called *Japan: A Paradise for Picking Up Women*.

3. To be honest, the exaggerations of these claims are also becoming well documented in the academic literature, both regarding language (e.g., Inoue 2006) as well as culture (e.g., Miller and Bardsley 2005).

4. There are certainly numerous books *about* Japanese women. Some of the general popular standards include Kondo (1990), Condon (1985), Sievers (1983), Imamura (1996), Rosenberger (2001), Birnbaum (1999), Smith and Wiswell (1982), and Lebra, Paulson, and Powers (1976). However, there are really few books in English in the social sciences presenting the full range of voices of everyday Japanese women: for example, Allison's (1994) ethnography focuses on women in the sex trade; Buckley (1997) restricts her interviews to feminist scholars; and Kelsky (2001) focuses on young "internationalist" women who see their futures lying overseas. There is indeed a growing body of translated fiction by and about Japanese women—including several dozen novels and classic story collections such as Ueda (1986), Tanaka (1987), Tanaka and Hanson (1982), and Lippit and Selden (1991)—but these of course suffer, or benefit, from literary and artistic license.

5. Actually, this is a subtle point and needs some clarification. We are not saying that the English language cannot be—or is not—oppressive. There is a vast literature that argues otherwise. To use an obvious example, does the use of the English word *fireman* subtly preclude women from wanting to become firefighters? Is the neutral *fireperson* really a better word? Is it fair that *he* is the default pronoun? These are controversial issues, and volumes have been written on this subject. What we are saying here is simply that compared to Japanese, English linguistic sexual dimorphism—to use a biological analogy—is less pronounced.

6. This particular table is based on Tsujimura (1996, 373), a standard Japanese linguistics text. However, such tables and their variants—some containing dozens of terms—abound.

1

LOOKING AT . . .

• 1 •

Marriage and Tradition

*O*h no, I'm married to your company!
Watashi wa kaisha to kekkon shitanoni
私は会社と結婚したのに

In this essay, Itoh describes the panic felt by a young woman who has just heard that her husband has decided to quit his job. Wives anywhere might feel a little insecure when a husband decides to change positions. But her husband's position is not *just* a job. He is what is known as a *sararii-man*, a term loosely based on English (i.e., "salaried man") used to describe the male white-collar workforce in Japan. He is on the Japanese career fast track and has lifetime employment at a large corporation with guaranteed raises and promotions.

His resignation would preclude him from working in the big corporate world ever again, as he would likely be seen as not only impetuous and selfish, but also somewhat disloyal. There is little mobility within leading corporations, so this is quite a drastic step. But why would a man even think about leaving such a secure occupational paradise? The reason is simple: the expectation of total commitment to the firm. While large Japanese corporations and "elite firms" (*ichiryū-gaisha*) give a lot, much is also expected in return. Saturday often means another trip to the office, and "overtime" is a concept that doesn't compute—that is, Japanese salaried workers do not expect that they will go home right away when the whistle blows (as opposed to many Americans who feel "work time," which is completely separate from time for one's self, ends at 5:00 p.m.). And many a *sararii-man* does not even take his allotted vacation days. Little time is left for family life or personal hobbies, as even recreational activities are often conducted with—only—coworkers.

17

Such a life is not for everybody and increasing numbers of the younger generation are expecting—or at least hoping for—a different lifestyle. And the phrase "death from overwork" (*karō-shi*, 過労死) is heard more and more these days. But what does the *sararii-man* who quits the rat race now do? He may do something like take up farming or open a restaurant. He may even start his own small company or become a freelancer (*jiyū-gyō-sha*) where he can be his own boss. In fact, the popularity of the famous long-running television show *Wataru seken wa oni bakari*, scripted by the noted screenplay writer Hashida Sugako, describes the trials of one such fallen *sararii-man*. The English translation of the title—"There Are Only Real Devils in the World," a pun on the Japanese proverb *"Wataru seken ni oni wa nashi"* (There are no real devils in the world)—shows just how much of a social problem this experience is in Japan.

The Japanese title of this essay is a little ambiguous, and Itoh is taking advantage of this ambiguity to make a point. The original could be translated as "I am married to *the* company," "I am married to *a* company," or "I am married to *your* company," all, of course, with slightly different nuances. These diverse connotations are discussed by Itoh in the essay.

Finally, we should add that Okazaki Hideko, the sociologist who is mentioned in the essay, was born in 1933 and is a visiting scholar at Hosei University in Tokyo. Her book *Han-kekkonron* (Anti-Marriage Theory) was published in 1972 by Akishobo in Tokyo. For more about the consequences of leaving your job in Japan, see the essay in this chapter, "When my husband lost his job, I thought, 'This is my chance!'"

When you first hear a woman say, "But I'm married to the company!" you might think she is simply concerned about her place of employment. However, a wife uttered this sentence when her husband told her of his decision to leave the elite firm he was working for and start his own small business by himself.

"Well, she is half kidding, but it is also probably half true," said her husband with a smile, reflecting the mixed emotions he was feeling. Whether the husband is right or not about this sentence being a joke, these words seem to tell us something significant about the true meaning of marriage in current-day Japan. More importantly, it also reveals something of how men can misunderstand their wives' values.

I run into men all the time who think that having social status means they also have a great personality, or that having a good salary is equal to being a good person. Some men believe that their title or affiliation is an accurate reflection of their personal worth and mistake the respect others give them due to their position for an assessment of their personal qualities. This belief is simply pathetic.

However, we can't just criticize men for this. There certainly are plenty of women who are quite content to marry men holding such titles, or to even just marry the title. Society's fetish for brand names seems not to be limited to watches or handbags; it also applies to marriages. Women can achieve social status by simply decorating themselves with these "brand-name" men. And having a "brand-name" husband is commonly believed to be the key to a woman's happiness.

This reminds me of the aphorism mentioned by Okazaki Hideko in her book *Anti-Marriage Theory*: "Men buy love with the power of money, while women buy money with the power of love."

I recall a woman who said with disgust, "What an egotistical female!" referring to a housewife who devoted her life to looking after her husband's health. "But since a woman's social rank depends on the social position or economic power of her husband, this is understandable. These days, love—a pure, innocent romantic feeling—has become something else."☙

*Y*our wife is bragging about her misfortune.
Kimi no tsuma ga fukō o misebirakaseri
君 の 妻 が 不幸 を 見 せ び ら か せ り

In this piece Itoh takes up an issue that will be revisited several times in this book: the position of the "other woman" in an extramarital relationship. While not as prevalent or socially acceptable today as in the past, the practice of maintaining a mistress was both institutionalized and common among the more well-to-do men in prewar Japan. Marriage was thought to be an arrangement between families as much as a bond between individuals, if not more so. Wives were chosen for their domestic capabilities; romance, companionship, and sexual excitement were often sought in the various kinds of pleasure quarters found throughout Japanese history. Of course, these different public and private personas sometimes caused conflicts for all parties. For example, men had to play the public role of devoted husband, and wives that of a heartbroken widow, even if their emotional attachments to their spouses were not all that strong.

The two poems in this piece are called tanka. Tanka is the most popular form of contemporary poetry in Japan, and millions of people have written poems in this style. The form has an ancient tradition going back some fifteen hundred years. As Japanese verse does not rhyme, meter is the most important element of structure. Tanka poems are short, usually written in five phrases of 5-7-5-7-7 syllables. Modern tanka poems, though written in the classical style, can often be about contemporary topics. Like haiku—its more famous poetic cousin—tanka appeals to the emotions and avoids overstatement. In the first poem below, for example, though not stated, the author is possibly the deceased husband's lover and is lamenting the fact that the wife can publicly grieve while she cannot. For more discussion of tanka poetry, see essays "Being the perpetrator is very hard," from chapter 6, and "Please don't tie me down," chapter 9.

The following tanka was written by the poet Nakajō Fumiko (1922–1954):

衆視のなかはばかりもなく嗚咽して君の妻が不幸を見せびらかせり
Shūshi no naka habakari mo naku oetsu-shite kimi no tsuma ga fukō o misebirakaseri
With no hesitation on her part,
your wife's tears proudly announce to all
the depths of her misery.

When I first read this poem, I was in my early twenties. At that time, I was a "wife" in my private life but nonetheless was still attracted to this poem that sharply criticized a "wife." I was drawn to this poem because I liked the implied criticisms of the wife's arrogance, insensitivity, and callousness; the wife who—after all—was playing on the publicly recognized social legitimacy of her position as a wife to gain sympathy.

Some years later one of my friends confessed to me that she was having a love affair with an older married man, a man well known in Japanese society.

She said, "If he were to suddenly die, I would know about it only through reading the obituaries in the newspaper. And when I would hear people speaking of his death—'Oh, did you know that Mr. So-and-so passed away?'—I would have to act like some disinterested party and show no emotion." She added that whenever they had to part, it never failed that this worry came to mind on her way home.

When I heard this story, I thought again about the "wife" in the earlier poem. Needless to say, even if she was in a mutually loveless marriage, she—and not the lover—would be informed immediately if her husband died, just because of her social standing as "wife." But I felt a pain in my chest thinking about the wife's humiliation knowing that the husband's body was coming back to her, but not the soul.

Nakajō Fumiko also wrote another poem:

とりすがり哭くべき骸もち給う妻てふ位置がただに羨しき

Torisugari naku-beki mukuro mochitamau tsuma to iu ichi ga tada ni urayamashiki

Seeing her publicly crying over his remains,
socially acceptable simply because she is his wife,
I can only envy her social status

After hearing my friend's confession, I could appreciate this poem differently, especially the part about "publicly crying over his remains."

When I was just casually talking about these things with my friends, one of them said, "These days 'illicit love affair' is becoming a fashionable word, but we can't blame the woman. It is not right to keep a marriage together if the couple does not have any feelings toward each other and are just sharing a house."

*W*e have to remember that it is our own fault because we raised them that way, didn't we?

Sō sodateta jibun ga warui to omowana-kuccha-ne!

そう育てた自分が悪いと思わなくっちゃ、ね

The word *maza-kon* in Japanese is an English loan derived from the Freudian term "mother complex." There are thousands of English loanwords used in everyday Japanese (see Stanlaw, *Japanese English: Language and Culture Contact,* 2004), and several more will appear later on. Regardless, being accused of being a "mama's boy," or a man suffering from a *maza-kon*, is an embarrassment in Japan. But, as the following piece shows, being spoiled by one's grandmother seems not so bad, as it usually can only happen when one is young. The burdock plant that is referred to is a long taproot that is a common food in Japan.

A while back, I was shopping at a vegetable shop around closing time, and a person came running in saying, "I was told I need to get a burdock." She needed this burdock to present as an offering to the gods at a local festival being held the next day. The shop owner told her, with some degree of instruction in his voice, "It doesn't necessarily have to be a burdock. As long as it is a root vegetable, it will do."

While I was overhearing this conversation I felt that it was interesting that some people are still giving these kinds of traditional gifts to the gods. This is getting to be rare these days.

Changing the subject to a more personal note, the customer then excitedly said, "Unexpectedly, we have decided to build a house together with my son's family." She added with some apprehension in her voice, as if to herself, "When we start living together, though, we will face many problems at first, don't you think?" She looked like she had mixed feelings, both of wonderment and worry.

The shop person responded well. He said, "It's nice that your place will be so lively with so many people."

Then the customer said, as if to remind herself, "Yes, and when we face an unpleasant moment, we have to remember that it is our own fault because we raised them that way, didn't we?" Her way of saying this made me believe that she had been saying these words many times to many people, as well as digesting them herself.

When I was chattering later with my friends, I told them this story. Many of them said, "It is hard to be a parent." But then one of them was reminded of a funny story about a quarrel she had with her husband. "Once when we were fighting, I had a slip of the tongue and shouted at my husband. I said, 'How can you be that way? Who raised you, anyway!'

Then my husband said, 'Don't talk that way about my grandma!' sounding just like a spoiled grandma's boy. I just burst into laughter. My husband also started laughing—in kind of an embarrassed way—and our quarrel ended there because it was so funny."

All of the people who were there said, "You were saved by a 'grandma's boy,' but if it had been a 'mama's boy,' you'd not be laughing now, that's for sure."✎

*I*t looks like she can't respect her husband anymore.
Mō go-shujin o sonkei dekinaku natteiru mitai nano yo
もう、ご主人を尊敬できなくなっているみたいなのよ

Maybe if pushed, most women in most cultures would say that husbands are a problem. They need to be pampered and flattered to keep up their self-esteem, but this can't be done too much lest their egos get inflated. Of course, husbands would take the opposite view. While Itoh's following essay has a light and humorous tone, she is actually dealing with a very serious subject: how couples can maintain respect for each other. In a time of an increasing divorce rate in Japan, such topics are more often being discussed.

A person who is a good friend of mine has an acquaintance who is having some marital problems. My friend said, "It looks like she can't respect her husband anymore."

Some other people who were around us, and heard her words, responded with sympathy. One person said sincerely, "It must be very hard to live with a person that you can't respect, right?" "You really think so? So that means *you* respect *your* husband?" kidded another back, feigning amazement.

After this, the topic of "respect for husbands" became the center of our discussion. Then somebody said ironically in reference to one of us who was not present, "Since *she* respects her husband so much, *she* is probably not able to join us!"

I think what the speaker meant was, she was so frustrated that this docile woman—our absent friend—just blindly followed her husband's opinions, and she resented the strong influence he had on her daily activities. And she ended up expressing these feelings in a rather sarcastic way.

I was very interested in the fact that, on one hand, we were discussing a woman who could not respect her husband anymore and wanted to divorce him. On the other hand, one of us was dumbfounded by someone who respects her husband too much, and believed that a woman who respects her husband actually has a problem.

So I tried to think about things by switching genders. I know many men around me who respect their wives and show their respect to their wives in front of other people. And I realized that such couples give me a warm feeling.

In addition, I remembered the words of a friend of mine who once said, "There are many liberal scholars and social critics around, but I don't value the opinions of these men until I know something about their personal lives and see how they treat their wives." ❧

*W*hen my husband lost his job, I thought, "This is my chance!"
Otto ga shitsugyō shita toki "chansu-da!" tte omottan desu
夫が失業したとき、「チャンスだ！」って思ったんです

As we saw in the first essay, until the beginning of the twenty-first century, the ideal employment trajectory for Japanese men was to work for life at a single big company right out of college. Job security was assured, promotion was more by seniority than merit, and raises were automatic. Of course, this was not an option for everyone. More than half of male workers found themselves working for smaller companies, some little more than glorified cottage industries. And as we saw, lifetime employment was not without personal cost. The company expected unquestioned devotion and commitment in return.

But these days the Japanese economy is stagnating, and many companies are now emulating the cost-cutting measures of American

businesses. Lifetime job security can no longer be automatically assumed, even at the largest firms, as seen in this essay. But sometimes,
with adversity comes opportunity

A friend of mine once said to me humorously, "When my husband lost his job,
I thought, 'This is my chance!'"

After she had graduated from junior high school, she had been working
ever since and had been supporting herself. But when she got married, she
quit her job. She told me that she had a pretty easy life: she would get fed if
she just took care of the house. But gradually she started to feel pain—her easy
life became torture—because she felt that it was not right to depend on the
income of someone else, even if that person was her husband.

Around this time, she attended a lecture held at our community center,
which was critical of gender roles. She decided that after all, "I was right! [I
should not be so dependent on anybody.]" So she told her husband about her
desire to work outside the house.

"We are not in tight economic circumstances, so you really do not need
to work. You don't need worry about just depending on my income," he said.
In other words, he did not understand her pain. She made us laugh when she
said in her own sweet humorous way that maybe he just misunderstood her.

However, she told us that later this husband suddenly lost his job, and she
had to go to work. But if she had not starting thinking about this before, she
might have become helplessly worried about their problems and would have
probably blamed her husband for everything, saying, "What are we going to
do from now on?" Or she might have felt miserable thinking, "Because of my
husband I have to go out to work now to earn our income."

But now she thought, "This is a great chance for us to change the
economics of how our house is run. We can go from a system where only
he works to one where we can both contribute to our household income,
and we can help each other out for a better life. This was a great chance
for us."

Later, he eventually found another job. However, this time, he did not
need to find a job that had to provide the entire household income and support for the family, so he could select an occupation from a wider range of
choices. As a result, he could select a job that he really wanted.

She said mischievously, "See, because I realized that the sexual division of
labor was a problem, this made my husband happy." All of us who were listening to her smiled and clapped our hands.✆

I don't like New Year's.
O-shōgatsu wa kirai
お正月 は き ら い

In Japan there are many "firsts" that can occur on New Year's Day, such as *kaki-zome* (writing the first calligraphy of the new year) or *hatsu mōde* (the first visit to a shrine or temple). *Hatsu hi no de* (literally, "rising of the first sun") finds many people watching the sun rise on New Year's morning, hoping to have a good year. Itoh describes some others here, including the first visit of the year with the in-laws. A daughter-in-law might not be looking forward to such a visit, and not just because she might not be particularly fond of them. A daughter-in-law, especially the woman married to the eldest son, is expected to work in the kitchen and serve the other New Year's guests. This can be a taxing all-day job and, as she is a representative of her husband's family, one that is particularly stressful.

For some women who work in the "water trades," New Year's can be especially depressing. Women in the "water trades" (*mizu-shōbai*) are the various cabaret hostesses, cocktail waitresses, bar girls, and *mama-sans* who serve drinks and lend a sympathetic ear to male customers at various drinking establishments. Because bars are frequented quite often by men after work, regular customers and their lady friends can develop close relationships.

See the essay in chapter 11, "Each individual's words gave me strength," for more on New Year's cards and "The *shujin* (literally, 'master') of the house is me" in chapter 4 for other discussions of New Year's. For more on the *mizu-shōbai* see "I am sorry that we women have to feel frightened when we go out at night" in chapter 8.

Today is the beginning of the year. The most important calendrical event in Japan is New Year's Day. However, this is neither a truly new time frame of reference nor a day especially different from any other. However, we do have little events—such as *hatsu hi no de* [seeing the first sunrise of the year on New Year's Day] or *waka mizu* [drawing the first (young) water on New Year's morning]—so we feel things are brand-new even though they are not, and it is a lot of fun.

Also, if I think about how we can keep connected with people through New Year's cards, then, in that sense, I like New Year's and feel it is worthwhile.

However, there are many women who say, "I don't like the New Year's." The reason they say this is that for some of them, they cannot make the usual excuses—like "I am sorry but our place is messy today" or "I'm sorry but we don't have anything special in the house to eat"—because New Year's Day is not a usual day. Some people say this is a big load.

The reason why others become depressed is that every year they have to go and see their parents-in-law at New Year's. They have to ride an extremely crowded train, packed with people returning home for the holidays, and what is waiting for them when they arrive is not especially pleasant. Also, single people say, "New Year's is the most lonely time of the year."

I have heard it said that "Even a man who spends most of his time at work—so much so that he forgets he has a family waiting for him—will faithfully spend time with his family on New Year's Day." Watching this guy leave for the holidays might remind a single female office coworker that, "Oh, yes, he really *does* have a family. And even though I am not having an affair with him, I realize he is a married man, and I feel a little left behind."

Others say, "The New Year's is the day when everybody gets swallowed by the black hole called the family. I feel that I am left out from the rest of the world. I don't know if this is true or not, but I have heard that women in the 'water trades' have a higher rate of suicide on New Year's Day."

Although it is said that the home is collapsing and that families are growing more distant from each other in the house, I wonder if New Year's Day has not lost its power to hold, or even reform, the family.

When I mentioned this, my friends around me responded nihilistically, "That kind of corny illusion is the essence of New Year's Day, isn't it?"❧

· 2 ·

Men

*M*en always want to lead women around.
Otoko-tte sugu onna o shidō shitagaru-none
男ってすぐ女を指導したがるのね

This essay addresses a complaint that is probably universal among all women—the tendency of men to try and dominate social situations. What is especially bothersome is when men attempt to boss women around. Women are not dogs and cannot be ordered around, as Itoh's friends plainly state here.

At a meeting a while back at the community center—attended mostly by women, but with a few men as well—the following discussion took place.

"Even when there are mostly women at the PTA meeting, a man will invariably try to lead the group." Right after she said this, many other women agreed, saying, "Yes," "Yeah," "That's right." Others continued, "They think that just because they are men, one of them has to take over, even if we don't ask them to."

"I wonder if they were taught to never play second fiddle to a woman."

It seemed that everyone had something to say about this, like "I don't like it when even women think that the leader has to be a man." And so on. One of the men, with a sheepish smile, admitted, "Yeah, the other day my wife told me to please not 'enlighten' her so much."

Such complaints are also found in the workplace. For example, these days we are seeing more and more male preschool teachers, and that's a good trend, I think. However, problems occur when these men try and pretend they are the big shots among all the other preschool teachers.

There are indeed some people who have great leadership qualities, and there are others who do not. But this does not depend on gender. Nevertheless, I wonder why men always think that they have to stand above women, always be the leaders, and always dominate society—just because they are male. It is not only a nuisance to have such men around, it can also be funny.

As I said, it can be a real pain if a man with no leadership skills tries to take over the group. But I also am not saying that it is just leadership ability that should be the criterion for leadership; sometimes there are situations where it is just that everybody is equal. In these cases it becomes a problem when a man takes over without asking, even if he is competent.

What I think is, that from now on, what is needed is not men who are competent leaders, but men who are competent partners, willing to associate with women on an equal basis. As for men, I wonder if it is really beyond them to enjoy associating with women—or even other men for that matter—on the same level and see people just as people. Although men try to appear smart and say, "Don't ask; just follow me!" they have to remember that we women are people, not Fidos. ✍

*M*en do not know the world."
Otoko-tte yononaka o shiranai-none
男って世の中を知らないのね

In this piece, Itoh and her friends—in a humorous way—talk about some Japanese men being old-fashioned and narrow-minded. Some men simply believe that their wives' lives should revolve around them, they lament. An interesting verbal and orthographic pun is used in the final anecdote. The Japanese word for society is *sha-kai* and is written in two characters, *sha* (社, public) and *kai* (会, meeting). The word for company is *kai-sha* and is written as *kai* (会, meeting) and *sha* (社, here meaning "institution" or "association" as well as "public"). The careful reader will note that these are actually the same two characters for *society* but in the opposite order. Imagining this written transposition of these two characters creates the humorous twist in the author's last comment.

Recently I've met many people who say that men don't know the real world. Until now it was always assumed that it was a woman's prerogative to say she didn't know the world. So I find it quite interesting that not one—but many—now say, "Men do not know anything about the world."

I heard a story from a woman who was very disturbed about the husband of one of the other women in the community center (a woman with whom she shares many activities). The husband thinks something like this: "A wife's first priority should be her husband. Therefore, at least while her husband is around, the wife should arrange her schedule around him."

Therefore, obviously, this woman cannot come to any of our meetings on holidays or at night, and she even hesitates to talk on the phone when her husband is at home. Although she tells him that other wives do not center their lives around their husbands, he just thinks that she has bad friends and they are a bad influence on her.

We had another case of a woman who wanted to get a job and go to work, but her husband disagreed. He said, "Other wives are quite satisfied being at home." He acted as if an unexpected disaster hit him: "Oh my god, my wife is starting to talk about going to work . . . what kind of selfishness is that!"

According to the wives of such husbands, these views are archaic. Some say, "These days women practice, and have come to accept, various kinds of lifestyles. Men, however, are restricted by society to being with other similar, like-minded men, and they cannot easily accommodate themselves to the new changes in women's roles."

Another woman said, "They think they are going to *sha-kai* [society], but they are really only going to their *kai-sha* [companies]. It is very comical." ❧

A man who is sleeping makes a great impression.
Nemutte-iru otoko to iumono wa hito o kandō saseru
眠っている男というものは人を感動させる

Most Japanese office workers and students commute by the very efficient and rapid public transit system. Subways, commuter trains, and elevated trains are ubiquitous, and usually crowded, and many members of an exhausted workforce fall asleep on the way home. Also, male office workers coming home late after drinking with their coworkers often sleep off a few on the return commute. Miraculously, however, no one ever seems to miss their stop. It is these images that Itoh's friend conjures up when she imagines a sleeping man in the following piece.

This phrase appears in Simone de Beauvoir's famous novel *The Mandarins*, one of my favorite books when I was a teenager.

The heroine Anne murmured, as she gazed at her lover's sleeping face, "A sleeping man makes a great impression. How innocent he is. His sleeping face makes me feel like I can accomplish anything—I can start from scratch and redo everything."

Was this passage lying around deep in my mind for many years? Sometime later these exact words came out of my mouth at an unexpected moment. It was when I had my first child. I said these words to my sleeping newborn son. The face of this newborn "sleeping man" was very impressive to me. I was surprised to find myself saying such a thing with a serious face.

I mentioned this unexpected incident once when I was chattering with some other women. One person said to me, "A baby's sleeping face is very impressive, isn't it?" Another explained, "Wondrously it brought out my dutiful side." And so it went on.

However, somebody then seriously asked, "By the way, how about a sleeping man? Is he impressive?"

"I think a sleeping man takes up space, but there is really nothing impressive about him," one person answered. "When I hear about a sleeping man, all I can imagine is some guy snoozing on the subway," another answered.

Our responses all contained such dull and pedestrian images. None of us could reach the level of what Anne felt.

Why was I attracted to these words when I was young? It could be that I was just longing to be a romantic adult woman like Anne. Whatever my reasons were, after talking about it here with my friends I now seriously wonder if a sleeping man's face has the power to impress? ∾

*I*t looks like people are now looking for "home cooking" outside the home.

"Ofukuro no aji" wa katei no soto ni motomeru-mono mitai-ne
「おふくろの味」は家庭の外にもとめるものみたいね

Japanese women, Itoh laments, are still expected to provide meals for their families regardless of their own careers and outside jobs. But, that said, Itoh also tells us that fast foods are becoming increasingly common, even among full-time housewives. The word used for home cooking here—*ofukuro no aji*—literally means "mother's taste." However, this term is used almost exclusively by adult men. Thus, the following story conveys how men feel about their wives turning to fast food or eating out.

We should mention, too, that miso paste is a very common food in Japan and is often used to make the famous miso soup, an essential course in most Japanese meals. In the past, each household or cook had her own way of making this soup. Throughout history, miso soup has been a symbol of the home, and a woman who could not make good miso soup was thought to be somewhat lacking as a wife.

The neighborhood pub or bar (*izakaya*) that Itoh talks about is ubiquitous in Japan. These are usually quite small, often having only three or four tables and a small counter. Besides drinks, the owner often also serves snacks or food made to order. These places are often frequented by male workers in the evenings after work. The proprietress of these establishments is often called *mama-san*, using the English loanword for mother (*mama*) with the suffix for proper names (*-san*) added. The connection between "home cooking" (*o-fukuro no aji*, or literally "mother's taste") and "mama" makes the last sentence of the essay a joke in Japanese on several levels, and Itoh uses this to make her point. First, she implies that modern housewives rely too much these days on fast or packaged foods rather than cooking from scratch, as women supposedly did in earlier times (no doubt, a debatable issue). Thus, for men to get the taste (*aji*) of their own mothers' (*o-fukuro*) real home-cooked meals, they must go out. Sometimes these dishes can be found at the neighborhood pub, and men here are being taken care of once more by another mother, a *mama-san*. On another level, then, Itoh is also poking fun at men, because they need to be pampered by some maternal figure.

Regardless of the rise of fast-food chains nowadays, there was a time when it was said, "To change the taste of the miso soup in each home is harder than starting a revolution." This was because back then people were particular about what they ate, and wanting to eat their own family's cooking, were not satisfied with the plain taste of fast food. Moreover, women felt guilty serving packaged foods, already made, on their own tables. If they did so, they thought of themselves as being a "lazy housewife" who was not working as hard as she should for her family.

However, these days I don't think that even women who call themselves full-time housewives cook meals three times a day at home. Fast-food shops are everywhere. I hear that it is not unusual to find many ready-made dishes purchased at supermarkets and department stores on the table. People are eating out more, too. I often see groups of housewives, or mothers and children, eating out at lunchtime. Also, people eating out at family restaurants on weekends has become part of our lifestyle.

Before, when people went out to eat, they looked for special professional tastes that they could not imitate themselves at home. But these days, people eat out regardless of the taste, just to take a break from cooking (even if the food is actually not so good!). Probably people's behavior has now permanently changed toward eating out more.

Interestingly, the foods we used to call "home cooking" are now served—not in the home—but at a pub or bar. I don't know if this is because society has changed, with people eating out only for convenience, or because of some other reason. But I was talking with my friends the other day and one said, "It looks like people are now looking for 'home cooking' outside the home." Someone responded saying, "Ah, I see now that since they are eating 'home cooking' in those places, the men call the owners '*Mama-san!*'" ∾

*O*nce a man becomes middle aged, he has to make a lot of female friends.

Otoko wa chū-nen o sugitara onna no tomodachi o takusan tsukuranakute wa ikemasen

男は中年すぎたら女の友達をたくさんつくらなくてはいけません

In this piece, Itoh discusses how hard it is for men to be just friends with women, rather than playing some prescribed social role such as husband, father, brother, or son. This is especially true for older and middle-aged men, who, she feels, use their social status and prerogatives to stereotype women. By social prerogatives, she means that men both use *their own* standards of what gender equality should be as well as believing that it is natural for men to be women's social superiors. Itoh argues that men must break out of their male worldview if they are ever to truly embrace egalitarianism.

We should make a comment about one of the English loanwords used in the essay, *walking democrat* (*wōkingu demokuratto*). This word is based on another borrowed term: *walking dictionary* (*wōkingu dikushonarii*). A walking dictionary, of course, is someone who knows everything, especially with regard to language. The English word *walking* (*wōkingu*) became a productive suffix in Japan for a while. A walking democrat, then, is someone who is a natural egalitarian, a true believer in equal rights and equality for all.

When I am working at the community center the overwhelming majority of people whom I am happiest to get to know are women. However, Mr. N is a rare exception. He is almost seventy years old, but he is not authoritative or formal. People call him a "walking democrat." A woman who is fond of him wrote the following analysis:

He has lots of female friends. This is very important for men. The offenses committed in national politics, by large corporations, by personnel in local government—all kinds of these funny things—are all based on men's logic; that is, obligating each other through old-boys' networks is unpleasant and patronizing and clouds political judgment. This is the root of social evils. Women have not been affected by this logic yet. Therefore, once a man becomes middle aged, he should try to mend his evil thoughts by making many female friends and talking with these women. The reason Mr. N has lots of female friends is that he does not follow this kind of perverted men's logic.

I agree with her totally. But once men pass middle age, it is not easy to make female friends. Men have difficulty viewing women at the same level because men inevitably try to stand in a superior way to women, and they grow up thinking that this way is natural.

I think many men have to start learning attitudes to use in their daily lives that would allow them to view women equally. But also, today's wise women think that since we are born as women, we do not want to stoop to the level of men. We don't want to have gender equality based on a men's standard.

Men have to know at first that they cannot make female friends if they are using their social prerogatives to do so.✍

• 3 •

Ourselves

*T*hanks for getting to the point where I cannot kill you anymore.

Watashi ga korosenai tokoromade seichōshita kodomo-yo, arigatō
わたしが殺せないところまで成長した子供よありがとう

In this essay Itoh talks about an important dilemma faced by all mothers: how to find a balance between protecting the child but not causing suffocation by holding on too tightly. In the phrase in the title—the first sentence of the poem discussed immediately below—the poet means she is grateful to her child for having survived being raised by her; in spite of all the lapses a mother has, her child has now gotten to the point where the mother no longer can do obvious damage.

There are several authors mentioned in this essay, the most well known among them being Hikari Agata (1943–1992), famous for her stories of mother-and-child relationships. Her novel *Wuh ho ho tankentai* (The Ha Ha Ha Expedition) was written in 1984 and published by Fukutake Shoten, Tokyo. Oka Yuriko's (b. 1943) *Boku wa 12 sai* (I Am Twelve Years Old), published by Chikuma Shobō, 1976, is the autobiographical novel of a famous Japanese radical of the 1970s.

The title of this piece comes from a poem called *Kisetsu* [The Season] by Kanazawa Hoshiko (b. 1927). It starts out with "Thanks for getting to the point where I cannot kill you anymore."

After this beginning Kanazawa continues on to the next line saying

わたしにとって保護するということは、逆に殺し得るという重さだった
Watashi ni totte hogo-suru toiukoto wa, gyakuni koroshieru toiu omosa datta
To me, the protection of children has the importance of life or death.

35

This reminds me of a section of the novel *The Ha Ha Ha Expedition* by Hikari Agata:

> A newborn baby . . . it is so fragile that I could crush it to death if I held it too tightly. Really, it is right next to me. I shudder at the thought that I could easily kill it with just my hands.

She goes on in another part to say, "I wonder if I can hold these two children tight enough, but yet not suffocate them?"

However, in *I Am Twelve Years Old*, the author Oka Yuriko asks herself, "After my son died, the feeling that keeps plaguing me the most is wondering if I held my son tight enough or not."

These two ideas stand as polar opposites. And yet, if you are a mother, you deeply understand these two feelings: the fear of holding too tight, and the guilt of not holding tight enough. For mothers who are responsible for giving children life and raising them, their world must be bound up in these two extremes.

The weight of holding the child is the same as the weight of his or her life. At the same time, for the mother—whose own life is interwoven with those of her children—that weight is upon her own shoulders. ๛

*I*t is always said that women's happiness is something that is made for them.

Sugu, onna wa shiawase ni sarete-shimau kara
すぐ、女は幸せにされてしまうから

What does it mean to be happy? Can a person in an inferior social position still find contentment if they are aware of their standing? Can happiness be given to the individual by the group, or is it something that individuals must acquire on their own? This is a perennial problem among all social activists—feminists or others—as Itoh describes in the following essay.

"It is always said that women's happiness is something that is made for them." These words were spoken by a woman some time ago at a meeting held in the community center where I work. The theme of the workshop was "Women's Issues as I See Them," and the proceedings were published by Miraisha as a book entitled *Housewives and Women*.

About twenty-five housewives met, and we spoke our opinions frankly, sincerely, and even painfully—every one of us focusing on how to discover the real issues underlying each of our problems. Many truths naturally came out. The above sentence was one of them, and even now I still cannot forget it. The woman did not say this phrase with any great forethought, but just uttered it naturally. I don't think she herself realized the significance of what she said.

There are at least three ways to take this sentence. First, it could mean that women can deceive themselves into simply being temporarily happy. Or it might mean that their happiness is made for them by tradition. Or it could mean that society says to them that they are happy—that is, someone else tells them they are happy even though they have little say about this in their own lives. This sentence has so many meanings.

But in moments of self-reflection, I have heard examples of true insight quite a few times among the women actively involved in the community center. For instance, "After I had a baby my life is really so easy now as I have less time to think about myself." Or "Because I spend all day long with my children, I cannot speak anything but baby talk." And so on.

Although the future picture for women is not yet bright in Japan, I want to believe that by women looking at their own situations through their own eyes, things are heading in the right direction. ๛

I do not like my age no matter how old I am.
Jibun no toshi-tte itsumo kini-iranai-noyone
自分の年っていつも気にいらないのよね

Japan has been stereotyped by many sociologists and anthropologists as a place where people can age gracefully. In Japan, the *otoshiyori*, or the "honorable elders" (Palmore 1975) are said to be well respected. In fact, the rapidity of physical aging may not be "solely a matter of physiological change, but reflects a social situation which encourages the mature person to reach out gladly rather than fear it . . . [because] . . . to enter old age early is to enjoy its advantages longer" (Plath 1972). But as Itoh shows, growing older for some Japanese is as dreaded as in any other culture. For more on aging on Japan see "What is a family? When we become ill, we find out very soon" in chapter 12 and "I am getting to know how to get along with my illness" and "I already passed the age when I should have died!" in chapter 13.

"When I became thirty-one, I felt it was better to be thirty. But when I became thirty-two, I thought that being thirty-one—which I used to complain about before—was better," said a woman acquaintance of mine. "It is not that you do not like your age, you just don't like getting old," others said with a smile. She replied bittersweetly, "But when I was young, I couldn't wait to be thirty, because in those days I thought being thirty would make me a little more mature."

I felt the same way when I was young. In my younger days, I thought once I got older I would be more mature. But it seems that everybody says, "Before, I thought a forty-year-old person was wise and mature, but once I became forty, I find I am still not an adult."

While talking about these kinds of things, one person said this to me:

> My child's art teacher always lies about her age. Every time I talk to her she gets younger and younger! When I first met her she knocked off a couple of years. A few years later she took off even more. Then after that she lost a few *more* years. Since she is the same age as my uncle, she should be fifty-one years old this year. But she wrote a letter to the newspaper and said she was forty. Though she is a very liberal person, it seems that when it comes to age she is worse than others. I feet sorry for her.

Some women think that lying about your age is bad for you in the long run: "If I tell someone a fib about my years and they think, 'Wow, she looks old for her age,' I end up feeling worse than if people knew how old I was in the first place." Upon hearing these words, a person who had kept silent until then muttered, "Wanting to appear younger than we are is an admission that we are really not young anymore." ∾

I was a cold person who tried to live a "faultless" life.
"*Ochido no naiyō ni*" *nante, watashi, tsumetai ningen datta*
「落度のないように」なんて、私、冷たい人間だった

In Japan, many large companies provide subsidized housing (*sha-taku*) for their employees. While the cost may be low, being in close proximity to other families in the company can be oppressive at times, as Itoh discusses here.

"That is, I didn't want anyone to be able to criticize me." This woman said that one of her guiding philosophies was not have people talk about her. As she moved around a lot because of her husband's job transfers, she had to live in various company-sponsored apartments, so she thought this was the wisest course. It could be that she was worried about people invading her privacy. However, she is not the only person who tries to live quietly and inoffensively, inconspicuously "flying just under the radar." In fact, this is how housewives live their lives.

However, many people say that they are scared that these habits will become ingrained into their character and personality: "I am talking to people through the chain on the door."

"And for me, even if I disagree with what the other person is talking about, I often end up just nodding my head, saying, 'Yeah. Right,' trying to be kind or sympathetic, I guess. But, maybe I am just covering myself."

However, there are women who are starting to see things differently: "After thinking about it, I would like to be more honest in my relationships with people. Otherwise, life is just too sad."

The following comments were made by a fifty-year-old woman who was trying to change the pattern of her married life: "Since my husband dislikes me going out when he is at work, whenever I used to go out I would make sure to put my outdoor shoes back in the shoe rack before he got home. But these days, I've stopped doing that."

With a fresh smile, she added, "Before, I worried about my husband getting all upset about me going out. But now, I want my husband to get used to it and not make a big deal about it anymore. Also, I have come to dislike myself when I act afraid of my own husband." ∽

I am a D student (literally, "I am a sixty-point person").
Watashi wa 60-ten no hito nanda-na
私は６０点のヒトなんだな

The rigors of the Japanese educational system are well known throughout the world. Six-day school weeks and hours of extra cram school in the evening are just some of the more notorious experiences of being a student in Japan. However, of course, not everyone goes to the head of the class. How do the less successful students feel? And do some of these feelings linger long into adulthood?

We had a lecture for young mothers at our community center a while back, and I noticed a woman sitting there the whole time with a blank expression on her face.

I was a little worried, so after the lecture I went over and asked her, "Do you have any questions? Was there anything you didn't understand?"

A surprised look came over her face as she replied, "You know, I have never been asked before if I understand anything or not. I have never even asked myself if I understood what I heard at a lecture."

Hearing her answer, I was surprised, too. I then asked, "What about when you were a student? For instance, if you only got sixty points out of one hundred on your exam, didn't you want to know what happened to those forty points? Didn't you want them to explain to you what you did wrong?"

She answered back, "When those things happened I just thought, 'I am a sixty-point person.' My teacher did not really care which questions were difficult or easy for students. I felt that after he finished marking the tests, he thought his job was done."

After I thought about our conversation, I realized many others I know say, "Hey, I was like her."

A while back the grade-school teacher Murata Eiichi (b. 1935) wrote a book called *Dono ko mo 100-ten o toru kenri ga aru* [Every Student Has a Right to Achieve a Hundred Percent] (Tokyo: Shufu-to-seikatsu-sha, 1981). In this book he said that it is the teacher's duty to explain the material to the students until each says, "I completely understand."

When I see how some of the women in our community center feel, I think that Murata's words are even more important now than when I first read his book. Even when people become adults, I wish we could all say that "I want to understand everything well" or "I do not want to be left in the dark." ∾

I don't have the word *criticism* in my vocabulary.
"Hihan" to iu kotoba o motte inakatta mitai
「批判」という言葉をもっていなかったみたい

No one enjoys being on the receiving end of criticism. Most of us, however, seem quick to criticize, or at least offer unsolicited commentary to anyone on anything. Itoh asks if we could eliminate the word *criticism* from our daily vocabulary. However, as she points out, being too indirect due to the fear of offending others also has a downside. As this—being excessively reserved—is often itself a criticism of Japanese social interactions, her remarks are all the more interesting. For more information on Yamashiro Tomoe see "Because I cannot see the faces of my audience . . ." in chapter 6.

The novelist Yamashiro Tomoe (b. 1912) said, "Criticisms should always be something supplemental. They should not be the main point of what you say." The essential attitude of criticism is that it should be something given in the spirit of teamwork and cooperation. Also, the person who is being criticized has to be in a position to be able to receive it. It is easy to get depressed or defensive when someone makes even a small negative remark.

"Comments" and "criticism" are often confused. The reason for this confusion is that people worry more about avoiding conflict and maintaining surface-level relationships and are willing to let the other person think they are right. I think that not being able to distinguish comments from criticism is not a language problem but is a representation of the society we live in.

I realized this when I heard a person say, "I never criticize anyone, even now. When I do, I feel like I am blaming the person, or meddling in their own affairs."

It is very interesting how a person's whole vocabulary—not just the word *criticism*—reflects their lifestyle, human relationships, and total being.

Someone said,

> I used to believe that the phrase "not misunderstanding" meant that instead of worrying about giving precise facts, things were fine as long as my words were not offensive to the other person. I think that I did not have any deep relationships with other people, and had no need to express myself precisely. Therefore, I didn't even realize that I didn't have my own words. ∾

*D*o not ask us to butter you up!
Tatsu nari suwaru nari jibun de sei
立つなりすわるなり自分でせい

There is a concept in Japanese psychology called *amae*—sometimes translated as "dependence" or "indulgence"—that many Western and Japanese social scientists feel explains much of the Japanese character. This term gained wide currency in Western academics with the translation of Doi Takeo's book, *The Anatomy of Dependence*, in 1973 (Tokyo: Kodansha). The idea is still often discussed. While we feel that the whole idea of a "national personality" or "character" is simplistic, crude, and reductionist—and that the concept of *amae* itself is too ill defined to be of much use empirically or as an operational definition—the notion of unconditional indulgence is not foreign in Japan. This is particularly true regarding males, some of whom expect to be mothered and indulged after marriage. Some of these notions of what it means to be a man in Japan today are the subject of the following essay.

"Do not ask us to butter you up!" This sentence was uttered by the feminist and Japanese-language scholar Jugaku Akiko (b. 1924) in a speech a while back.

This comment was a big hit with the women in the audience, who acted as if they all had gotten something big off their chests, as the waves of laughter and agreement washed across the hall.

It is often said that men are supposed to be buttered up, but I hate the phrase *butter up*. The concept of buttering up is actually an insult to the person being buttered up. It is very indulgent to expect to be buttered up all the time. Instead of asking to be buttered up, he or she should earn our respect.

During an election we always hear some candidate begging, "Make me your man!"—even though none of them looks like a woman. What else would he expect us to think? He does not look like a woman, but asking us to "make" him a "man" sounds like he is not certain of his gender. And there are also men who, during the course of their magnificent rhetoric, suddenly gesture dramatically and pause, saying, "I am a man."

"So what?" I think. How I am supposed to react? I wonder if they know how it sounds when we hear men keep saying, "I am a man, I am a man" all the time, in their attempts to use their gender for obtain faint respect.

There are still many men who go around saying antiquated phrases like "Once a man gives his word . . ." or "A man would never do such a thing . . ." or "A man has his pride . . ." or "That's beneath a man's dignity . . ." and so on. And there are even more men who think these things but do not say them.

But these attitudes could also be the fault of women as well. This is because we have let men believe this is how men are. After all, the person who first gave men these ideas was a woman: the mother who nursed him. ∾

I have a pet monkey who knows how to tie a necktie very well.
Nekutai o jōzu ni shimeru saru o kau
ネクタイを上手に締める猿を飼う

Senryū are short, humorous Japanese verses, similar to English limericks. They have been around since the Edo period (1600–1868) and are still a popular satirical medium. Like their more serious cousins (such as the famous haiku and tanka) *senryū* poems rely heavily on innuendo and implication to make their point. For example, in the poem that is the title of this piece, we do not yet know who the monkey really is. However, because this monkey can tie a necktie, an allusion to a Japanese "salaryman"—a white-collar office worker—comes to mind. See "Far away, far away, cherry blossoms are falling" and "The winter chrysanthemum is not pleasant" in chapter 14 and "The abundant seeds of grass that don't know national boundaries are cast upon the ground" in chapter 10 for more about *senryū*.

The above line is a *senryū* poem by Morinaka Emiko, a modern poet. What severe critics women are as they look at men! I think even men would burst into laughter to hear themselves criticized in this manner. When I read this poem the first time, I laughed heartily at the poem's images.

However, later, upon a second reading, I suddenly realized that this poem might mean something different than what I had first thought. Perhaps it isn't a critique of men so much as it is a critique of women.

In this poem Morinaka does not say, "*There is* a monkey who can tie a necktie well"; instead, she says, "*I have* a monkey who can tie a necktie well." This implies that the woman—the "I" in the poem—is living with the monkey. If this is so, this means that from the woman's point of view she sees the monkey as her husband, and this pet monkey—who can tie his necktie well—is supporting her.

This reminds me of a story I once heard about a precocious little girl. If I remember correctly she was in sixth grade, and the parents had been having marital problems for a while. She said to her friends, "Although my mother looks down on my father, she is financially dependent on him. But because of this, she is always frustrated."

When I first heard this story I, myself, as a mother, was thrown off by the fact that a grammar school girl could already see her parents in this way and talk about these things with her friends; however, I was also impressed by her sharp insight.

If this little girl's observation was correct, I wonder if her mother was frustrated because she herself was being sheltered by a monkey. ∾

*I*s *honne* (showing one's true colors) such a good thing?
"Honne"tte sonna ni īkoto nanoka-nā
「本音」ってそんなにいいことなのかなあ

Honne is another one of those Japanese words that has no exact counterpart in English. It means the act of revealing or disclosing one's true feelings or intentions (as opposed to notions like *tatemae*— outwardly expressed emotions or motivations). Depending on the nuance, we have colloquially translated it here as "showing one's true colors," "being frank," "speaking from the heart," or "giving oneself away." Most Americans might say that always being honest is a good thing, but a moment's reflection would indicate that things aren't so simple. As seen in this essay, Japanese also have concerns about what this word really means.

A woman said to me the other day, "Even if I am speaking on principle, if someone says to me, 'Let's be frank,' or 'This is how I really feel' [that is, using the word *honne*], I end up totally accepting their opinion. Then somehow I feel strange. I then begin to wonder if *honne* ["speaking from the heart," or "showing one's true colors"] is such a good thing?"

That's right, I think. The word *honne*—like when someone says, "Because I feel I can talk to you frankly"—sometimes carries a strange power and can have an absolute and irresistible effect on us. However, when I look at how people sometimes use this word (*honne*), they often use it to fulfill their own desires or priorities, or their own narrow-minded interests. If used in this sense *honne* is just a synonym for a selfish request, self-protection, or dependency.

I believe the real value and meaning of *honne* is in dynamically getting to know people's personal qualities. The social situation is not good, however, when people abuse the word *honne*—the result being that the users of the word and people who hear it relate to each other on a lower human level rather than trying to really understand each other. This is what happens when *honne* is used to pursue trivial requests by people who have little self-respect. I think that it is despicable—even scary—when *honne* is not used correctly to create something truly meaningful. The important thing is not whether or not people use the word, but rather, the real quality the word *honne* is meant to convey.

These days, words like *rirakkusu suru* (from the English *relax*), *kiraku-ni* (take it easy), or *kigaru-ni* (lighthearted) are very often used in our conversations. But again people should not abuse these notions. For instance, even though we might say that it is good to relax, we should not do so without constraint. I hear younger people say, "When middle-aged women chatter loudly on the train or in a coffee shop without thinking about others, that is not relaxing; that is simply being inconsiderate." ∾

*I*s a woman's identification card her husband's business card?
Onna no mibun-shōmei-tte otto no meishi-nano?
女の身分証明って夫の名刺なの？

In Japan, the idea of having an ID was very different than in the United States until recent times. People generally were listed on their family registry and no special identification card needed to be carried. For times when something like an official signature was needed, people used their *hanko*, a personal carved stamp or seal.

Japanese people still are not asked to show their ID cards as often as Americans. Nowadays, people do have company employment cards or insurance cards and the like, but these often expire after retirement. And not everyone has driver's licenses, either, as having a car in Japan is very expensive.

However, while official IDs are not as prevalent, printed business cards are ubiquitous and are ritually exchanged upon first meeting someone. It is these things that Itoh and her friends are talking about in this essay.

Historically in Japan, women were often known only as somebody's wife or mother or sister. Women did not generally identify themselves in public using their own names. Even Murasaki Shikibu, the author of what many consider to be the world's first novel, *The Tale of Genji*, written over a millennium ago, is known to us only through the department her father and brother worked at in the court (*shikibu*) and the nickname of one of the main characters in her book (*murasaki* or "lavender child"). The women in Itoh's essay here suggest that perhaps this has not changed so much in the last thousand years.

The other day, a housewife was asked to show her ID card, but she didn't have any. She said, "A person who does not go to school or work in a company does not have any ID card, right?"

Another woman, a shopkeeper, added, "Yes, that's right. When I was walking down the street in the middle of the night once, a policeman asked me who I was. I found that I didn't have any ID card." Another woman said, "I usually show my husband's health insurance card." And so our topic for discussion (for the afternoon) became, "What's wrong with this picture?"

One woman started by asking, "What is 'identification' anyway?" Another said, "I do not understand why the way to let people know who I am is to show proof of which organization I belong to."

Then another woman added, "And by the way, I know the name of my husband's company and his position there, but I don't actually know what kind of work he really *does* every day." Another said, "Introductions among women are the same way. Some women think that if they state the names of their husband's company or their children's school, they have introduced themselves."

Someone asked, "Is that the way we women introduce our own social position, I wonder . . ." Another replied, "In that case, our social positions are defined by our husbands or children."

Another woman added, "We tend to feel that when the rank of our children's school or our husband's social rank is higher or lower, we wives and mothers ourselves likewise feel we are women of higher or lower rank.

However, I'd like to think that I am not that kind of person." Someone then asked, "Well, that means our ID cards are just our husbands' business cards or children's school grades, right?"

Hearing this last comment, all of us cried, "Oh no!" ∾

*W*hat did I want to be, I wonder?
Watashi, nani ni naritakatta-no kashira
私、何 に な り た か っ た の か し ら

Both in the United States and Japan, women's roles and expectations are changing radically—as well as ideas about what is expected of them. New opportunities may become available, and previous options become viewed in different ways. More professional career opportunities are now available in addition to the traditional role of housewife and mother. But perhaps some things have not changed as much as we think. In this piece, Itoh tells us that in Japan many women are indoctrinated—by both society and the mass media—into becoming housewives even before they have a chance to dream their dreams.

What was that TV commercial we had a while back? In that commercial there was a little child who asked her father what he wanted to be when he grew up. The dad said something like, "Papa wanted to be artist." The child asked the same question of her mother, but the mom did not have an answer.

After a silent pause she muttered to herself, "What did I want to be, I wonder?" She still looked pretty young, but yet, she already could not remember what it was she wanted to be. The impression she gave was that this dream disappeared a long, long time ago.

What did I want to be, I wonder? This question does not necessarily refer to occupations. However, in the case of many women, things like dreams and ambitions become diluted as they become housewives, as such things are so easily lost in the rhythm of everyday existence taking care of the household. Is that the real reason? Or is it that many women are just taught to simply be housewives even before they find their life's dream?

When I saw the woman asking herself, "What did I want to be, I wonder?" in the TV commercial, I was very impressed that this short vignette precisely captured the description of so many women's lives. But at the same time I felt very sorry to hear her say the words "What did I want to be, I wonder?"

I believe that some people who see this commercial think that the mother is such a fulfilled person that she does not even need to remember her dreams or think about anything else. In fact, I think this interpretation is what the producer intended. I do not know if this commercial was made by some naive people who simply knew nothing about a woman's happiness, but I am afraid that this type of mass media brainwashes women into believing that being a mother and housewife is a woman's only true joy. ∾

> *T*here are more people these days who don't feel ashamed about being highly educated.
> *Kōgakureki o hajinai hito ga fuetekita-ne*
> 高学歴を恥じない人が増えてきたね

Historically in Japan, women's education was something that was suspect. Not only could it be dangerous to society, it was thought to be personally unfeminine and unbecoming. After Lady Murasaki—the author of *The Tale of Genji*, the world's first novel (which we talk more about in the next essay)—picked up faster the lessons she overheard her brother being taught, her father lamented sadly, "Oh, if only she could have been a boy!" However, Itoh tells that these days women no longer feel ashamed at being highly educated; but, as always, actions speak louder than words.

A woman the other day said, "There are more people these days who don't feel ashamed about being highly educated."

This was not a mistake. She didn't mean "uneducated." She was lamenting the fact that people these days do not have the ability to put their higher education in perspective and have no humility about being highly educated.

This woman, who is now fifty-five years old, says that when she was young there were still not so many people who went to college, especially among women. Under this kind of social and academic climate, she felt she was very lucky to have been able to attend college. But there were many other women around her—some much more intelligent than she was, or with a much stronger desire to learn things—who did not go to school.

They couldn't go to college because of finances or tradition: "Why do women need to have a higher education?" But her social and economic circumstances allowed her to go on to school. This fifty-five-year-old woman felt very bad about her receiving a degree without having any particularly great scholarly aptitude or any particularly strong academic curiosity. But she always felt she rode on the shoulders of those who didn't make it.

Also, she feels shame when she thinks about people who go to school for no reason and don't want to cultivate their humanity. When she thinks about the meaning of her college degree, she says that although she was in school for a long time, she found she was not especially competent and did little to improve herself. This makes her feel ashamed. Many other people like her used to feel this way, she claims. However, currently young people don't feel ashamed if they haven't learned anything. They are proud of their education, but they aren't shy about their incompetency.

This kind of thinking makes me reflect upon my own everyday experiences. I often see situations where we could say "High education, little competency."

For instance, I hear people say things like, "My major was history at college . . ." and then go on to tell us all kinds of stuff that is clearly wrong. Though they proudly make all kinds of pronouncements, the rest of us laugh behind their backs. When I hear them spout off all these wrong opinions my frustration makes me sweat and my face turns red. ✿

*I*t was punishment for being an ideal, perfect, good wife.
*Risō-teki na, kanzen ni manzoku na, yoki tsuma de atta koto no mukui
de atta*
理想的な、完全に満足な、良き妻であったことのむくい
であった

The Tale of Genji, written around 1000 CE by Lady Murasaki—or Murasaki Shikibu—is Japan's most famous literary masterpiece, as well as the world's first real novel. Its thousand pages tell of the intrigues and everyday concerns of medieval Japanese court life. Even today, references to it abound everywhere in Japan, even more than to Shakespeare in English.

The author of the novel was not actually named Lady Murasaki. But as discussed in "Is a woman's identification card her husband's business card?" women—having no legal name in medieval Japan— were often labeled in terms of a male relative. In her own time she was known as Tō no Shikibu (a reference to the Shikibu-shō, the Ministry of Rites where her father and brother worked). One theory claims she is known to us today as Murasaki because of the name Murasaki no Ue, a major character in *The Tale of Genji*. There may be another connection, however. The color purple (*murasaki*) was a color reserved for royalty, and many ladies in the Fujiwara court used some version of *purple* in their names. The powerful Fujiwara family dominated imperial life during the Heian period (794–1185), basically controlling the throne through various alliances and intermarriages without actually occupying it. The wisteria plant (*fuji*), from which the Fujiwara family name is derived, exemplifies the purple color (*murasaki*) in Japanese. Thus the "name" Lady Murasaki—or Murasaki Shikibu—presumably comes from two sources: the name of the title held by her father (*shikibu*, or "minister of rites") and the color purple (*murasaki*). We should note, too, that purple is considered to be a very elegant color in Japan. For example, it is the color of the robes of the highest-ranked Buddhist monks.

For more about Genji and Lady Murasaki, see "Women are thought to be just the place where men sleep" in chapter 3.

I recently read an interesting book that made my heart pound with excitement. It was *The Tale of Genji: Its Women and Author* by the social activist Misao Fukunaga (1907–1991). Fukunaga was in the Communist Party before the Second World War. When she was twenty years old she was arrested under the Maintenance of the Public Order Act and spent some time in jail. While she was in prison, she asked for a thick book to pass away the time in prison. That book was *The Tale of Genji*.

Before I read Fukunaga's book, the image I had of *The Tale of Genji* in my mind was that of a great classic, but one we are hardly able to understand in the twenty-first century. I now think it is a story I can really relate to very deeply. Although I had avoided reading Lady Murasaki because I was intimidated, I have now come to like her very much.

The reason for my newfound appreciation has to do with Fukunaga's view of *The Tale of Genji*. She reinterpreted the female characters in approachable ways, capturing what Lady Murasaki wished to describe in this story in terms we can understand today. Her surprisingly fresh and unique interpretation was based on logic and her deep observation of the human condition. Fukunaga is very convincing in her arguments, which makes her book so attractive.

My title for this essay is taken from a phrase Fukunaga used when she was writing about the woman Murasaki no Ue, the major character in *The Tale of Genji*: "I think what Lady Murasaki is trying to do through the character of Murasaki no Ue is to get us to realize how in vain it is for a woman to have only one purpose in life, to be one man's ideal wife."

After reading Fukunaga's book, the thing that I was so wonderfully impressed with was how respectably—as a woman herself—she treated women in the story, rather than being bound to traditional scholarly interpretations. Because she was not influenced by the so-called conventional wisdom of the so-called specialists, she could really enjoy reading *Genji* on her own terms. ❧

*T*he people who dress up to go to a reunion are pitiful.
Dōsōkai ni kikazatte kuru hito-tte, kanashī
同窓会に着飾って来る人って、哀しい

In English we simply say that "The clothes make the man." Itoh here tells that for women in Japan, things are a bit more subtle. Linguists and semioticians—those who study the messages of signs—argue that clothing is a "language" with all the complexity and nuance of the spoken word. What is the appropriate thing to wear on a particular day, at a particular time? While this question is universal, Itoh is critical of many Japanese female politicians whom she feels have answered it badly.

There a few things in this essay that might need explanation. The Diet, which Itoh mentions, is the Japanese parliamentary legislative body, similar to the Congress of the United States. Japanese also love proverbs, and Itoh uses several in this book. The one she mentions in the third paragraph—*Bōzu nikukerya kesa made nikui*—literally means, "If you hate a monk, even the sight of his robes will offend you." We have left this translation in the text, but a colloquial English equivalent might be something like, "He who hates Peter, hates his dog."

"Instead of dressing up to be happy seeing their old friends, people who dress up to go to a reunion—who dress up just for appearances' sake or to show how successful they've become—are pitiful. Without my being aware of it I was that kind of person, too." These were the thoughts expressed to me by a woman who had recently attended her reunion.

I feel the same way, when I see people who vainly overdress, trying to show off. I really feel sad for them. But I also understand their feelings of insecurity and why they might sometimes want to cover themselves up for protection or encouragement.

Style of dress truly represents our feelings as well as our character. Also very interesting is that the impressions of a person's dress change depending upon the relationship between the dresser and the observer, or the feelings of the observer. In this sense, the old Japanese proverb, "If you hate a monk, even the sight of his robes will offend you," has a deep ring of truth.

By the way, these days, the clothes worn by women running for the Diet are quite gaudy. I don't know why, but we nickname these candidates "Madonnas," and somehow most of their suits are shocking pink. I understand that wearing such showy clothes is probably an election strategy, but what do they want to express to us by wearing such clothes? Do they wear them just to make themselves stand out? To me I feel it is ironic that all these women share the same fashion sense. Oddly, by trying to show how especially unique they are, they have all become the same by adhering to the same "unique" fashion.

I do not know how I feel about their clothes. I do not like these spoiled "Madonna" women who take advantage of their status in society without having any second thoughts, so maybe that is why I hate their clothes. But maybe it is because I can't wear these kinds of clothes, given my age and my body, that I hate the women? I wonder which it is? ✷

> *W*omen are thought to be just the place where men sleep.
> *Onna wa otoko no shinjo toshite ninshiki sareteiru*
> 女は男の寝所として認識されている

In this piece Itoh addresses the problem of how words unconsciously reinforce our thinking and behavior. She packs a lot of punch in this short essay, deftly establishing connections between medieval times and the present day with confidence and aplomb. She makes the important—but often neglected—point that just because some particular individuals do not feel they have been discriminated against does not mean that institutionalized discrimination does not exist. Lady Murasaki, whom she mentions, is the name of the author of *The Tale of Genji*, the great classic novel of Japan written about a thousand years ago, which we talked about in the previous several essays. See "It was punishment for being an ideal, perfect, good wife" in chapter 3 for more information on this book, perhaps the most important in Japanese literature. Komashaku Kimi (1925–2007), whose quote begins the essay, teaches modern literature at Hosei University. Her book, which Itoh refers to—*The Message of Lady Murasaki*—was published by Asahi Shimbun Publishers, Tokyo, in 1991.

The phrase "Women are thought to be just the place where men sleep" comes from the book *The Message of Lady Murasaki* by the literary critic Komashaku Kimi. She goes on to say:

> [During the Heian period (794–1185) of medieval Japan] a woman who gave birth to a child of the emperor was called *miyasu-dokoro*, which literally means "a place where the venerated emperor sleeps."... This word precisely points out the fact that at this time women were defined in terms of where a man would lay his head, where he would sleep. From the earliest beginnings of Japanese society, then, men and women's gender relations were such that a woman is located under a man in the social structure.

Although not as obvious as the previous example, there are numerous words that indicate men's dominance and authoritative power in Japanese society of this time. And words that treat women as sex objects are commonly seen in even today's society.

For example, one phrase that carries such stereotypes is *nyōbō yaku*, or "the role of a wife." Even in social discussions among men, this phrase is used. *Nyōbō yaku* itself consists of three roles: *ukeru yaku*, or the "role of the receiver" [such as one who always listens]; *sasaeru yaku*, the "role of the supporter"; and *naijo no yaku*, or "role as inside assistant" [one who works behind the scenes]. These are the roles that from the beginning were expected of a woman in traditional society, especially a wife. Even though this expression is thought be just "common sense," it is actually very discriminatory.

The descriptions and metaphors associated with the word *shojo* [virgin] is another example. I can't stand how insensitive the tone of some of these are. Consider the term *shojo-hō* (literally, "Mount Virgin" or "Virgin Peak"). This phrase places a value on the sexually inexperienced woman. Moreover, a woman's virginity is thought to be something that is to be scaled or conquered by men. Such insensitivity just makes my skin crawl.

I often hear men say, "There is no gender discrimination in our company," or women claim, "I have never been sexually discriminated against." However, the essence of gender discrimination is not such that it lies on the individual level.

There is an important difference between "I *personally* do not feel discrimination" and "There *is* no discrimination." The problem is, discrimination is structured into people's relationships and is deeply embedded in our cultural and moral behaviors. People sometimes do not recognize discrimination in daily life.

I think, however, that such unconscious discrimination in society can obviously be seen in our daily vocabulary, which we use without thinking, without considering the problems that exist in the social structure. ✎

*I*t is hard to see someone having to smile all the time.
Itsumo egao de inakutewa ikenai hito-tte taihenda-ne
いつも笑顔でいなくてはいけない人ってたいへんだね

While the facial expression of a smile is universal, the meanings attached to smiles can vary somewhat from culture to culture. Here Itoh is talking about some of the manifestations of the "Japanese smile," which sometimes puzzled early Western observers of Japan. Besides smiling to showing delight and happiness, Japanese people will often smile to hide embarrassment or shame, or smile just because it is expected. These different kinds of smiles are discussed in the following piece.

I once said to a group at the community center, "When I see people on television talk shows and variety shows, I sometimes feel it must be a hard job." Someone commented, "I wonder how they can always be so cheerful and bubbly all the time."

Another person said, "I wonder if after work when they go home they have to look in the mirror and peel off their smile 'facial mask.' Do they feel released seeing their real face?" And we all started chattering about this. Someone else said, "I don't think those kind of smiles are limited to businesspeople or people in special occupations."

We all started talking about things like the social role of the smiles, or how some people try to just get by in life on a smile.

One woman said, "A housewife is the sun of the home! So I guess that means I always make an unconscious effort to be cheerful and have a sunny smile on my face." Another said, "Although I am not the center of attention of the workplace, I still always try to be nice to people with a smile." Still another added, "Since I do not want people to think I am conceited, I smile a lot, which is kind of a tool to protect myself from people saying I am arrogant."

There were also some opinions about fearful smiles. "Since I cannot tell what a person really means by smiling, I am always a little afraid of people who are always smiling." Someone else added, "Some people try to distract you by smiling and just try to close the deal. That kind of smile is very manipulative, fascist, even."

Also we tried to analyze the real meaning of smiles. One person said, for example, "I don't like a smile that is just used to flatter, but I dislike more the insincere charity smile that bosses, celebrities, or politicians—for example—give you."

It is often said, "A smiling face is a good thing." Especially for women, they tell us, "You should always have a smile on your face." Therefore, I now think that smiles also reflect a person's social position and lifestyle. ✿

I wonder if even the wife of a guy like that thinks he's OK?
Anna otoko demo oku-san niwa yoku mieru-no kashira
あんな男でもオクサンにはよく見えるのかしら

In the war between sexes, there are the minor everyday skirmishes as well as the occasional ruthless battle. In this essay, Itoh gives us the color commentary on one such after-action report. Great fun is had by all until one woman cautiously mentions that perhaps there are other women someplace saying the same things about them and their husbands. This gives everyone pause . . .

One type of man they discuss is the *boku-chan*. In Japanese, the first person pronoun, *I*, for boys is *boku*. The suffix -*chan* is a diminutive marker for children. To call someone *boku-chan*, then, suggests that the man is still behaving like a spoiled and indulgent little boy.

When we old friends got together the other day after not having seen each other for a while, the focus of our chattering went from recent events to catching up on the latest criticisms of our male coworkers.

We went through some of the different types of men we knew. There was the high-maintenance *boku-chan*. This kind of man is sulky if he is not constantly flattered.

Another type is the sycophant, who acts like he is a great guy to your face but is really only skin deep. Another is the country bumpkin who thinks he is so sophisticated. And so on and so forth. We almost started competing with each other to see who could come up with the worst kind of man.

For instance, one would say, "I know this shabby guy at work . . ." and somebody else would top that. It was a lot of fun to see who had the best worst-man story.

After truly amazing ourselves at the depths to which a man's behavior can sink, and sympathizing with each other for having to work with them, we gradually calmed down.

Then one woman said with some curiosity, "By the way, I wonder if even the wife of a guy like that thinks he's OK?"

"Well, I would wonder about the *wife* of a husband like that!" another said in reply.

"Maybe even their own wives gave up on them," someone said coldly.

The topic of our conversation now became one about wives not knowing how their husbands are seen by their female colleagues at work and their not knowing how their husbands are looked down upon and hated.

While we were actively talking about our male colleagues behind their backs, the conversation was so lively, with lots of laughter. However once someone said, "But maybe my husband is one of those guys?" things became more somber.

"This means, then, that we might be one of those wives . . ." As they say, what goes around comes around. Everybody became silent.

The day's "Let's Cut Up Our Male Colleagues Club" ended with us learning that probably our own husbands are receiving the same kind of pointed criticism by their female coworkers that we had just been dishing out, which was certainly food for thought. ∾

*E*ven though she is a healthy adult, only a wife gets categorized as a dependent.

Kenkō na seijin nanoni hi-fuyō-sha ni sareteiru nowa tsuma dake
健康な成人なのに被扶養者にされているのは妻だけ

There are two words for part-time work in Japanese. The older word *arubaito* (from the German *Arbeit*) now refers to the work of college and high school students who work extracurricularly. The newer term *pāto taimu* (a borrowing from the English *part-time*) is used for people—usually women—who work at an extra job outside the home. While *arubaito* carries positive connotations, *pāto taimu* usually suggests only a middle-aged or older female worker. Part-time work usually carries no benefits, often with erratic hours. And "part-time" could actually be regular jobs for many people. Part-time workers are those whom Itoh and her friends are talking about in this piece. For more on the use of English loanwords in Japanese see "We have to remember that it is our own fault because we raised them that way, didn't we?" in chapter 1, "It's become a case of 'the weak fish eat the weaker fish,' hasn't it?" in chapter 4, "They can't stand each other unless they change their surroundings from time to time" in chapter 5, and "This is a town that keeps the worst of the country and has lost the best of the country" in chapter 11.

We also need to explain one other pun that appears in the essay. The characters of the Japanese word for dependent (*fuyō*, 扶養) literally mean "to be fed" or "to help feed." When the women are complaining about how poor their dependent benefits are, they joke that there is really not enough in them to "feed" anyone.

There are a quite a few women who work part-time but need to carefully count their hours so they don't overstep the limit of income that a dependent can bring into the household. Even a woman who wants to work more hours will admit to people, "It is silly to lose dependent benefits just to gain a little more income."

People say these things as if they were the wisdom of the housewife.

At first some friends and I were talking about a woman who didn't go to work because she didn't want to overstep her hours. Then the topic of our conversation went to the amount of benefits a dependent receives from her husband's company. We talked about how even though "They call it 'dependent' there is really not enough there to 'feed' anyone," and we started complaining about how low dependent benefits are.

But then by and by the conversation changed direction and someone said, "Even if the amount of benefits would become higher, it is still humiliating to be relegated to the social status of being a 'dependent.'"

When we heard this we all looked at each other, as we felt she hit the nail on the head, and many started talking:

> Until now I thought "dependent" was a kind of handling fee given to me because I am helping my husband. I understood this to be my reward for this work. However, now I think that dependent benefits are given to the husband so he can feed his wife.

> Because I am looking after the home and doing domestic chores and taking care of our children, I am not just fed by my husband. *My* work allows him to do *his* work. But in society there is no social recognition for such a thing.

But then one woman suddenly realized that "I am not in between jobs, or sick, or too old to work. Doesn't it seem like even though she is a healthy adult, only a wife gets categorized as a dependent?" "This just means that society naturally accepts the fact that a woman is fed by her man," added another woman, strongly. Our conversation slowly revealed the ignoble position of women in the world.

Once we take off the veil to reveal the gender inequality that lies hidden under the system of benefits for dependents, problems of the social role and social position of women become visible. It was fun to discover these kinds of things by talking together. No, it was not! It was not fun at all to have such social inequality pointed out. ∾

My days go by with me only speaking baby talk.
Aka-chan kotoba shika tsukae-nai kurashi nan-desu
赤ちゃん言葉しか使えない暮らしなんです

In this essay Itoh confronts an interesting, though often unacknowledged or unexplored, linguistic issue: how might the use of women's language weaken one's sense of self-worth, or even personality? Of course, these things are very hard to test empirically; we can only rely on anecdotal evidence such as that presented here. Nonetheless, Itoh makes a case that the quality of our language reflects the quality of our personal relationships. And she is not impressed with what passes as communication these days. If we can just pass off our feelings as language, does this mean we deal with each other on an equally superficial level? If so, Itoh claims, our social problems may be much deeper than we originally thought.

"My days go by with me only speaking baby talk. Therefore, I feel like my intelligence level is becoming like that of a baby." These words were once said to me a by a young housewife who spends every day only with her young children. She expressed these sentiments after realizing her social situation. When I heard these poignant words a long time ago, they stuck deep into my heart.

But what about women whose children have grown up? Well, here are some reasons people gave for joining in on the activities at the community center:

> All day long I am looking after my family store, but all I do is greet customers or talk to them about the weather or exchange innocent gossip. I do not have many chances to talk with anybody about any serious topics, so I felt I should do something about it.

> I felt shocked when my daughter said to me, "Mom, you often say just what people on TV say. Are those really your own opinions?"

When these people looked back on their life as expressed through daily language, they felt the weakening of their personality. When I heard these stories, I felt sympathy for these women's language-life.

I mention these things because recently it seems that people rarely think about their own language. I have not heard many say that they have reconsidered the positions of their lives based on a reconsideration of their daily language.

For instance, there are many kinds of expressions used today such as, "Well, like, you know . . ." which are very commonly used. The meaning of *like* or *you know* is empty and does not precisely convey what we are thinking. These days it seems as though you can simply pass off your feelings as language, and if the other person just gets the general idea, that's fine. This is what passes for communication these days. But if we don't have any human relationships, our language ability and our ability to think will deteriorate.

If that is so, then our current linguistic fashions are not just a simple matter of claiming "this is just how we say things these days." If this is true, our problem is not just with the current language but goes much deeper than that, doesn't it? ∾

*I*t's kind of nice to be able to feel happy about someone else's happiness.
Tanin no koto o ureshī to kanji-rareru jibun ga chotto ii na to omō
他人のことを嬉しいと感じられる自分がちょっといいな
あと思う

In this essay—as in the last—Itoh again addresses the issue of the quality of human relationships as expressed through language. She suggests that some of the causes of alienation are the modern media—as people are encouraged to digest information individually rather than collectively—and the educational system, as schools foster competition rather than cooperation. Thus, ironically, instead of unifying people, language can also separate them. She ends on a positive note, however, demonstrating that the power of human empathy can overcome alienation. This facility, she claims, will ultimately make society livable.

In the current social climate these days it is common to think that "respect individuality" is the same thing as "you are you and I am I." That is, we think that respect for another person is the same thing as not interfering in another person's business. In reality, people confuse *kyōkan* (compassion) with *dōjō* (feeling sympathy or pity) and do not know how to distinguish *kyōryoku* (co-operation) from *kanshō* (interference).

When I talk to young mothers whom I meet at the community center, I feel they experience shallow human relationships and tend to associate with people only on the surface. I take this to be a result of the educational system, which has taught them only competition. They do not know how to connect with others, and they do not know how to appreciate real human relationships. This kind of society, where people are separated individually like grains of sand, is great for those who control and use people. People can float around in a world of information controlled by the media and believe what they are given, without uniting or cooperating to stand together for the same purpose.

Around the time I was thinking about this kind of dangerous situation, everyone at the community center noticed the change in one of the members:

through her participation at the center, her attitude toward learning had changed greatly, and she grew to be a sparkling person. One person said this about her:

> Until now, although I liked and admired the things that other people did—and thought they were great—I never really felt happy for them. But this time, when I see her changes and achievements, it's kind of nice to be able to feel happy about someone else's happiness. I felt happy for her change and growth. At the same time, I feel good about myself to have such a feeling for others.

When the others heard these words, they were happy, and needless to say, I was impressed, too. This is because cultivating such feelings develops our compassion for others and is a very important thing in the kind of society we have now. ✿

That woman is like an obstinate, grumpy old man.
Ano onna wa marude kuso-jijī-da
あの女はまるでくそじじいだ

There are a pair of words that are quite common in Japanese that are used to refer derogatorily to (often older) men and women. The first, *kuso-babā* (literally "shitty granny") is a biddy, old hag, bitch, or grumpy old woman. The male equivalent, *kuso jijii* (literally, "shitty grandpa"), means an old geezer, old fart, or grumpy old man. What is funny about the title of this piece is that the woman under discussion is not called *kuso-babā* (grumpy old woman) but is called *kuso jijii* (grumpy old man). The reason why is explained below.

We should mention, first, a few geographical facts: Nagano is a mountainous prefecture near Tokyo and hosted the Olympics in 1998. Kyushu is the southernmost of the four main islands of Japan. There is a saying about the men on Kyushu, especially those from Kagoshima Prefecture: 男尊女卑 (*dan-son jo-hi*), or "men dominant, women inferior," which, as we will see, is an example of what Itoh is talking about in this essay.

For more on the "comfort women" issue see "We can't conduct a conversation equally when we only use women's language" in chapter 6, "This is a town that keeps the worst of the country and has lost the best of the country" in chapter 11, and "The most important thing about being a human being is to learn about the world by ourselves" and "I think it is so good that I am not a Japanese" in chapter 13.

The day when the "comfort women" issue hit the newspaper, my friend, who is a reporter there, lamented that they received a phone call from a woman who really bashed "comfort women" and Koreans, using some pretty colorful discriminatory language. She said, "Because that phone call was from a woman, I felt worse. She sounded just like she was an obstinate, grumpy old man, I think."

Her words gave us a great laugh. They were funny because she did not say "obstinate, grumpy old woman" but instead said "obstinate, grumpy old man." The implication behind her words was, we would expect such an opinion from some man, but we would not expect it of a woman.

But there are, indeed, women around me who have very extreme opinions like this woman had. They have their own prejudices, often based on where they are from, and say things like, "Men from Kyushu are stupid and silly," or "Men from Nagano Prefecture are awful."

When I tease them about this saying, "What about the women from Kyushu or Nagano?" they say without any hesitation, "All women are wise no matter where they are from."

Interestingly, many of these people who are firmly convinced of such opinions also have sons. But based on their observations and experiences, they say things like, "Girls my son's age are much more mature, without exception." They claim with true conviction, "Women are superior to men."

I am sure they are just kidding, but still, I am very interested in seeing that women have the confidence in themselves, of being women, that they can rate women as superior to men. Until now, we women unconsciously looked down on our own gender and believed stereotypes about ourselves like, "Women are ditzy," or "After all, men are smarter . . . " When I think about it, this newfound confidence is really delightful.

Furthermore, I am so happy to find that this is not just theoretical but can be found in everyday experience. When I hear women at the community center talking about the activities of their groups, they say things like, "We have a bunch of really talented people on board."

Hearing this, I am truly happy. Why? Because I have directly watched them *make* themselves into "talented" people. ॐ

· *4* ·

Other Women

*W*omen don't need their own names, do they?
Onna niwa namae nante iranain-desu-ne
女には名前なんていらないんですね

As we mentioned earlier, it was common in tenth-century Japan for women to be known only by association with some male, usually a husband or other relative. Here Itoh argues that things might not be that different even in twenty-first-century Japan.

Choosing a name, of course, is not really so simple an exercise for a woman as we might think. For example, in China, and lately often in the United States, married women will keep their so-called maiden names. Sometimes this is done as an intentional statement of social independence; sometimes it is a matter of professional convenience. Regardless, a Japanese woman is legally obligated to take her husband's last name and become officially listed on the husband's family registry (and never the other way around).

However, as Itoh mentions, Japanese women will even often refer to themselves using their husband's full name rather than using their own given name. An English counterpart, for example, would be like saying "I am Mrs. John Smith" instead of "I am Jane" or "I am Jane Smith."

The book that Itoh refers to in the beginning of her essay— *Kagerō nikki* (literally, "The Diary of the Shimmering Waves of Heat")—is the personal journal of a Japanese noblewoman in Heian Japan covering the years 954 to 974 CE. It tells of her unhappy marriage to Fujiwara Kaneie (the Fujiwara being the most powerful family of the time). She is known to us today only as the mother of her son, Michitsuna. *Kagerō nikki* was translated into English by the famous

61

American Japanologist Edward Seidensticker as *The Gossamer Years* (Tokyo: Charles E. Tuttle Co., 1964). For more on the "Kagerō" diary see "When men are around it is happy and cheerful" in chapter 10. For other examples of women's names in medieval Japan see "It was punishment for being an ideal, perfect, good wife" in chapter 3.

When I started out reading classic Japanese literature in high school, I detested hearing about court ladies who had no other names besides the identities given to them historically through their association with some man. For instance, the author of *Kagerō nikki* (the Kagerō diary) was only known as "the mother of Udaishō Michitsuna."

The Letters to the Editor column in the newspaper that I read every day often gives me this same feeling. Most of the time the contributors are men, but sometimes I find a woman writing in. However, when they do write, they only identify themselves as so-and-so's mother or somebody's wife. That is all; they do not give their own names directly. They let their own names lie in the shadows.

I started looking around, and every day I find that women are nameless everywhere, even when they are alive. For example, many women at the community center where I work tell me that they are so often only called so-and-so's mother or somebody's wife that when they are addressed by their own names, they feel refreshed. About twenty years ago I heard a young housewife mutter with some self-effacement, "Women don't need their own names, do they?" I couldn't answer; I was speechless. Even after twenty years, this situation has not changed. Moreover, it seems that even the Japanese women themselves have forgotten their own names.

When I asked a woman to fill out an application for a library card where I work, as she began to fill out the space for "name" she asked me, "You mean my husband's name?"

I heard of a woman who started to write down her husband's name on the visitors' book we had at the reception desk for a quilt exhibition. And even though all the participants at a kindergarten PTA meeting a while back were mothers, somehow the names written on the attendance list were all fathers. Also, when women order clothes from the local boutique and have them delivered to their homes, they give their husbands' names to the clerks.

I wonder what women are getting in return for giving up their names? ∾

The *shujin* (literally, "master") of the house is me.
Go-shujin wa, watashi-yo
ご主人は、私よ

There are many words for husbands and wives in Japanese, both as terms of address and terms of reference. Here, Itoh talks about two of them: *shujin* (husband) and *oku-san* (wife). The Sino-Japanese characters for these words, however, literally mean "master" and "the person in the back," respectively. Thus, these apparently neutral words have some subtle connotations, which is the subject of her essay below.

Yamazaki Tomoko (b. 1932), whom Itoh mentions in this essay, is a women's studies historian. Her most famous book in English is *Sandakan Brothel No. 8* (Armonk, N.Y.: M. E. Sharpe, 1999), about poor Japanese women sold into prostitution in Southeast Asia in the 1930s and during World War II.

Even among young people, there are still many who call their husbands "*shujin*" (literally, "master"). Even if they do not call their own husbands *shujin*, I still often hear them casually call others' husbands "*go-shujin*" (an honorific form of *shujin*).

Yamazaki Tomoko told me that when she is asked about her "*go-shujin*" she replies, "It is I who am the master of the house." I think this makes perfect sense. Yamazaki told me, "My good friends ask me, 'How is your husband (*go-shujin*) today?' I tell them that the '*shujin*' is me! They then say, 'Ah, yes, . . . of course.'"

Here is something I recently heard from my newlywed friend. Her husband is a student, so she is the one who is supporting the family. After I heard about her situation, the other meaning of "*shujin*"—which Tomoko translated somewhat in jest as the "master" being herself—began to ring true.

When we talk about these kinds of things, this reminds me of problems with another word that I often hear. A single female friend of mine said, "When I go out with an *oku-san* ("wife," or "a married woman"), I feel I have to be very careful."

What she is saying here is that when she goes out with people who are not living on their own salary, she always worries about spending a lot of money in front of them on lunch or dinner or trips.

> I do not worry at all about spending money in front of women who have their own income, but I worry about spending money on food and travel in front of women who are using their husbands' money to buy things for themselves. They have a different way of handling their household budgeting than single people. Therefore, I always ask them to pick first, and I just follow their lead.

I wonder how *oku-sans* would feel if they knew their friends were seeing them like this? ∾

> *I*t is not because I am afraid of my husband.
> *Shujin ga kowai wake dewa nai-noyo*
> 主人が怖いわけではないのよ

In this essay Itoh tackles a very tough subject: how should a wife "handle" her husband? There are many alternatives, of course, but a common device that she sees the women around her use is to be especially accommodating. That is, if you try to anticipate any problems before they occur, things will go smoothly. But Itoh wonders if this just isn't a kind of sly manipulation, and if it is, is it healthy for the relationship? Is a relationship that simply runs smoothly necessarily a successful one? And isn't there a double standard here, if husbands can get angry but wives cannot?

As soon as our nighttime meetings are finished, the woman dashes home by bicycle, and her speed makes me wonder if she obeys all the traffic lights . . . or not. Her children are all grown, and she does not have an elderly person that she has to look after. It is not that she cannot be away from home. When I asked her the reason why she had to always take off so suddenly, she said that her husband gets cranky if she is not at home.

As we watched her back as she was hurrying home one night, someone who was in the same situation said sympathetically, "It is not that she is afraid of her husband; it is just that she is uncomfortable when she sees her husband's sour face."

Since the old days in Japan a proper housewife should be expected to welcome her husband home with a smile, even if he is staggering in late. We don't say anymore that this is a necessary requirement to be a proper housewife, but it is the wise woman who knows how important such things are in keeping the peace.

But if this was really a recipe for a happy relationship, then you would think that when the wife comes home late, the husband should be there to welcome his wife home with a smile. However, in reality, this is not what happens. Always the husbands come back home late, and always the wives welcome them home with a smile. Even now there are still many men who think that wives should not come back home later than they do, and they view such things as simply inexcusable.

I wonder why many women still believe that they should not give their husband a sour face. I am also very concerned about women who say, "I am not afraid of my husband; this is just the best way to manipulate him." They think that if they can somehow keep their husbands from having sour faces, they are handling their relationship well. This makes me worry about our futures.

It is often said that a couple who do not quarrel do not necessarily have a solid marriage. Is the woman who agrees with her husband on everything just so she doesn't have to see his scowl—even if she does not have the same opinions—really that wise?

If that is the kind of wisdom the wife has, I think that she is really cold and insincere. I am afraid of the woman who tries to avoid seeing the truth by saying, "I am not afraid of husband, but . . ." ❧

*O*ne always has to make sure to speak logically.
Ronriteki ni iwanakute wa ikenai
論理的に言わなくてはいけない

In this essay, Itoh addresses a very common quandary in the (actually!) complex process of daily discourse that all of us face at some time or other: How can we distinguish our *own* words and thoughts from the words and thoughts of others that we have simply heard? Are we even aware of the difference? There is probably nothing new under the sun, so when can we claim originality? We can't recite a bibliography, after all.

But here Itoh also shows that there is another side to this as well: many times, she says, Japanese women will simply attribute their own thoughts—however creative and new they may be—to someone else. Often this is a husband or some other male. The question is, is this just a sociolinguistic rhetorical device—that is, a mere stylistic convention of discourse—or something more profound? Do these women want to avoid taking responsibility for their own ideas? If so, Itoh suggests, then much of their woman's voice has been effectively silenced.

Once when I was chairing a meeting at the community center where all the participants happened to be women, I said, "Women are not allowed to use the power of logical expressions." However, I later heard some women say that "Mrs. Itoh said we women have to speak more logically."

I think that when I said the above sentence, my listeners thought that I was saying that women do not speak logically and was arguing that we had to. Apparently they did not understand what I was saying but only stuck to their own preconceptions. In other words, their thoughts and what they heard were conflated. I could argue, I think, that they could not separate themselves from others or could not recognize fact from fiction.

And I also thought that it was a shame that although women might have their own deep thoughts, when they say something, without thinking they always attribute it to having heard it from someone else. I think there are lots of women who have these kinds of experiences. This seems typical.

For example, there are lots of women who begin a conversation with, "My husband says . . ." and do not add anything of their own. Her husband said something. So what? Doesn't she have her own opinion? Don't they have any opinions about their husbands' opinions? Are they trying to be one with their husbands? Or are they hiding behind their husbands and not taking responsibility for their *own* words? Do they think that if they say their husband said this or that, everybody will then agree with them?

It seems very simple—but it is actually very hard—to distinguish our own words and thoughts from the words and thoughts of others, even though it is very important to do so. ✍

> *W*e can see very well the home life at the other end of the phone.
>
> *Jūwaki kara, sono hito no katē ga yoku miete-kuru*
> 受話器から、その人の家庭がよく見えてくる

While the *keitai-denwa*, the ubiquitous cell phone that every Japanese teenager possesses, has not yet penetrated the middle-aged and older market, telephone manners are still an important part of daily life. Itoh here claims that how family members answer the household phone says much about the quality of the human relationships within the home. This is one more example, presented many times in this collection of essays, of the presentation of self to outsiders—the inside, the private, the withheld (*uchi*) versus the outside, the public, the exposed (*soto*).

When people call up when I am out and they see me later, they often say something like, "The person who answered the phone was your son, wasn't he?" Even before they tell me why they called, I immediately ask, "Did he answer the phone abruptly, or was he impolite to you?"

Here's what it is like when I call: Let's say I call my friend, for example, but I do not know her other family members. If a family member answers and tells me he or she will make sure that my friend will get my message correctly without fail, I think, "This family communicates very well and they respect each other. They must have a great relationship among themselves." And I really I hope my family is like that.

Now when I say that someone has a "nice response" over the phone, this is a little different from what I would call "well mannered." I am not talking about "telephone manners" like being polite and using appropriate language and being amiable. What I am talking about is this: the good human relationships of people inside the home will be naturally reflected in the outside public activities of the family (even in answering the phone). Especially for housewives.

We can see very well the home life at the other end of the phone. For example, when I am calling someone and a man—most likely the husband—answers with an unwelcome voice and yells "Phone call!" to the person I am calling, this leaves a bad impression.

Or if someone I am talking to suddenly hangs up in the middle of the conversation saying, "I gotta go. My husband is back," even though she called me, this is also disturbing. Then at such times I can really see where the wife is located in their family—and the relationship she has with her husband in her daily life—over the phone.

Also, yesterday, when I ran into a close friend on the street, she told me, "I just called you at home and your husband answered and he told me, '*Again* she is out' with a laughing voice." Oh, well, how shameful I am. ✒

*T*heir double income has been in vain.
Zuibun muda ni tomobataraki o shitekita mono-ne
ずいぶん無駄に共働きをしてきたものね

Again, Itoh addresses the problem of equality in marriage. Here we hear the story of a woman who held a responsible position outside the home, but her talents and contributions were underappreciated by her husband (to phrase it kindly). But Itoh suggests that possibly this was a failure on both sides. The wife, too, simply fell into a traditional role in spite of changing realities. Neither accepted or appreciated the privileges *and* the responsibilities when people work outside of the home.

I knew a woman who was a schoolteacher for twenty years but recently retired. She is a leading figure in our local community and is always looking after the people around her very conscientiously. But this woman always worries about her husband's moods. Thus, even if someone has something very important to talk about with her, she won't let them call when her husband is at home. I heard that among her female friends he is well known as being very narrow-minded and conservative.

One day people were talking about them, and someone said, "Because he is so unreasonable, she can't even reach half of her full potential even though she is very talented."

People were quite sympathetic. Another woman, when she heard this story, was amazed. She asked, "Why? She has been working outside the home just like he has, right? For him to behave this way implies that there is no importance to her contribution or that all her work has no meaning. She was working outside the home for no reason. Their double income has been in vain."

The other friends who had been just listening to the story so far, thinking that this was just a case of an obstinate husband and pitiful wife, suddenly changed their countenance. You could see the "wait a minute" expression on their faces.

How come, during her long marriage, didn't she ever just tell him that she had her own job and her own social life? When both people work outside the home every day, whether by preference or not, men and women must be on an equal footing, and it is inevitable not to share even the housework. And yet, she never talked about such issues with him seriously. His attitude, then, is simply a reflection of their lifestyle.

That woman's words, "Their double income has been in vain," points out that because the wife didn't talk things out with her husband, it might even be her fault that this couple ended up in this kind of relationship.

I think that the value of a man and a woman working outside the home is to force them to reconsider the traditional roles couples usually have and to get them to think about new roles. Only people who practice new kinds of relationships will appreciate the value and meaning of the wife working outside the home. ❧

Housewife is just the pronoun for *stupid*.

Shufu-tte, "baka" no daimeishi mitai ni iwareru-none

主婦って、「バカ」の代名詞みたいに言われるのね

Women everywhere probably get offended by the label *"just* a housewife," implying that raising a family and managing a household are nothing more complicated than getting up in the morning and fixing coffee. And the Japanese media still often portray housewives as *just* silly, self-absorbed, or stupid (if not desperate, in the American sense). But, as one women in the vignette below argues, perhaps some of this is self-inflicted. Being *just* a housewife can also be a way of avoiding confronting unpleasantries or taking responsibility for their thoughts and actions, which, after all, are just assumed to be mainstream.

At our community center the other day a woman I know, who is also a housewife, said with some degree of sarcasm, "*Housewife* is just the pronoun for *stupid.*"

Hearing this comment, another woman said truly angrily, "That's right. That makes me sooo mad!" According to them, in television shows and in newspapers they often see things like the following:

主婦にも分かるように
Shufu nimo wakaru yō ni
Try to make it so even housewives can understand it.

主婦向けに易しく
Shufu muke ni yasashiku
Try to make it so simple that it is housewife-proof.

Those who use these words demean housewives by believing they are too stupid to understand anything except the simplest of explanations. This is an issue that I always feel uncomfortable about, too.

I said, "There are, in fact, many different kinds of skills a housewife must have, and there are even specialists among housewives. Also, it is not right to believe that just because someone does not work in public, they don't know anything. Isn't it simply old-fashioned to believe that people who work at home have narrow minds?"

After I said that, the other women all agreed. One said, "Probably today's housewives know more about the world than those tribes of husbands who stay in their companies all day long."

Others nodded. When men describe issues like taxes or prices they promote rotten stereotypes in the mass media by saying things like, "Housewives get headaches trying to make ends meet," thereby reducing big public issues to the level of the household. Therefore we should say in order for men to understand these big issues we need to use footnotes.

But while we were talking, we heard a different opinion from another woman:

Some women bring this on themselves saying, "But I am just an ordinary housewife." They say this as if normal housewives are naively innocent and have no ideologies or philosophies or no political leanings. Furthermore, they say such things as if they are claiming to be good moral citizens. By saying "I am just an ordinary housewife," they think they are saying something like, "I am a housewife who does not have any dangerous ideas," or "I am just an ordinary housewife and therefore my opinions are mainstream." Not only do I not like such people, I feel they are more harmful than men.

I think she is right. We all agreed that men's opinions toward housewives are, in general, pretty bad, but the way some housewives justify themselves can be much worse. ∾

*A*lthough she talks big, her house is probably still a mess.
Erasō na koto itteru kedo, ie no naka wa kitto, torichirakatte iru-noyo
えらそうなこと言ってるけど、家の中はきっと、とりち
らかっているのよ

As we saw in the previous essay, there is a certain degree of self-imposed guilt by housewives who do not work outside the home. In this vignette we hear of a student who took offense to what she perceived as a snide criticism of her stay-at-home lifestyle by a successful and public career woman in a lecture. She sarcastically rates the lecture on the "house-messiness scale," the ultimate litmus test of post-teenage Japanese femininity. Itoh also finds herself being defensive or apologetic about the condition of her home. However, she seems to have trouble explaining how internalized and insidious this notion is to others. Her unspoken question—Is it true that women are women's harshest critics?—is left unanswered.

This is a story that I heard from my friend who is a student at a school of social work. My friend told me that her school has students of all different ages attending, and there are many housewives like herself in class. In one class, a female instructor was discussing the social problems of housewives who don't have jobs.

During the lecture, a student sitting next to my friend—another house-wife—whispered, "Although she is talking big (*erasō na koto itte iru-kedo*), I bet her house is probably still a mess." I guess this student took the point the instructor raised as a personal criticism—that is, that she didn't have a job—rather than seeing it as a social welfare issue.

If this student had an opinion or disagreement with the teacher, I think she should have brought it up in class. Instead, she whispered to my friend that "her house is probably still a mess" behind the teacher's back, which had nothing to do with the social issue being discussed. I think it is unfair of her to do this, in order to justify herself for not having a job.

How dare she attack someone without understanding the theme of the argument? Hers was just an emotional reaction supported by the "common-sense" notion that women should attend to housework first. What kind of argument is this, especially among women?

"Isn't that awful? I feel disappointed as a housewife myself," said my friend. I agreed with my friend's opinion, but at the same time, I thought about how messy my house is all the time. Without thinking I said the following words:

> I have a friend who is a great person. Even though her house is very messy she never says, "I am sorry my house is a mess," or "I am ashamed how messy my house is." I myself always give some kind of excuse for why my house is a mess. I wish I could be calm about it just like her. Don't you agree?

My friend—who is very serious and conscientious—was surprised by all this. The expression on her face said, "Oh, again, you are . . . that's not what we were talking about . . ." ❧

*W*ith much difficulty, she had a baby when she was older.
Sekkaku no kōrei-shussan nano-ni
せっかくの高齢出産なのに

In the United States—and as we see here, increasingly, in Japan as well—many women are marrying later and raising their children well into late middle age. The age at which one has one's first child is also increasing. And there are many established career women who now seek to have their first baby in their forties. While most Americans are probably neutral about this at worst—or even encouraging at best—in Japan not everyone is so approving. As Itoh implies here, work experience and a higher education do not necessarily translate into good parenting.

We also need to mention an interesting Japanese orthographic convention to explain Itoh's comment in the first paragraph about the word *maru-kō*. In the United States or Europe a picture of a dog circled with a red line across it means, of course, "No dogs allowed." In a similar, though opposite, way, Japanese conventionally circle things that they want to draw attention to. *Maru-kō* literally means "circle-high," though perhaps a better rendition would be "*circled-high.*" That is, what we are referring to here is the character for *high*, 高, with a circle drawn around it (see below). This image, which would be conjured up by any Japanese hearing *maru-kō*, means someone who has a child later—high—in life and is much more euphemistic than saying an "older" birth.

These days there are more people having their first child later in life. There are several commonly used new words to reflect this, such as the formal *kōrei shussan* (delivering a baby in old age) or the informal *maru-kō* (literally, "circle-high" [age]).

But concerning this new social phenomenon, I heard the following remarks from a preschool teacher: "However, when I hear, 'With much trouble, she got a baby when she was older,' I am disappointed. Since these people are in their forties, I thought they would be more mature, but actually they are very immature."

I always felt strongly that I became a mother while I was still too young, and I always thought my friends who waited to give birth later in life were better mothers. I always felt that it was preferable that people become parents at a later age. Therefore, her words were unexpected. This got me to start listening around about these kind of things, and I often heard comments like the following: "There are many mothers who are not reliable. I can't believe these people have been in the workforce for a long time."

Another said, "Although they were toughened up working in a company, the power of their training is not directly connected to child-rearing skills. Is this because, unlike office work, raising a child does not have an organized structure from start to finish? Unlike the workplace, caring for a child does not have a manual that people can just follow without thinking; you must be flexible." These are the kinds of things that preschool teachers and kindergarten teachers say.

I think that life as a career woman or a student does not necessarily make people into mature adults. Thus, the issue is not just one of people having children when they are older. Doesn't it also represent a more general problem that our current society is not fostering people's character? I wonder if society is twisted and is becoming a poor place to foster people's character? ∽

*A*s a housewife and mother, I am proud that I have done my
duty.
Shufu toshite haha toshite, nasu-beki koto wa shite kita to jifu shite orimasu
主婦として母として、なすべきことはしてきたと自負し
ております

In this essay Itoh again asks us to think about what the role of
women should be in modern Japanese society. She argues that there
is blindness by both radicals and conservatives. Traditionalists, by
definition, accept the professed values of the established social order
and pride themselves on living up to these expectations. Thus, they
miss or dismiss evidence of gender discrimination around them.
Career women, however, often feel themselves to be somehow
different from—or even superior to—the typical housewife. Thus,
gender discrimination doesn't apply to them, as demonstrated by
their own public success. Both groups are confident of their position
in life, however they conceive it to be. But this confidence, Itoh
claims, often prevents people from seeing the obvious.

On the first day of the administrative meeting I attended of the Committee on
Women's Policy Issues, one committee member introduced herself and confi-
dently said, "As a housewife and mother, I am proud that I have done my duty."
"Oh my god!" I thought. When I heard this I did not know what was going to
go on with this committee, and I sat back and took a deep breath.

Her words tell us that she has lived her life without any uncertainty about
what is the traditional "women's way of life." Furthermore, she seems to never
have had any doubts about this conventional way of life for women herself, and
even now it does not appear that she recognizes essential gender issues.

That a member of the Committee on Women's Policy Issues has this kind
of attitude is a problem. However, isn't this just a typical example of how hard
it is, ourselves, to recognize problems of gender discrimination? Everyone has
to rethink their values, virtues, and way of life. In that sense, we essentially have
to critically examine ourselves. This must be very hard to admit to—and to
understand—for women who have lived what they felt was the "right way" as
a woman and who have prided themselves for following such a path.

Also, career women (who work hard to compete with men) find it very
difficult to understand, too. This is because these career women think that they
are different from the average woman. They have a bit of a superiority complex
and find it hard to admit they are facing some of the same problems together
with average women, and this disturbs them.

In other words, it seems like the more confidence someone has, the harder it is for women to recognize their own problems. ∾

At the workplace she still acts like a housewife.
Shokuba de shufu yatte kurechatte-iru
職場で主婦やってくれちゃっている

Again, in this short essay, Itoh is really asking us to think about the proper role of the housewife—and by extension, the proper role of the woman—in Japanese society. Generally, housewives who dote on guests or family are held in high regard. But in the workplace, some of her friends claim, it is possible to be too kind or too diligent—to the point of interference. Itoh says these comments have made her reconsider how women should work with others.

There is always a woman at a potluck party who conscientiously asks for the recipe of a dish that she liked so she can make it herself. These women are very good at cooking—unlike me, who is lazy with no cooking ability and who just looks forward to the chance to eat others' good food. People who cook these delicious dishes are very eager to do research about food, and most of all, they are diligent about cooking.

For whatever reason, I am kind of dumbfounded at how lazy I have always been. Of course, housework is a chore, but I have even come to hate doing other daily tiny things that I think are a nuisance, and I can't move swiftly.

I think that laziness and idleness, of course, affect our social relationships and affect our personality and character. When I said this, it was not to try and improve myself, but to simply put myself down.

When my friend heard this, however, she said, "It is too late to know yourself. But some people are annoyed by others' diligence, so I wouldn't worry about it."

She said this to try and encourage me in her own strange way. When I made a puzzled face, she continued,

There are women who can be diligent to the point of being a real nuisance. They think that just running around is the same thing as work. We have one of those at work. At the workplace she still acts like a housewife. Those people are annoying.

Other people agreed with her, all chiming in saying, "Yeah," and "That's right."

And one said, "For instance, these women disturb important conversations that others are having by jumping in and asking if anyone wants any of the coffee she has just brought." "And if we are working on a group project, this kind of woman works devotedly by herself without consulting with the others," added another.

Their opinions cannot justify my own laziness, of course, but it was a bit of a shock for me to hear these words and made me reconsider a woman's way of working with others. ⌒

*P*lease discriminate against women.
Jōsei sabetsu o shite-kudasai
女性差別 を し て く だ さ い

In 1989 several changes took place in the Japanese imperial family. Owada Masako (b. 1963) became engaged to Crown Prince Naruhito with a fanfare that rivaled that of Prince Charles and Lady Diana in the United Kingdom. Masako worked in the Japanese Ministry of Foreign Affairs, was a member of a career diplomat family, and was educated at Harvard University and the University of Tokyo. People expected that such a strong-willed and accomplished young woman might transform the imperial family. So far, not much has changed. That same year, the Japanese emperor—known in the West as Hirohito (1925–1989), but referred to as the Showa Emperor here—also died, raising many questions about Japanese war guilt and the role the imperial household played in the Second World War. Both these issues are still quite controversial and are the subject of Itoh's essay. For more discussion on the role of the emperor in Japanese society, see "The winter chrysanthemum is not pleasant" in chapter 14.

Around the time when Masako's impending marriage with the crown prince was reported all over the world, and the Japanese mass media was going crazy, someone wrote the following comment in a newspaper column: "Becoming a member of the royal family is like saying 'Please discriminate against women.'"

Around this same time in 1989 the Showa Emperor also passed away. The country went into a national self-imposed mourning period of self-restraint and self-sacrifice. In such a social climate, I thought it was healthy that a newspaper journalist could still be critical of the imperial family by writing remarks like that.

However, what happened later? Where did such insightful criticisms go? Soon after, when we heard stories in the mass media, all they talked about was

Masako's clothes and it appeared as though each was trying to outdo the other in finding a silly topic to report about.

I was so amazed at this stupidity. I read somewhere, "Masako is going to use her experiences as a foreign diplomat for the benefit of the royal family in their international social relations." But I heard little real criticism, and no one raised questions or warnings about social manipulation by the media.

Feminists who had been actively campaigning against gender discrimination were happy about Masako becoming the crown princess and compared Masako to the American president's wife: "Now a real career woman has become the 'first lady' and member of the royal family. This is a great, epoch-making, heroic event." Or, "With this action, career women are now becoming publicly accepted."

Everybody knows, even without thinking about it, that the imperial throne is passed on patrilineally only to male heirs. In that sense, the emperor system is predicated upon gender discrimination. But society and the public make a virtue of this obvious discriminatory practice and accept it in the name of tradition. The royal family, then, is the "symbol" of gender discrimination. How could people not focus on this issue when they talk about gender discrimination?

However, that said, I am worried about feminists who praise career women in this way. They might say, "Someday even a woman can become emperor," but I think basic rights are more important than symbolism. I think that by saying things like that, they are missing the real measure of gender discrimination that exists in society, and this worries me. ✎

It's become a case of "the weak fish eat the weaker fish," hasn't it?
Soredewa jakuniku jakushoku janai-no
それでは弱肉弱食じゃないの

The title of this essay contains a pun based on a famous Japanese proverb: 弱肉強食 (*jaku-niku kyō-shoku*, literally, "The big fish eat up the small fish"). What this means is that in life, the strong prey upon the weak. The quote inside the title changes one character in the third position that also puns with the first character—that is, 強 (*kyō*) becomes 弱 (*jaku*). This changes the phrase to 弱肉 弱食 (*jaku-niku jaku-shoku*, literally, "The weak fish eat the weaker fish"). The meaning of this humorous (at least in Japanese!) phrase is the point of the following piece.

We also should mention one last thing about gender references in this vignette. We know from an earlier essay ("Even though she is a healthy adult, only a wife gets categorized as a dependent" in chapter 3) that *"part-time* worker" here refers to females, because the English loanword *pāto taimu* is used. For more information on other English loanwords in Japanese see "They can't stand each other unless they change their surroundings from time to time" in chapter 5, "This is a town that keeps the worst of the country and has lost the best of the country" in chapter 11, and "I wonder when a home became a thing that can be bought and sold" in chapter 12.

There is a woman I know who finished a postgraduate program but has not yet been able to get a permanent job. She gives lectures and workshops to housewives at community centers and women's centers.

She once said to me, "I am rather critical of the activities of the Such-and-such Section of the So-and-so Women's Association, but since they pay well, I agreed to give a lecture there." When she saw my surprised face, she explained, "When we are asked to lecture we have to do it. Otherwise we cannot eat; we can't be choosy." She also talked about another person in a similar situation as herself, a Ms. X. She told me, "Ms. X said to me that 'K-city is my territory so please do not go there.'"

Right after I heard such a distasteful thing, I myself received a phone call from a community center from a nearby prefecture inviting me to give a workshop there. I asked the person who called me up what the theme of the lecture was to be and why they were inviting me. The caller said, "I was just asked to call you, and I really do not know the details, but someone gave me your book."

However, after talking to her and asking for more information, I found that they had not read my book at all. They just saw my name on the cover. In other words, anybody would have been fine for them.

Unfortunately, these kinds of things are not unusual. It looks like women who are seeking their own position in society are hired by administrators for the convenience of the executives; and later, in turn, these women also use other women.

When I talked about the experience of my acquaintance—that part-time lecturer—to some of the active female members of my community center, they were outraged. One of them said, "We are all women, but she is looking down on housewives from the start." Another said, "I cannot excuse the kind of woman who acts like that. Does she think that she is different from these housewives and even the other part-time instructors?" Someone deplored, "It's now become that 'the weak fish eat the weaker fish,' hasn't it?"

I wonder if this is only an issue we find at the individual level? I think women do not realize that they are all tethered together by the same yoke. I think we should direct our anger at the social system instead of each other. ✎

2

HOW TO DEAL WITH . . .

· 5 ·

Families, Parents,
and Parents-in-Law

I always feel "Thank god we have TV" during mealtime.
Gohan no toki, itsumo "Terebi ga ate yokatta" to omō
ごはんのとき、いつも「テレビがあってよかった」と思う

Here Itoh addresses a complaint that is becoming more and more common in the Japanese media these days: housewives who hate to have their newly retired husbands lying around the house all day. Because the "salaryman" has devoted most of his time and energy to the company, and the wife to the children and homemaking, they often find themselves thrown together for long periods of time with little in common after the children have left home. But she also talks about the importance of the Japanese family meal and sharing food with another person (even if they need a television set to make it happen).

I have heard that the meaning of the Latin word *convivo* is "eat together" as well as "live together." In an essay actually called "Convivo" by Kawazu Chiyo, she says,

> [After I lost my husband and started living by myself] I did not feel I ate well. While my husband was around I was—surprisingly, I think—a very good cook. But after he passed away, I hardly cooked at all. I would go for days on end just eating rice topped with a little flavoring, like sesame and salt. I felt this way not just about my diet, but for everything in my daily life. Still now this feeling of depression has not left me. (*Kagetsūshin*, 1984, 3)

Moreover, reading this, one thing stuck out in my mind: she said that when she lost her special "someone" she also lost the special "someone whom she ate together with."

However, the other day I also found a woman who said just the opposite. She said that when she is eating a meal with her husband, she feels she is suffocating and doesn't know what to talk about. "Thank god we have TV," she admits.

Now that her husband has retired and is hanging around the house all day, she has come to despise his presence, which fills her life with a heavy cloud of gloom. They do not have anything in common to talk about, but at the same time she feels uncomfortable with their table being silent when they eat. Their relationship is held together—just barely—by television.

When I told this to one of my single friends who is about the same age as this woman, she was deeply moved and said, "Once I felt so empty about eating alone that I started thinking about getting married. But I never thought about what she said, that eating together could be a burden rather than a blessing."

Eating together every day seems just to be one of life's ordinary pleasures, but I guess this simple pleasure is one of the hardest things to obtain. ∾

I am nice (*yasashii*) to elderly people whom I don't know . . .
Yoso no o-toshiyori niwa yasashiku dekiru-noni
よそのお年寄りにはやさしくできるのに

As we have seen, one of the most sensitive of relationships in Japanese society is between daughters-in-law and parents-in-law. While these are often fragile in many places in the world, because of patrilineality—that is, tracing inheritance and family membership through male relatives—and patrilocality—living with the male relatives—the Japanese case can be especially tense. Typically, in historical times the eldest son would eventually inherit the land and house from his parents, and the new bride would come and live with him immediately after marriage. She would someday become the mistress of the home. However, this would not happen until after the son's parents died. Until then, she was often little more than a glorified servant in the eyes of her husband's mother, who invariably found fault and foibles on a daily basis. Yet, in spite of this, she would be expected to loyally take care of her mother-in-law once she became old and feeble. Japanese literature and film are rife with tales centering around mother-in-law/daughter-in-law conflict.

Though things have changed greatly since World War II, these practices and expectations are still not uncommon in modern Japan, and Itoh shows us in the following essay. While individual cases may vary, generally a Japanese woman marries *into* her husband's family and *leaves* her own. Upon her death, she will lie with her husband's relatives in the family gravesite. She is expected to view her husband's relatives as her new family. This naturally can cause mixed feelings in the daughter-in-law's heart.

The Japanese word *yasashii* is really very hard to translate, as is the case with many common and everyday words in Japanese. We have translated it here as "nice" or "kind." For more about this word see "Kindness just because you're a woman is a real pain" in chapter 7.

A young housewife who lives with her husband's extended family said, "Although I am nice [*yasashii*] to elderly people whom I don't know, I'm not nice to my parents-in-law who live with me. This part of myself scares me."

I also heard this from a woman who works in a nursing home:

> People often ask me how can I look after elderly strangers. However, since they are total strangers, I probably can be more open-minded looking after them. I do not know their pasts so I can accept them as they are, right at this moment, without any reservation or feeling of hesitation.

However, there are people who feel miserable about not being able to look after their own parents. One woman I know said her own parents are much older than her parents-in-law. She lives far away with her in-laws, and when she goes back to visit her parents, she is not able to look after her parents-in-law. After she got married, she sensed an invisible conservative chain binding her to her parents-in-law as she now was a member of her husband's family. She feels an obligation to look after her parents-in-law exclusively and even feels guilty even wanting to go and visit her own parents.

Her biggest complaint is that she cannot get any support from her husband when she wants to make up some excuse to go to see her parents. She said many times, "I cannot do anything for my *own* parents. That is very painful."

However, when I told this story to a friend of mine, she told me about her mother who lives back in her hometown rather far away. The mother always says to her daughter, "When you are nice to the elderly people who are around you, you do not need to come all the way back home just to look after me. Someday, someone who is around me will repay that kindness and do the same thing for me."

I was touched by her mother's warm words. Then I thought, "I wonder if this is what social welfare is supposed to be all about?" ❧

*B*ecause I don't need to do anything while I am walking, I love it.
Aruiteiru aida wa nanimo shinakute īkara suki
歩いている間は何もしなくていいから好き

In this poignant vignette Itoh talks about ways of coping—whether with the loss of a husband, or being forced to live with one. Perhaps, she asks, "killing time" is not necessarily a "waste" of time.

Walking is often said to be good for the health, and it prolongs our youth. There are many people whom I know around me who walk for their health. However, I usually ride a bicycle because I am a little lazy, even to places that are close by or I don't need to get to in a hurry. Thus, I really respect those people who have the discipline to walk religiously.

One day an elderly woman and I were talking. She liked to walk ever since she was young, and she told me the reason: "I like to walk because while I am walking, I don't have to do anything else." I was very surprised by these words.

She had lost her husband during the Second World War while she was still young and had to raise her four children all by herself. Thus, she had to work day and night, but it still wasn't enough. She had to work even more. She said with a bitter smile, "In those days, I wouldn't even go to the bathroom before I went to sleep, so I wouldn't oversleep." That's how hard she worked in those days.

These days "walking" and "power walks" are all the rage in women's fashion magazines. Regular walking is thought to be an indication of self-discipline. Thus, when I heard this elderly woman's comment, "I like to walk because while I am walking, I don't have to do anything else," I was quite shocked.

But then the words of another woman came floating over my memory like smoke across the air. She is a housewife whose children are now gone, and she did not know how to kill time since she and her husband don't seem to communicate well.

"I do difficult embroidering, with as complicated a stitching as possible. While I am embroidering I am satisfied that I am doing something, and since I am focusing on it I do not need to think about anything else." ∾

My children are my life, but my work is my life's purpose.
Kodomo wa inochi, shigoto wa ikigai
子どもはいのち、仕事は生き甲斐

In this essay Itoh tackles a question that American working women also continuously face: what is the happy balance between career and family. Does—or should—the job come first? Or should raising children take priority over everything else? Is it even possible for a mother to work and raise a child properly? But will a woman with career ambitions eventually feel stifled if she cannot pursue an occupation outside the home? Itoh suggests here that a career outside the home can make a woman a better mother inside the home.

The above words were said to the media by a musical star who wanted to make a full-time return to the stage after her divorce.

I am certain that she has been receiving lots of questions from people about why she chose her career over having a happy life as a homemaker. These kind of "hand-grenade" questions are asked not only to stars like her. Even if an average woman who has children—and who is not divorced—wants to keep working outside the home, everyone always says that she is choosing work over their children. But that is just not true. Both are important for us. Many women are bothered when no one understands this. I think for these women, hearing those words of that musical star was something they clearly wanted to say themselves.

I am not simply saying, "I have children, and I work, too," and that that is necessarily a good thing. However, I do not think it is right that society believes as if child care should be a woman's career. The issue is how we balance child care and our job in our daily life. When I look around me, is it a coincidence that the people who do best in their life find a balance between the rhythm of child care and work?

For example, I once knew a woman who said, "If I were not working, I would have become a women who lives only around children." Another said, "If I did not have children, I would become a slave to the company, just like a man." Still another reported, "Because I have children, I have discovered the value of work in my life."

From these voices, I think that "work" saves women from the danger of being only devoted to child care, and "children" allow us to find a way of living as true human beings. ✎

*I*t would have been better if I had liked my mother-in-law.
"Shūtome" o suki-dattara yokattan desu keredo
「姑」を好きだったらよかったんですけれど

As we just saw in the third essay before this ("I am nice [*yasashii*] to elderly people whom I don't know . . ."), daughters-in-law and mothers-in-law in Japan can have quite contentious relationships. As we see in this piece, this fosters no small amount of cynicism when everyone tries to put on the best public front (in spite of private feelings to the contrary). The Japanese word *ie* literally means "house" but also refers to the patrilineal family and its main branch. For more on the *ie* and the traditional Japanese family see "The woman who lies here by herself prays for peace" in chapter 11.

Our local community newspaper reported on a housewife and her mother-in-law who worked at the same shop. The story said, "These two have a great relationship, just like a real mother and daughter."

One of my friends who read this column said, "Why does everyone try to pretend that they are a real mother and daughter?" "I don't think these are just old-fashioned banal platitudes. I feel that they are remnants of the traditional family [*ie*] system," suggested another. Another criticized the article: "In the narrow world of the countryside, this type of story is fostered by the local administration as the ideal model of the family; I think it can be governmental pressure. We have to pretend we have good familial relationships to get societal approval."

While I was listening to the critical comments in this conversation, I recalled the lament of a housewife I once knew. She had a reputation as being a good person, and everyone said how wonderful she was because she looked after her husband's mother. Even after her mother-in-law became bedridden she had continued to look after her mother-in-law very well. People often said that even a biological daughter might not have looked after a mother like this.

After her mother-in-law passed away, she said, "It would have been better if I had liked my mother-in-law. I kept thinking, I wish I could have liked her."

I think what she meant was that had she liked her mother-in-law better, she could have done a better job taking care of her. She would not have had to push herself if she had liked her more . . . looking after her mother-in-law would not have been such a chore. These are the thoughts she kept having while she was looking after her mother-in-law, so she kept saying, "It would have been better if I had liked my mother-in-law."

When I heard these words I thought, "How sweet, how sincere, but how distressed." However, now when I think about it, her words were not telling me that she tried hard to "like" her mother-in-law but say clearly that she "couldn't like" her mother-in-law no matter what she did. She was focusing on the idea that she was not able to like her instead of the fact that she made no effort to like her. The moan in her words could be the result of the pain that people feel when they have to live with those they dislike but are under social pressure to act like they like each other and give the appearance of being a good family. ❧

$\mathcal{S}$ince I am the eldest daughter, my father is not immunized yet . . .
Watashi wa chōjo dakara o-tō-san wa men'eki ga nain-desu-yo
私は長女だからお父さんは免疫がないんですよ

Here Itoh is talking about the road to adulthood in Japanese society. Generally, young people—both males and females—are not thought to be full adults (*shakai-jin*, literally, a "public/social person") until they get married. Until this time, young people—especially women—will likely live at home (unless they are at a school dormitory), even if they are working full-time. What the father is "not immunized against" (*men'eki ga nai*) yet is his grown daughter's increasing independence.

Ms. A got a job right after graduating from college. I could see from each word she said that she had been raised by her father, who protected her while she grew up. However, I was surprised to hear what happened each time she did not come straight home from school and got in a little late.

Her father would ask her to come into the den and say, "Excuse me, but I'd like to talk with you a moment, please. Where did you go? Who were you with? What were you doing?" According to her, although her father never got angry and did not scold her, he wanted to know every little thing about what she was doing.

Even though she is an adult now, he still treats her the same way he did when she was in college. When she comes back home after a few obligatory drinks with her friends at work, he says, "Excuse me, could you come into the den for just a minute?"

Because I thought young women were living a much more free lifestyle these days I had not expected to hear something like this. I felt it curious that she was not annoyed by her father's attitude toward her. So I asked, "Why don't you just tell your father, 'Please do not ask me such questions'?"

She then said, "Well, because I am the eldest daughter, my father is not immunized yet . . ." I burst into laughter with her way of saying this, like she was building up her father's immune system step by step.

However while I was laughing so hard, I became confused. I didn't know if she was not mature enough to come out from under her father's protective umbrella, or if she was a much more mature adult than her father, since she was trying to get her father gradually used to the idea that she was growing up. ❧

$\mathcal{T}$hey can't stand each other unless they change their surroundings from time to time.

Fūkei ga kawara-nai to, motanaku natteiru-noyo
風景が変わらないと、もたなくなっているのよ

What is the secret to a healthy, long-lasting relationship? The question is no doubt universal. One solution is a getaway. In Japan, there are now "full-moon" trips for older married couples—comparable to honeymoon trips for newlyweds—which have become quite popular, as Itoh's friend explains. Again, as is often the case in Japan today, an English "made-in-Japan" loanword is used to label this. For more on English in Japan see "Even though she is a healthy adult, only a wife gets categorized as a dependent" in chapter 3, "It's become a case of 'the weak fish eat the weaker fish,' hasn't it?" in chapter 4, "This is a town that keeps the worst of the country and has lost the best of the country" in chapter 11, and "I wonder when a home became a thing that can be bought and sold" in chapter 12.

I met my childhood friend a while back after not seeing her for a long time. Her parents and I were very close when I was a child, so naturally I asked right away, "How are your parents doing?" She said, "Oh, they're fine. These days they travel quite often. I heard the other day they were going somewhere on the *Queen Elizabeth II*."

Wow, I thought, an old couple who can enjoy a luxurious cruise trip. What an ideal life in the twilight years!

I said softly, "It's wonderful, isn't it, that after all these years they are still the same and have such a good relationship." But she answered coolly without any hesitation, "Not really. They can't stand each other unless they change their surroundings from time to time." When I heard these harsh words, I tried to understand them as the remarks of a bitter daughter. But her words stuck in my mind and they wouldn't go away.

When I was talking about this later with my friends, all the middle-aged women understood what she was talking about.

One said, "Older couples who tend to travel a lot do so not because they have lots of money or free time; they do so because they need to change their physical environment. Travel agencies understand this and are making many 'full-moon' tours for these kinds of couples."

Another woman said as if to try and heal a wound that was deep in her heart, "It could be that in order not to look directly at each other in their twilight years, they have to stand side by side and look at something else. That is, they stand shoulder to shoulder rather than facing each other."

Since I did not want acknowledge this bitter reality directly, I said with some hesitation, "Isn't that saying a bit much?" One sharp, mature lady kindly said, "Yes, it is not nice to say that they always have to be in a new place in order to stay together. Maybe we should say instead that these elderly people have become pretty smart and have developed a strategy to keep up the good relationship that they built up over the course of their marriage."

Ah, a strategy to maintain a good relationship, huh? Although at that moment I felt kind of a relief, these words still stick in my mind and have never left me. ∾

· 6 ·

Life and Society

We should only have surface-level associations with others.
Dare tomo asaku tsukiau koto-desu
だれとも浅くつきあうことです

In this essay Itoh claims that it seems nowadays that people only want casual relationships instead of deep friendships. This is reflected by the conventional topics of everyday conversations she sees all around her. Japanese housewives, especially, want to avoid not only confrontation but also forming too-close relationships with others. People should not delve too deeply into others' affairs. To Itoh, such attitudes are the norm, the default style of discourse chosen by many. While she is sympathetic with those who feel the necessity of having only casual relationships, she also wonders if society as a whole even is aware of this phenomenon.

On a TV show about life in a nursing home a while back, a female resident said that in order to get along in a nursing home, a person "should only associate with people on a surface level."

I could not stand to hear this. However, when I think about it, she is not the only person who has this kind of attitude toward life. I think the majority of housewives have these kinds of relationships with others. They choose harmless topics of conversation. Even when the other person says something they disagree with, they just say, "Uh huh," or "Yeah, that's right." It is said that having relationships where we don't delve too deeply into each other's business is just common sense and is the best way to run our lives.

I feel sympathetic for people who feel that they have to behave this way, following this kind of "guideline for living" even though they may not like doing so. But increasing numbers of people seem to be perfectly comfortable having these kinds of relationships and do not even question them.

Before, many people used to say, "I want to have friends with whom I can talk sincerely, just like the friends I had back in my student days." But this generation seems to think that the casual relationships that they have had since childhood are actually very deep. They think they have intimate friendships even if all they ever do together is just go shopping or eat out.

These days I think the idea of friendship is becoming less serious. I cannot stand the opinion of that elderly woman who said, "We should only associate with people on a surface level." But I wonder if society is aware of how shallow it is becoming? If this is true, then things are worse than I thought. ✎

*B*eing the perpetrator is very hard.
Kagaisha-tte tsurai-ne
加害者ってつらいね

In this piece, Itoh asks us who suffers more—the victim or the perpetrator? She proposes an answer via a poem by Yosano Akiko (1878–1942), a famous pre–World War II tanka poet and feminist. She was noted for her sensual, and sometimes erotic, verse describing the passions of young womanhood. Though her poetry often shocked traditionalists, she and other writers of the early twentieth century revitalized the classical tanka form. For other discussions of Yosano Akiko see "Far away, far away, cherry blossoms are falling" in chapter 14. For more on tanka see "Far away, far away, cherry blossoms are falling" in chapter 14 and "Please don't tie me down" in chapter 9.

Itoh also refers to some comments Takenishi Hiroko (b. 1929) made about this poem in her book *Ai suru to iu kotoba* (The Words Called "To Love," Tokyo: Shinchosha, 1980). Takenishi, a survivor of the Hiroshima atomic bomb, is a noted novelist and literary critic. Much of her creative writing is based on her wartime experiences.

If a person is a victim, they can cry out about the injustice done to them and pity themselves for their poor misfortune. However, the perpetrator has to just patiently stand there and feel the guilt for the crime that he or she did.

I heard a woman who lost her child due to her own carelessness say, "Being the perpetrator is very hard, isn't it?" The woman who said this did so rather lightly, but I could tell from her eyes she was truly sad. She used the word *perpetrator* as if she was trying to punish herself.

I like many of Yosano Akiko's poems. My favorite poem changes depending on my age. My current favorite is

いさり火は	Isaribi wa
身も世も無気に	mi mo yo mo muki ni
瞬きぬ	matatakinu
陸は海より	riku wa umi yori
悲しきものを	kanashiki mono o

"Because the fishing fire does not flicker and has no influence from anyone, the land is much more sad than the ocean."

The novelist Takenishi Hiroko had this to say about this poem in her book *The Words Called "To Love"*:

You must stand with your own two feet on the ground, and even though you want to cry, but cannot utter a sound, you must live for tomorrow. This poem captures this feeling of sadness and grief very rhythmically, but it is presented from the third-person point of view. I think poetry is a marvelous invention. I also think the beauty of a person who lives through words is seen through this poem.

The first time I read Takenishi's book I was immediately struck by the phrase, "The beauty of a person who lives through words is seen through this poem."

When I saw my friend who is suffering and punishing herself—calling herself a "perpetrator"—these words by Takenishi crossed my mind: "You must stand with your own two feet on the ground, and even though you want to cry, but cannot utter a sound, you must live for tomorrow."

"You must live for tomorrow." This grief must be the human condition. ∾

*B*ecause I cannot see the faces of my audience . . .
Minna no kao ga mien-kara
みんなの顔が見えんから

Effective communication is thought to be important in almost all walks of life. But just what does it take to be an effective communicator? In this piece on Yamashiro Tomoe (1912–2004), Itoh shows us that truly effective public communication is not necessarily based upon being glib or smooth, but something more modest.

Yamashiro Tomoe was a novelist noted for her writings on rural farm women and socialist causes. She and her husband, both Communist sympathizers, spent World War II in prison for alleged subversive and antipatriotic activities. These experiences radicalized her and affected her later writings. For more on Yamashiro Tomoe, and her comments on criticism, see "I don't have the word *criticism* in my vocabulary" in chapter 3.

The reader should be reminded that Japanese people often use titles instead of names as terms of reference and terms of address. The title *sensei* literally means "teacher" but can be used for anyone accorded a certain amount of respect, such as doctors, lawyers, politicians, professors, maestros, accomplished artists, etc. Now, even most non-Japanese already know that the honorific suffix -*san* is attached to names as a sign of respect in most utterances (e.g., Kimura-*san*, or Ms. Kimura). But other titles like *sensei* can be used in similar ways (e.g., Kimura-*sensei*, or Prof. Kimura). In this essay Itoh is referring to her guest speaker as Yamashiro-*sensei*, indicating how she holds her in high regard as an elder spokesperson for civil rights and as a social activist, but because she does not have an academic position we used the neutral *Ms.* Yamashiro here so as not to confuse Western readers. For more about the common suffix –*san*, see "We should not use titles on the rooms of nursing homes" in chapter 11.

I was so happy that the story "Chiyo's Adolescence" by the novelist Yamashiro Tomoe was serialized in the journal *Haha no tomo* (Mother's Friend) in 1989. Because of my work at the community center, I have been influenced by Ms. Yamashiro in numerous ways. Many of the phrases in her works have become part of my life's philosophy and goals. These include aphorisms like

"Even in our everyday lives we have to think of human rights."
"We have to combine sensation and philosophy."
"We have to practice a pragmatics based on theory."
"We have to go to the future with the wisdom gained from the past."
"Criticisms should always be something supplemental. They should not be the main point."

We asked Ms. Yamashiro to give a talk at our community center. It was good to see her again after such a long time. Her talk was titled "On Everyday Human Rights."

If I remember correctly, Ms. Yamashiro must have been at least seventy-six years old at that time. She was not healthy. Thus, I said to her, "Please remain seated if you would like while you talk." However, she replied with a girlish face, "If I sat, I wouldn't be able to see the faces of the audience." She kept standing for two and a half hours, and she paid attention to every single person in the audience while she was speaking. Her talk was very impressive and I was touched by her attitude.

Among the people who are called *sensei* there are many who do not pay any attention to what the audience wants, or if its members are understanding, and they just give their own speech regardless of what the audience is feeling. I call these kind of speakers the overconfident or "sprinkler" types, spraying their information over the audience. There are quite a few of them. They can be very interesting, and their style of presentation can sound quite polished in the lecture hall. But their words do not stay in our minds. A speaker has to communicate with the listener before a talk can finally become complete and make a lasting impression. Ms. Yamashiro was such a speaker; her sense and attitude were very precious. ❧

*W*e can't conduct a conversation equally when we only use women's language.

Onna kotoba dewa taitō ni hanase-nai
女言葉では対等に話せない

In this essay, Itoh clearly argues that the Japanese language is hardly egalitarian. In any conversation, two people may use different words, honorifics, and grammatical forms reflecting differences in age, gender, or social position. Phrasing requests in Japanese, for example, can be very complicated, as the language marks levels of hierarchy and politeness in many subtle ways. Certainly Japanese men *can* use polite forms when making requests, and many do when speaking to their male social or occupational superiors. However, the *degree* of politeness, and the frequency and expectation of the use of polite forms, is far greater among women than men. In general, women use more polite forms when speaking to men than men use in reply (or in speaking with other men). This is Itoh's main point.

Itoh discusses the language used by some women wanting to present a petition to the emperor. The petition is on a very sensitive topic in Japan and elsewhere these days: the treatment of "comfort women"—Korean and poor rural Japanese women who were enlisted (or more often, coerced) into working in the sex trade for the Japanese military during World War II.

When native Japanese speakers read these demands, they sound very harsh and unfeminine. The reason why the three demands sound so strong in Japanese is because of the imperative grammatical ending *-shiro* (literally, "DO!") found at the end of every sentence. Such forms rarely appear in writing and are only used in speech by men. To see such forms not only uttered by but also written by women made a very deep impression on Itoh, motivating her to write this essay.

For more on "comfort women" see "That woman is like an obstinate, grumpy old man" in chapter 3, "This is a town that keeps the worst of the country and has lost the best of the country" in chapter 11, and "The most important thing about being a human being is to learn about the world by ourselves" and "I think it is so good that I am not a Japanese" in chapter 13.

A Japanese friend of mine who is married to a Swede said to me the other day with a smile, "When I argue with my husband, especially when we really quarrel, I use Swedish instead of Japanese." According to her, this is because we cannot conduct a conversation equally in Japanese when we only use women's language.

This is true. To articulate one's own opinion clearly and equally in Japanese using women's style of speech is very difficult. For example, in Japanese the way a woman must word a request is by using the terms *shite kudasai* (literally, "could you please do") or *yamete* (literally, "please don't do"). These are then no longer requests but become begging for *o-negai* (favors).

However, I think this problem is not just a matter of grammar or terminology. Japanese society has never encouraged the notion that people can associate equally without falling into hierarchical levels based on differences in gender and social status. The social environment is reflected in the style of speech, using such particular phrases.

The other day I was reading something translated into Japanese that really brought this home. Last May just before the president of South Korea visited Japan, various Korean women's associations, including representatives from Ewha Woman's University, submitted an official declaration to the South Korean president to present to the Japanese government. Its tone and articulate style, representing their determined and dauntless attitude, made a big impression on me. Here are some passages from the section "Our Requests." The person who translated it from Korean into Japanese is a Korean woman in her forties:

> To the emperor: We demand that you officially apologize in public and in writing for Japan's criminal actions during World War II.
>
> To the Japanese government: We demand that you stop denying the existence of Korean "Comfort Women" sent overseas for the pleasure of Japanese soldiers.
>
> To the people of Japan: For those of you with a conscience, we implore you to take the initiative and force your nation to investigate the criminal actions of your country during the Second World War.

一、日王（天皇）は、日本がしでかした犯罪行為に対して公式に
謝罪し、文書化しろ。

Hitotsu, Nichiō (tennō) wa, nihon ga shidekashita hanzai ni taishite kōshiki ni shazai-shi, bunshoka-shiro.

一、日本政府は挺身隊「従軍慰安婦」に対する卑劣な隠蔽を中
断しろ。

Hitotsu, Nihon-seifu wa teishintai ("jūgun-ianfu") ni taisuru hiretsu na impei o chūdan-shiro.

一、日本の良心的な勢力は、日本がしでかした犯罪行為の解決
に先頭にたって努力しろ。

Hitotsu, Nihon no ryōshin-teki na seiryoku wa, nihon ga shidekashita hanzai-kōi no kaiketsu ni sentō ni tatte doryoku-shiro. ✎

I am a kind person on the outside who really just disposes of people.
Yasashi-sōni misuteru
やさしそうに見捨てる

Once again Itoh returns to one of her favorite topics: how the handling of individual human relationships reflects greater social concerns. As a case in point she speaks of how to care for elderly patients in hospitals or clients in nursing homes. Some caretakers say that it is easier for the staff, and better for the patient, to simply accommodate them in any way possible. Others say that it is better to try and get the patients to make lifestyle changes and realize that they may not be able to control their lives in ways they had done in their earlier years. But the question of who knows best—the "insider" individual or the "outsider" institution—is not an easy one to answer.

A friend of mine who is a nurse at a hospital where many elderly people stay long term told me some of her thoughts.

She said that patients bring to the hospital many of the same habits they previously followed in their everyday lives. For instance, when an elderly gentleman coughed before he went into the hospital, his wife or sons' wives would bring him tea. These elderly male patients think such a way of life is normal and expect nurses to do the same things. And elderly women who have obediently depended on their husbands—while at the same time blaming all their problems on them—act like they don't know what to do about even their own health.

When nurses who look after elderly people talk among themselves, they always end up arguing about what is the best way to care for them. Some say,

"It is too much to ask for them to change their attitude at this stage in their lives." These nurses, then, try to fulfill their patients' expectations as much as possible. Other nurses say it is better to try to get them to foster a healthy attitude while taking care of illnesses and infirmities of old age.

In other words, the issue is whether nurses should accept their patients for who they are or support their patients by getting them to foster better human relationships. That is, from a nursing point of view the problem is how best to respect a person's lifestyle.

My friend said to herself,

> If I just accede to my patients' whims without reflection, am I a kind person on the outside who really just disposes of people? That is, do I make my job easier by just giving them what they want? However, I also don't want to be too pushy and just impose my point of view on them.

While I was listening to her talk and considering her opinions, I was thinking that this is actually a huge social issue—not just an issue for nurses or the elderly, but for all human relationships every day. ∾

I cry because there is nothing I can do.
Dō suru koto mo deki-nai kara nakunja nai ka
どうすることもできないから泣くんじゃないか

In English we say "boys don't cry," and nor do "big girls" if the old 1960s rock group the Four Seasons is to be believed. In this piece Itoh asks us to consider the role sensitivity plays in our daily lives and wonders if we can be *too* sensitive?

There is a vast literature in psychology, cognitive science, and anthropology about the cross-cultural universality of emotions—or the lack thereof. There are probably at least several thousand papers and books comparing *just* Japanese and American emotional behavior. Needless to say, we can give no definitive verdict here. But—speaking in very broad and dangerous strokes—Japanese probably tend to be less emotional, especially in public, than Americans (though they are hardly as inscrutable as American stereotypes portray them). Thus, Itoh's husband was probably a little baffled at her tears, as described in this vignette.

The children's book Itoh refers to in the beginning of the essay, *Non-chan kumo ni noru* (Non-chan Climbs upon a Cloud), was written by Ishii Momoko (b. 1907), a noted author of children's stories, and was published by Fukuinkan-shoten in 1967 in Tokyo. There is no English translation, but one of her books is available in English, *The Tongue-Cut*

Sparrow (published in 1987 in New York by Lodestar and translated by Katherine Paterson).

Once an influential person in our community center had to move far away. The day I heard about her moving away, this shocking news made me cry. Because I was crying so much my husband was amazed, and he probably did not know what to do. He tried to comfort me saying, "You really can't change things even if you cry."

However, when I heard these words, I felt as if I had been struck by lightning. I thought to myself, "What are you talking about? Because there is nothing I can do, I do not know what else to do *except* cry!"

The words "I cry because there is nothing I can do" are spoken by the main character—the elementary-school girl Non-chan—in the famous children's book *Non-chan kumo ni noru*.

Adult logic or common sense might be to think that even if we cry it would not help, so why should we cry over things we can do nothing about? But while I was crying I thought that Non-chan was really right, and I kept on shedding tears.

Even now I have a soft spot for the words of Non-chan. However, at the same time, another side of me thinks that I cry too much, and I am ashamed of myself for crying so easily. I cry over small things. I sometimes beat myself up because even though I realize this, my mind and my emotions do not always come together.

A forty-year-old friend of mine who like movies once related to me the following thoughts: these days, she says, little girls and young girls cry so easily. When I was their age, she said,

> I especially told myself with pride, "I am not going to cry over something so small." I get surprised these days over these young girls. They cry over a scene where there is nothing to cry about. I am surprised, she said, and worry a little about the future.

I heard her words as if she were talking directly to me. This made me reconsider the value of being sensitive, and at the same time made me realize that we also have to cultivate a sensitivity to different kinds of emotions. ❧

3

THINKING ABOUT . . .

• 7 •

Women's Social Roles and Our Behavior in Men's Society

*K*indness just because you're a woman is a real pain!
Yakuwari de suru yasashisa-tte, tsumaranai
役割でするやさしさって、つまらない

This title is terrifically difficult to translate. As we saw in "I am nice [*yasashii*] to elderly people whom I don't know . . . ," the Japanese word *yasashii* is ambiguous, and it is this word (in its noun form *yasashisa*) that forms the basis of the above title. Depending on the context, *yasashii* is variously glossed as "kind," "sweet," "gentle," "tender," "graceful," "soft," "meek," "mild," "delicate," or "affectionate," though probably none of these captures the whole range of connotation the word has. We have translated it here as "kind" or "gentle" or "sweet" or "considerate" depending on the sentence. As we will see in this piece, when men are *yasashii* it often means something different from when women are *yasashii*. For more about this term see "I am nice [*yasashii*] to elderly people whom I don't know . . ." in chapter 5.

Tanikawa Shuntarō (b. 1931) is one of Japan's most well-known contemporary poets. The son of a philosopher, his work often seems to have an underlying metaphysical edge. Considered to be one of the "New Age" poets who rejected the existential angst of poets of the 1940s, he has also written essays, children's books, and scripts for radio and documentary films. He is a prolific translator (whose translations include the American *Peanuts* comic strip). His book *"N" made aruku* (Walking until Omega) was published by Sōshi-sha in Tokyo in 1985.

At the community center, a woman recently told us the following story of a great discovery she made:

103

When my husband and I were quarreling the other day he said to me, "Although you are a woman you are really not very *yasashii* [gentle]." I see now what he meant. Although I didn't really feel like being *yasashii* [sweet] to him, I felt that being a woman, it was my obligation to be *yasashii*, regardless of how I actually felt. Though I didn't get it at first myself, I now understand what he meant.

Hearing her words, some of the other women said that their being *yasashii* (kind or sweet) just because it is expected of them is not fulfilling. For us to be *yasashii* (sweet or gentle) is meaningless if it only comes from a gender stereotype. We all agreed that we didn't like be defined as *yasashii* just because we are women.

The poet Tanikawa Shuntarō wrote in his book *Walking until Omega*:

I do not think there is any difference between *yasashii* for women and *yasashii* for men. There is only one *yasashii* and it is not male or female. *Yasashii* as a feeling represents a person's actions. In other words, sweetness does not have femininity or masculinity, but always humanity.

I want to be a considerate [*yasashii*] person. Although it is a little late in my life, I really think this is the kind of person I want to be. I want to be a person who can be sweet, kind, and considerate to people from deep within my heart. This is the kind of person who would make a rich and fulfilling partner.

Therefore, I respect those women I was talking to who resisted being stereotyped and who could see if their actions came from gender obligations or not. They recognized that they would not feel fulfilled if they did something only because of their social role. If in our hearts we, ourselves, do not know the difference between "have to" and "want to," how could we really be a "*yasashii*" person? ❧

*W*e can't stand by and let women's sincere good intentions be exploited anymore.
Onna no kimajime o riyō sarete tamaru mono-ka
女の生真面目を利用されてたまるものか

In this piece Itoh addresses some of the issues of early Japanese feminism. But as we will see, one has to be very careful whom one follows lest one end up at a place not intended.

The two women whom Itoh speaks of in the beginning are extremely well known in Japan. Hiratsuka Raichō (1893–1971) was one of the earliest feminist activists in the country, and Ichikawa Fusae (1893–1981) was a women's activist and was one of the first women elected to the national Diet in 1953 when she was sixty years old. She and Hiratsuka often worked together. For more on Ichikawa Fusae see "The woman who lies here by herself prays for peace" in chapter 11.

The following incident happened a while back at a lecture series on women's history at our community center. The theme of the workshop was "Mothers and Women: Perspectives from Hiratsuka Raichō and Ichikawa Fusae."

These were two leading figures in the early days of the women's revolution in Japan and today are thought to be divine heroines of the feminist movement. Through these lectures—and walking in their paths—we were trying to learn how their feminism first developed and how they found the courage to act. We also wanted to study their faults and mistakes in an objective and detached manner.

When we started the workshop, many people were frequently surprised by the things they were learning. I heard, "I did not know such a thing" many times. We were also getting interested in the history of the topic.

Many said things like, "I always thought history was just the memorization of facts that happened in the past. I now believe that through history, we can see ourselves today." Others added, "At school I always studied just to get good grades, but now there are numerous things I want to research and to know just for my own curiosity."

While we were studying more and more, we began to focus in on one important question and lesson: "How did even these great people get caught up in the political and social system and, as a result, get taken in by the militarists during the war? We should learn this point firmly, and we should use our learning for our future, shouldn't we?"

One person said, "I really feel it was a pity that the goodwill of the Ichi'i City women—who during World War II served soldiers hot tea, thinking, 'This is the least we can do for the young men who are going off to fight'—was co-opted into national politics when the Ichi'i City Women's Association became part of the National Guard Women's Auxiliary."

Someone else replied, "These days the government administration is often encouraging us to take up volunteer activities, but—as we have just seen—we have to be careful about this." Another also said, "Yes, if we are not careful, and we get caught up in slogans like 'governmental revolution' or 'women's participation in society,' we will be the new National Guard Women's Auxiliary."

We all nodded in agreement, saying, we cannot be stereotypically feminine and gentle and stand by and let women's sincere good intentions—notions like "I also want to be useful"—be exploited anymore. ∾

*W*omen, please don't become a person who is "female on the outside but male on the inside."

"Sukāto o haita o-ji-san" ni naranai-de

「 ス カ ー ト を は い た お じ さ ん 」 に な ら な い で

The Japanese phrase for the words "female on the outside but male on the inside," which are actually used in the above title, is *sukāto o haita oji-san*—literally, "a guy that wears a skirt." Such a skirt-wearing guy is really a woman who actually believes, acts, and thinks like a man. The reasons why we find such women in society are the point of Itoh's following piece.

The television commercials that Itoh refers to later on in the article hawk numerous health drinks and energy boosters that Japanese workers are encouraged by advertisers to take to maintain their health and increase their productivity.

The freelance journalist Yanson Yumiko (b. 1943) often uses the expression "she is 'female on the outside but male on the inside.'" She uses these words to criticize women who accept the values of men's society and are slaves to trying to achieve things within the male-defined version of success.

Until not too long ago, society felt that women who actively worked outside the home were either unfeminine or women who "worked like crazy with their tangled, messy hair" [that is, women so devoted to their work that they didn't have time to take care of themselves]. However today, women who work are called career women and the image they present is fashionable. They can manage well both career and housework, and they are mild, gentle, and humble to others. Yet they are always gallant. People praise women who look womanly on the outside but inside can do the same work as men, or even better.

However, this image of a career woman (who is "outside-feminine, inside-talented") and the word *guy* (in the phrase "skirt-wearing guy") don't match together. This is because this notion of femininity that supposedly a career woman has is really nothing but the notion of femininity that is made by—and already exists in—male society.

The harder women work, and the more they polish their "femininity," the more they become "female on the outside but male on the inside." Actually, that's not true; it's more than that. These women have to endure and strive harder than the "guy," and I find that rather pitiful.

Recently, "female on the outside but male on the inside" kind of women often appear in TV commercials and the other media. They are portrayed as wives, mothers, and section chiefs at work. Thus, they have to always be pretty and neat and must have smiles on their faces. Therefore, they should buckle down and do it, even if they have to take a vitamin supplement to keep up their health. How cruel this is, I feel. This is much worse than the depictions of the plight of the male eager-beaver company employees.

Although women these days seem to be pleased by their brilliant abilities, in fact women are having a much harder time than they used to have. This is because they are now separated into two categories: capable or talented women versus regular, ordinary women.

Currently it is fashionable—and this is fanned by the media—to try and raise the social status of women. But I think it is dangerous to act if we do not consider the heavy burdens we place on women, and we don't know what their loads are. ✿

*T*oday I have to go intimidate men.
Kyō wa otoko o iatsu shinakute wa ikenai-kara
今日 は 男 を 威圧 し な く て は い け な い か ら

A stereotype, to be sure, is the often-thought idea that women pay much more attention to their appearance than men. While this could be attributed to mere individual vanity or conceit—or to social institutions that reinforce certain notions of femininity—Itoh says that it *is* true that women are judged by their appearance more often than men. Women know this, and dress can be used as a weapon to wield power or deflect criticism. But in either case, Itoh argues, attention to appearance is a necessary defense mechanism for women.

Itoh gives an example toward the end of the essay when we hear of a woman who wore a kimono when she was giving public presentations on feminism. A kimono, of course, is the traditional formal garment worn by Japanese women on certain special occasions, even today. By speaking to her audience in a kimono, the speaker appeared to her listeners as a rather formal, even conservative, person. This ameliorated any preconceived notions people may have had about radical feminists and helped the audience focus on her message rather than her own personal attributes.

A group of us old girlfriends met at a hotel lobby coffee shop after not seeing each other for a while. One of us, a lawyer, arrived a bit late and walked in, in a stately, gallant manner. She looked very nice and sophisticated. But because she is tall and has a good figure, her dress looked especially great. All of us couldn't help but notice and gazed at her with astonishment.

She was slightly embarrassed and said shyly, "After this little get-together, I have to go intimidate men today at a business meeting, so I am all dressed up." Ah, I see. "To intimidate men." With that kind of strategy, I guess.

While we were all talking I found out from the others that when they have to confront men on business, every woman tries to dress up, as if she were wearing armor to either protect herself or encourage herself.

While we were talking about this I was reminded of a woman I knew who once said that she dressed up to "avoid resistance" from others. During the women's lib movement in the 1970s she was an activist, and extremely radical.

She told me that at that time, "When I gave a talk about gender issues, I wore a kimono." The reason for this was, "I didn't want to compromise my beliefs, but I wanted the listeners to be on my side. So, in order for people to accept me and listen to what I had to say, I tried to use my appearance to dampen their resistance."

This was about a quarter of a century ago. Today we find women who delightfully claim that they are "dressing up to intimidate men." Probably both opinions—to impress men or avoid resistance—are women's wise defense mechanisms to get men to listen to them. But what makes the difference? Is it just a different situation? Is it a personality difference between individual women? Or are the times different? ∾

· 8 ·

Social Attitudes toward Women

*M*en don't work for free, do they?
Otoko no hito-tte, tada no koto wa shinai-desho
男の人って、タダのことはしないでしょ

In this vignette, Itoh describes a plight—and complaint!—probably common to women in all cultures: the fact that women's work is often undervalued and underappreciated, to say nothing of undercompensated, even though about half the workforce in Japan today is female. In Japan, women earn substantially less than men in all age-brackets and occupations, with the average female wage at 66.8 percent of the average male wage (*Japan Almanac* 2005, 88). In 2003 only 3.1 percent of company department heads were women, as were only 4.6 percent of all section chiefs. Only 15.6 percent of all physicians are women, as are only 10.7 percent of accountants. Only 10.2 percent of the legal profession is female (*Japan Almanac* 2005, 210).In addition, Itoh and her friends claim that much of women's work is either expected to be done gratis or is not well-thought-of enough to earn compensation. In contrast, as the title here says, men don't work for free.

The poet Yoshihara Sachiko, whom Itoh mentions, was born in Tokyo in 1932 and died in 2002. She won the Murō Saisei Prize in 1964 with her first poetry collection and continued receiving awards (the last was the Hagiwara Sakutarō Prize in 1995). She is noted for her poems on life, love, and betrayal, all lyrically depicted from a woman's point of view.

"Men don't work for free, do they?" This was said to me by a woman friend of mine during one of our citizens' activism campaigns. She is not a radical

109

or one to see deep hidden meanings in things. Rather, because she was such a good-natured, innocent housewife, her words stuck in my mind.

I guess that she felt that even though everyone—as concerned citizens—was supposed to be working toward the same goal in the campaign, she sensed a strange desire in the men in the group to make things turn out to their own benefit. They would try to use this social activism as a stepping-stone for their future career advancement.

Of course, I know that not all men are like this. But when I heard this woman make the above generalization—together with her matter-of-fact comment that "Men don't work for free"—somehow she sounded very convincing.

When I look around, trying to see the world through her eyes, women's work has always been for free. Running the household, nursing, looking after old people and sick people . . . such very important daily chores have been done by women without pay. Why are women to do all these things for free? Society has always justified this by saying that a woman's calling is to do this free work; it is a mission of a mother's love or her respectable volunteer spirit or her upbringing or the way of her virtue. Social tradition would never ever let men do the same work for free.

When you categorize jobs into women's work or men's work, there really are no differences except that one gets paid for one kind of job but the other does not. The poet Yoshihara Sachiko summed this up succinctly saying, "Women's jobs are the kind that do not provide unemployment insurance." ๛

*M*other is waiting.
O-kā-san wa matte iru-no
おかあさんはまつているの

In this essay Itoh once more laments how poorly society views the work and contributions of housewives. She is especially perturbed by the idea that housewives sit around idly all day doing nothing. She cites a scene from the French novelist Simone de Beauvoir's (1908–1986) novel *La femme rompue* (Paris: Gallimard, 1968), which was translated into English by Patrick O'Brien as *The Woman Destroyed* (New York: Putnam, 1969), in which the errant husband accuses his wife of laziness. Itoh suggests, then, that this may be a universal failing of the male heart.

When I just moved into this town, a neighbor's little girl came by to peek in our house. I asked her a couple of the usual questions like, "What's your name?" and "How old are you?" When I asked her, "Your father is . . . ?" she quickly answered, "A carpenter." But when I asked, "And your mother is . . . ?" she said, "She is waiting for me at home."

Later on after I got to know the child's mother, I discovered she is actually quite busy at home every day, far different from the impression I got when the little girl told me that her mother was just waiting for her children to come home. I was disappointed to find that her kids felt their mom was just "waiting at home" for them to get back, just because she was physically in the house.

I was reminded of this child when I read a letter to the editor in the newspaper today. A wife wrote saying that her husband did not appreciate all the work she did around the house. He was always complaining that "You get to stay at home and play around all day" or "You don't have to do any work."

Thinking about this, I am also reminded of a scene in *The Woman Destroyed* by the French novelist Simone de Beauvoir. The heroine was a woman who protected the home and was devoted to raising her children and was proud to be a housewife. But after twenty-two years of marriage, one night she found out that her husband had a lover. The lover was a well-known beautiful and intelligent lawyer. Because of her jealousy, the wife bad-mouthed the lover shamelessly. The husband's response was incredulous: hearing her criticisms, he said, "A woman who does nothing can't stand a woman who has a job."

A woman who does nothing! Someone thinks that a housewife is a person who does nothing? I am sure many women would become furious hearing these words. ∾

*B*ecause she gives me money, she is tricky.
O-kane o kureru kara zurui
お金をくれるからずるい

There have been scores of books written about Japanese notions of obligation and duty. Many key words describe the various shadings and nuances of the debt owed, the ability to ever possibly repay it, the appropriate level of gratitude, and so on. As Itoh shows us here, the Japanese themselves are also puzzled about these things, even in their own families. And apparently mothers and daughters in Japan can misunderstand themselves in ways similar to Americans.

We should mention, too, that in terms of pharmacies Japan is currently going through a transition. American-style drugstores are becoming increasingly popular, unlike the dispensaries of the past that were usually found inside most hospitals and clinics in Japan. Patients now more commonly take prescriptions to independent druggists rather than getting them directly from the hospital or physician.

This is a story about one of my childhood friends who used to be a pharmacist before she got married. Her parents own a large medical clinic. Since she lives in the neighborhood, she goes and helps out at the pharmacy of her parents' clinic sometimes. Not only that, when her parents are away she also helps out at the reception area and even cleans the office sometimes.

Talking with her after not seeing her for such a long time, I felt warm knowing she was working for her parents. I had lost my parents long ago when I was young. So I told her, "How nice it is that a daughter and mother can help each other out." "Not necessarily!" she said in an unhappy tone. "When I help my parents, my mother usually gives me money. She's pretty sneaky, isn't she?"

I was not sure what she meant. Why was this not nice? Seeing my confused face she said,

> My mother gives me money because she does not want to owe me anything. She is really sneaky. When my mother helps me, I do not pay her. Thus, I am obligated to her. My mother has always been this way ever since we were little kids. I don't like that at all.

But I don't know if her mother really thinks that way or not. Maybe her mother just wants to help her daughter out a little with her finances. Perhaps giving a little money is a sort of symbol of her true appreciation of her daughter's help. Nevertheless, her daughter thinks her mother is being sneaky.

This is a case of a daughter and mother misunderstanding each other's feelings. But in everyday life, many people try to handle relationships with money. Although some people will feel that this is being a little sneaky, not everyone would think so. ∾

*W*omen can't be unemployed, right?
Onna wa shitsugyō-sha nimo narenain-desu-ne
女は失業者にもなれないんですね

Here is another description of how hard it is to be a working woman in Japan. While more and more women have jobs outside the home—almost half of the workforce is now female—there are still institutional barriers and cultural attitudes that make this difficult. If a woman *is* working, many feel it is because she *has to*, which reflects poorly on the husband's ability to provide for his family.

Things are also hard for women who want professional careers. Some suggest that their teachers and supervisors would rather help them find husbands than jobs. One comment should be made about this, however. Unlike the United States where most professors would never interfere in the personal affairs of even their closest graduate students, in Japan it is rather common for a teacher, department supervisor, shop foreman, or friend or relative to become involved, at least casually, with helping a person—female *or* male—find a marriage partner. The complaint made here is that some women feel that this is the *only* thing done by supervisors for their female underlings.

This following incident happened during a meeting of the young housewives group (women about twenty years old) at the community center.

When I inquired about one woman who was not there, someone said, "She has some family problems now, and it turns out she has to go to work."

She said this very sympathetically. I could tell she was not saying this with any ill will, but nevertheless I was not comfortable with the phrase "and it turns out she has to go to work." This stuck with me because it sounded more like she was saying "and she has fallen into a lower social class than the one she used to belong to."

I wonder if Japanese women think that women who stay home and depend on their husbands' salaries have the ideal way of life. While I do sympathize with a struggling family that is facing financial problems, I do not think "work" itself is a pitiful thing. Isn't it natural that an adult would work?

Maybe I am making too much of this, but there is a philosophical reason why I am bothered by these comments. Recently women have started to go off working—entering the men's world—yet we women are often still struggling to overcome the thick wall of tradition, a society that still thinks this is a difficult thing for us to do.

For example, there are many women who graduate from college, or even graduate school, and cannot get any full-time jobs at all. These women often complain about this, but the rest of society does not seem to understand.

One college women said furiously, "Although our supervisors try hard to find jobs for their male students, they do little for the female students. Some teachers—kindly, they think—even try and find them a marriage partner instead of a job. Isn't that just too much to take?"

Another women said with a bitter smile, "If we are married, they say we don't need to have jobs because we have husbands. They don't accept our wish to be employed. But we women can't ever be unemployed, right?" ❧

*M*others are mothers of children, but at the same time mothers
   of the nation.
Haha wa ko no haha taru to tomoni kuni no haha
母は子の母たるとともに国の母

Here is another sensitive issue tackled by Itoh. Simply put, who owns the womb? A mother raises her own individual child, of course, but by doing so, she is also contributing to society. Thus, in some ways, mothers have social obligations beyond their own homes, while society also has a special and vested interest in motherhood. And yet, even though everyone grants the social importance of motherhood, these words are vacuous. Not only are the social contributions of motherhood often downplayed, individual rights can also be superseded.

The other day someone showed me a report from a committee that was studying women's issues. One phrase from their discussion struck me.

Somebody said, "We should reconsider the social role of motherhood. Mothers not only raise the next generation of people, but they also raise the next generation of leaders." Because the word *reconsider* was used, I suppose this group was trying to be "liberal" in advancing the protection of motherhood. "But this seems to me like they are saying 'for the nation.' That sounds like something they would say during World War II," one of my friends said, quite offended.

She showed me an article written in 1942 by the journalist Ifukube Toshiko (1899–1970). Ifukube argued,

> A child is a child of its parents, but at the same time the child is a child of the nation. A mother is a mother of a child. But at the same time a mother is the mother of the nation. Thus, an individual mother's power is both public as well as private.

Why, yes, I thought, that does sound very similar to what that committee was saying in the report.

When people say, "What you are doing is very meaningful for society," we tend to feel important—that we are making a contribution. However, when people say, "We respect motherhood because of its contribution to society by raising the next generation," that is less flattering.

Then consider the logic behind a phrase like, "Because mothers are doing their social duty of bearing and raising the next generation, people should respect them." This ignores the fact that there should be respect for both the public rights of *women as mothers* and the private rights of *a woman as a mother*.

Some say, "Because you are useful to society, society should protect you." Using this logic, then, what is the difference between saying this and saying "Your womb is not your own, but only borrowed"?

My friend was furious. I think that everyone has basic human rights, and society should protect you just for that reason alone. Why isn't this the basic principle we all follow? ∾

$\mathcal{I}$ am sorry that we women have to feel frightened when we go out at night.

Kowai to omō koto ga kuyashī

怖いと思うことが悔しい

A perennial problem for women—probably in every culture—is safety. Even in spite of the growing success of "Take Back the Night" movements, in the United States people often feel that if a woman is approached indecently, or is sexually assaulted, it is somehow her fault.

As we see in this essay, some of these same thoughts are prevalent in Japan. In fact, there have recently been public service campaigns encouraging men to behave more carefully and women to be more cautious. The "Beware of lechers" sign mentioned in this piece refers to the practice of inappropriate "accidental" touching that some women experience on crowded commuter trains, especially by men who have had quite a bit to drink after work on their way home.

That said, we must in all fairness be careful not to overstate this problem. There are many public service signs put up by the police in Japan, encouraging people not to leave their valuables behind on the subway or to beware of pickpockets in certain areas. And generally speaking, compared to America, the level of safety of the public transportation system in Japan is extremely high, and most women are quite comfortable—and secure—coming home alone at night, though there is always the occasional uncomfortable incident or crime.

Toward the end of the essay we see the phrase *mizu-shōbai*, or literally "water trade." This is a term that is applied to women in the sex and entertainment industry, such as bar hostesses, etc. For more about *mizu-shōbai*, see "I don't like the New Year's" in chapter 1.

One day a friend of ours came up to us in great agitation. She told me, "When I get in a taxi these days, the driver always starts chattering about stupid things to me." She said that according to the driver of her last cab ride, he has noticed that recently he has quite a few female customers, even in the middle of the night. The driver said with amazement that these female customers are not only those who work in the *mizu-shōbai*, but even university students and office workers. "That's terrible!" the driver said. He added, "I don't like a young woman who is not afraid to go out at night."

My friend then commented,

It is men's fault that we women are frightened to go out late at night. It's a pity, and it's not fair, that we have been given this fear by men. However, men say it's not good if women are not afraid of the dark, like it is kind of an attractive thing. That is too much to take, isn't it?

Another added, "That's right. We are not asking men to take responsibility for this situation, but men need to be more considerate about this."

Thinking about this issue, I began wondering if signs like "Beware of lechers!" are written by men? I felt such signs were like a thief telling me to be careful of robbers. It is fine with me if women say, "We should watch out for lechers," but I think men should instead say, "We men should be careful not to be lechers." But I felt that that, too, was a little funny.

Regardless, recognizing the irresponsible attitude of some men is very a serious issue. When a woman is raped, they act as if it were her fault, saying things like, "She shouldn't look like such a tramp."

Tradition maintains such unjust attitudes toward women. That is why the cabdriver could say, "If something happens it is a woman's fault that she goes out late at night." This is just one small example of this attitude. ᔆ

*W*hen they found she was defective, they naturally returned her.

Kizumono datta to wakattara hempin sarete tōzen-tte wake-ne
キズ物だったとわかったら返品されて当然ってわけね

In Japan, marriage has always been a rather complex thing, closely involving the families as much as the couple. Even today—though hardly as commonly as before—private detective agencies will sometimes be hired to investigate the background of prospective spouses, looking for hidden skeletons of all kinds, from past financial improprieties to insanity or illness in the family. As we see here, a perceived lack of full disclosure can cause some serious problems for a marriage.

Recently I heard two very similar stories. The first one was about a woman who just delivered her first child. Because she had a severe intestinal problem that was discovered, she had to stay in the hospital for a while, and we didn't know when she could be released. According to her, no one knew about this problem before, including herself, and the doctors told her this was a lingering problem she must have had for a long time.

Later, when her mother-in-law found out about this, she said, "Because she married my son without honestly revealing everything about her health, she should go back to her natal family, and they should obviously take care of her and the children." Because of this, her mother and father were put in the middle and placed in an extremely difficult situation. Her husband, however, just sat on the sidelines and didn't say anything.

The other story is also about a woman who recently found out about a serious chronic disease. She discovered this in a manner very much like the woman in the first story. Until not too long ago, she didn't have any symptoms.

After she found out about her illness, she said, "I feel bad that my husband didn't know I had a serious illness before we got married. Do you think I should let him divorce me?" She became preoccupied with this notion and still has not yet been able to tell her husband about her illness.

What kind of stories are these! The other women who were listening to these accounts felt sympathy for the health problems of these two people. However, the more they heard, the more they were amazed by the reactions of the families.

Some were furious and shouted, "What time are we talking about here, the Dark Ages? Some people spoke even more plainly: "When they found she was defective, they naturally returned her."

Hearing these stories, I felt that we heard the real opinions many people have deep down in their hearts about the significance of marriage and the social status of wives. ❧

· 9 ·

How We Are Seen

*W*hy do mothers threaten their children so much?
O-kā-san-tte, dōshite annani kodomo o kyōhaku surun-darō
おかあさんって、どうしてあんなに子どもを脅迫するん
だろう

Here Itoh addresses an issue that is of concern to all mothers everywhere: child rearing and discipline. We remember that Western social scientists a while back often praised Japanese mothers. Many of the standard texts of the 1980s and 1990s on Japanese sociology and anthropology, for example, remarked that Japanese mothers generally avoided two self-defeating behaviors often found in American mothers: corporal punishment and being overly rational with a child and reasoning with him or her as an adult. Instead, it was argued, Japanese mothers used techniques like distraction to stop children from misbehaving. But according to at least one woman at the community center, such an optimistic assessment is exaggerated.

When a women took her son to the barber, she told me that she overheard him say, "Kid, if you move I will cut your ear off." Of course what he meant was, "If you move, I might cut your ear off by accident, so don't move around." However, when I heard him say that, it sounded to me like, "If you move, I will cut your ear off!" I almost said, "Please don't threaten my little boy."

But then she grinned and added, "But if I really would have said that, everyone would have thought, 'Yeah, it's just like a mother to think such a thing.'" With an ironic smile she went on, "I am very sensitive to the things strangers say to my son even though I often say awful things to him myself."

As soon as she said this, another—single—woman said, "I always wonder why mothers threaten their children so much." She kept on talking even though there were other mothers around making faces, saying, "Threaten?" or "That's not true."

But the young woman continued,

> When I am walking around, or riding the subway, I see lots of mothers who threaten their children. Even I get scared sometimes. For instance, I hear them say, with these frightening expressions on their faces, "I will leave you if you do not listen to your mother" or "I won't let you go outside and play unless you finish piano practice" or "I'll hit you, if you do that again." It's really scary. Really scary.

After hearing these words, all the mothers looked downcast and guilty. I guess they were ashamed by the words they themselves sometimes used for their children. ∾

*P*lease don't tie me down.
Watashi o tabane-nai-de
わたしを束ねないで

A recent phenomenon in Japan has been a special type of juvenile delinquency among young girls. An increasing number of girls in their midteens—often coming from well-off middle-class families—solicit "dates" from older men using cell phones or the Internet. These affairs usually involve some sort of sexual activity in return for money or expensive presents. Itoh's explanation as presented here is too anecdotal to hold up to strict sociological scrutiny. Nonetheless, it is suggestive about how at least some young Japanese women might be viewing their future.

The poet Shinkawa Kazue, who wrote the title poem of this essay, was born in Ibaraki Prefecture in 1929. She is noted for her verses on women's issues and the longing for freedom in a confining modern world. She was the first woman to become president of the Japan Modern Poets Society in the mid-1980s. The poem can be found in her book of the same name, *Watashi o tabane-nai-de* (Please Don't Tie Me Down), published by Dōwaya, Tokyo, in 1997.

I had a conversation with a student counselor at the junior high school the other day. She told me, a little reluctantly, that society tends to idolize teenage girls for their beauty and innocence, but many of them are actually quite cynical and worldly. I asked her what she meant. She said feels very sad when she hears female students not respecting themselves and saying things like, "We will just end up being housewives anyway."

She heard from one student she was counseling, for example, that she slept with a man for money. The student said, "I did not do anything to cause problems for anybody else. What I did is no different than what my mother does. By sleeping with my father, my mother is fed by him." She wasn't giving any excuse; she just acted as if it were strange for her counselor to see anything wrong in what she was doing.

Hearing how this student felt about her own mother—and her seeing the same future for herself when she becomes a woman—my counselor friend said she felt a cold chill go up her spine. She also said, however, that at the same time she felt guilty that we adults were not able to give much hope to these girls for their future.

There is a poem written by Shinkawa Kazue entitled "Please Don't Tie Me Down":

わたしを名付けないで	*Watashi o nazu kenaide*
娘という名 妻という名	*musume to iu na, tsuma to iu na*
重々しい母という名でしつらえた座に	*omo omo-shii haha to iu na de shitsuraeta za ni*
座りきりにさせないでください	*suwari kiri ni sasenaide kudasai*
わたしは風	*watashi wa kaze*
りんごの木と	*ringo no ki to*
泉のありかを知っている風	*izumi no arika o shittte-iru kaze*

"Please don't name me
with the name called 'daughter,'
or the name called 'wife,'
or with the social position decorated with the solemn name called 'mother.'
Please do not keep me sitting here.
I am the wind,
the wind who knows where the apple trees and springs are."

This poem has the fresh sense of girlhood. Now don't girls have this feeling of freedom, to fly away in their own imaginations? If we adults have dried out the flower of fresh girlhood, our crime is very deep. ❧

*C*ongratulations on not being the eldest son.

Shōnan de nakute yokatta-wa nē

長男でなくてよかったわねえ

As we have seen in several previous essays, problems between mothers-in-law and daughters-in-law are probably a cross-cultural universal, but in Japan, with its vestiges of Confucian patriarchy, life can be awkward for the woman who marries the eldest son. Traditionally, she becomes a member of the husband's family and because the eldest son—at least as was true in the past—will become the next head of the family line, her responsibilities are huge. But she will not become the matriarch until after her husband's mother dies, and until then she is closely supervised—and often criticized—by her mother-in-law. This is the topic of Itoh's essay.

However, things are changing rather rapidly now in Japan. These conditions are not as strictly enforced as before, and it is not unheard of, for example, for the second son to take over the family. Also, there is a trend now starting for the wife's elderly parents to live with the daughter (making houses having "two family nameplates" increasingly common).

In the late 1960s I went back to tell my favorite junior high school teacher about my impending marriage. The first thing she asked me was, "Is he the eldest son?" Upon hearing my negative reply, she said with a sigh of relief, "Oh, that's good. You wouldn't want to be married to an eldest like son I am."

When I heard this at the time, it stuck in my mind. And ever since then, whenever her words pop into my head, I get a prickly feeling, like someone is sticking me with a thorn. Occasionally, when I think back, I am disappointed about her character, because instead of first asking me about my husband's personality, she focused on whether he was the eldest son or not. At other times I feel sorry for her, discovering that being the bride of an eldest son was the cause of so much pressure and unhappiness for her.

However, we can't just dismiss her feelings as being the concerns of "a traditional old woman." This is not something that was only civil law in the recent past. Quite a few people, even young wives, say things like, "It is good that my husband is not the eldest son" or "My husband is the eldest son, so I am at a real disadvantage." Why do such traditional types of social pressure persist in everyday life in Japan, even into the twenty-first century?

Also, I must say that I would feel miserable if this is how my eldest son's wife also sees me.

And it is impossible to ignore things people say, like, "I want to live separately from my parents after we get married as it is so difficult to adjust to each other if we live together." Once these children marry, however, many of these people—who now have become parents and parents-in-law themselves—often change their minds and choose to live together. I wonder why? I really can't overlook this problem. ❧

It looks like I'm an auntie now. Hah!
Oba-san de aru-rashi okashi
おばさんであるらし可笑し

> The Japanese word *oba-san* literally means "aunt." However, this word is often used as a fictive kinship term of address for any woman of mature age by younger people. Before this age is reached, she is often called *o-nē-san* (elder sister). The time of transition from *o-nē-san* to *oba-san* can be somewhat shocking to Japanese women, and this transition is what Itoh is writing about in this piece. The poem by Kawano Yūko appeared in her book *Hayari* (In Vogue) published by Tanka-Shimbunsha, Tokyo, in 1984.

When does a woman realize she has become an *oba-san* ["auntie" or "middle-aged woman"]? I wonder if it usually happens when some children outside the home call her that on the street for the first time?

That was how I discovered it: I was shopping, and an amiable junior high school girl who happened to be helping her mother shop asked me, "*Oba-san*, do you prefer to have a boy or girl?"

She asked me this because it was obvious that I was pregnant as I had such a huge stomach. Nevertheless, I was still in my midtwenties, and I thought, "What? *Oba-san*? Me?" But then I saw the shape of my body and said to myself with a bittersweet smile, "Oh, yes, with this stomach . . ." and accepted the fact.

This was an old buried memory. But when I read the following tanka poem by Kawano Yūko (b. 1946) this memory came flashing back to me:

子の友が	*Kono tomo ga*
三人並びて	*san-nin narabite*
おばさんと呼ぶから	*Oba-san to yobu-kara*
おばさんであるらし	*Oba-san de aru rashi*
可笑し	*Okashi*

"My child's friends, three kids who line up addressing me as "*oba-san*": it must be because I *am* an *oba-san*. Hah!"

I could imagine the author's feeling in this situation, saying at the end of the poem "*Okashi!*" ["Hah!" or "That's pretty funny!"]. Me, too. It was really not unpleasant for me when I was first called "Auntie" [*Oba-san*]. However, I also felt something like "Hah!" [*Okashi*]. I felt a little silly at my own ignorance about myself. I felt the gap between my own self-recognition and the view of a second person was interesting.

Thinking about this, I find there are many other such things in life. We only find out for ourselves the first time someone else points them out to us. Sometimes I am surprised to find that such gaps are not just "*okashi*" but can also be rather serious.

When I think about how my words or actions must appear to another person, I realize that another person is our mirror of reality. ∾

*W*hat is your social status?
Go-mibun wa
ご身分は

As we have seen in several of Itoh's essays in this collection, rank and social status in Japan are much more complicated affairs than in the United States. The Japanese language is grammatically marked for several levels of honorifics, and words for titles abound. Even choosing a first-person pronoun (*I*) is hard, as there are at least a half-dozen choices available, each reflecting subtle nuances of hierarchy and position. As seen here, on first meeting, Japanese people often have to negotiate a complex nexus of cultural and sociolinguistic variables—such as age, gender, or occupation—before being able to utter a single word. Though times are certainly changing, these things are still factors that enter into every Japanese conversation.

Here are a few specific references in the piece that should be noted: While *emeritus* is used for any retired professor in the United States, it carries more status and prestige in Japan, and to be called an "emeritus professor" is really, in a sense, a promotion. The University of Tokyo is establishment-Japan's equivalent of Harvard, Yale, and Princeton—combined. For those who desire a job in the diplomatic service or government judiciary, for example, attending the University of Tokyo is almost required. Uno Kōzō (1897–1977) was one of Japan's most influential postwar economists. Though a Marxist by training and belief, he sought to ground economic analysis in pragmatism rather than reducing it to class-struggle ideology debates.

An academic I know told me the other day that she ran into a female colleague at a protest meeting a while back. Although they knew each other's names through their publications, they had not met in person until then. So they introduced themselves to each other.

Then the second scholar asked, "By the way, what is your social status?" Although the person who was asked this question couldn't figure out the meaning of it immediately, it dawned on her that she was being asked something like, "Which university do you work for?" or "Are you associate or assistant professor?"

The people who were listening to this conversation smiled with amusement. One exclaimed, "What an anachronism!" "Yes," added another, "I am surprised that she calls herself a feminist. But she sounds like she has almost the same kind of hang-up about social hierarchy that men traditionally do."

When I heard this story I was reminded of the following anecdote. The famous Japanese economist Uno Kōzō was a full professor in the economics department at the University of Tokyo. In a journal article an editor once referred to him mistakenly as "Emeritus Professor" at the University of Tokyo. The editor was very apologetic over this careless error. But Professor Uno said mischievously, "Did you make me emeritus just to give me more authority, or were you trying to give more authority to the University of Tokyo instead of me?"

Even if people are not outspoken and do not ask us directly a question like, "What is your social status?" people commonly judge others by which institution they belong to and the position they have there. I actually think that a question like, "What is your social status?" is not anachronistic but rather, in fact, reflects the social hierarchy of our world.

I was told about another woman who works in an office. She was fed up with her female manager who always was saying things like "my people" (referring to those who are working for her) or "The big boss needed to talk to me about . . ." Another friend of mine mentioned that when she was transferred to another section in her company, nobody asked what she was now going to do. Instead everybody asked, "Is it a promotion?" She was very disappointed by these people.

I think that if women do not come to recognize how social structure warps our consciousness—and if we don't try and change society, as women, but just absorb the ready-made social values already given to us—the future of the women's movement is very dim. ∾

· *10* ·

What I Want to Be

A "Ms. Ditz" cannot remain a "bachelorette."
Baka dewa hai-misu wa tsutomara-nu
バカ で は ハ イ ・ ミ ス は つ と ま ら ぬ

In this essay Itoh ponders what life is like for the Japanese single female. But by implication, she also asks if certain women simply *need* a husband and lack the ability to live by themselves. She starts with a quote by the famous novelist and scriptwriter Tanabe Seiko (b. 1928) from her book *Mado o akemasu ka?* (Do You Wish to Open the Window?) published by Shinchōsha, Tokyo, in 1972. Tanabe won the Akutagawa Prize in 1963 (see "Why did you get involved with *that* kind of woman?" in chapter 12 for more on this award). An Osaka native, she is noted for her colorful and blunt writings in this dialect (rather different from the supposedly more refined "standard" speech, based on the Tokyo dialect). For more on Tanabe see "When men are around it is happy and cheerful" in chapter 10. The Akutagawa Prize is Japan's most prestigious literary award and was established in 1935. It is awarded semiannually to new writers by the Association for the Promotion of Japanese Literature.

Tanabe Seiko has the following passage in her novel *Do You Wish to Open the Window?*:

> In my opinion, if I were so immature as to not know how others see me, or if I was not able to see myself objectively, I could not stay single. The tension over how others see you makes an unmarried woman appear beautiful. A "Ms. Ditz" cannot remain a "bachelorette." That is, a stupid woman who cannot think about anyone but herself is unable to get along by herself and must find a husband simply in order to survive.

I definitely agree with Tanabe's opinion. I think it is true. I have quite a few women friends who live by themselves. When I see them, I think Tanabe's words really apply.

I imagine that living by yourself is not so easy—especially when people see you and think that that kind of lifestyle is wonderful. But the really mature single woman understands that we cannot live only our own way and realizes that we, as members of society, are always under others' scrutiny. She is sincere to herself, keeping her course; she does not drift endlessly with the changes of the wind but is flexible and true to herself when necessary. Such is an enjoyable way of life, one that only an adult woman can achieve. A stupid woman cannot live this way.

I see quite a few single, competent women these days—more than you would think—and as a woman myself, this makes me feel satisfied.

Generally speaking, well-adjusted single people living alone have the ability to take care of themselves as well as others. These people are especially good at social relationships because they know the appropriate social distance to maintain in the traffic of life.

I do not necessarily want to live by myself, but I always admire the abilities of those who are able to do so successfully. ✆

A person who does not have some inferiority complex is weird.
Rettōkan no nai ningen nante, iyarashī-yo
劣等感のない人間なんて、いやらしいよ

In this vignette Itoh talks about a problem everyone faces: how to handle our inadequacies, especially in that proverbial and universal terror, gym class. However, she shows us that we all can inadvertently make assumptions about people's feelings, even those we know well. Sometimes these are quite incorrect, as we might add our *own* fears and feelings of inferiority into the mix.

Decades have passed since my second son was born with a slight handicap in his leg. All this time I had been wondering if he would develop an inferiority complex over this handicap, and I felt regret about this possibility. One day I was talking about this to my friend, and she said, "A person who does not have some inferiority complex is weird."

That's right! Her words hit me as if I had just stepped into a spotlight. If a person's character becomes warped due to an inferiority complex this is, of course, a problem, but a person who does not have any inferiority complex at all surely is strange. Not only that, such a person is even a little scary.

Several years later, when my son became a student in elementary school, I innocently said, "Although you might not be good in gymnastics class, you . . ." He stopped me saying, "No, I am OK in gymnastics."

Even then it dawned on me: I had assumed that "bad grade" was equivalent to "not good at." But for him, "good at" or "not good at" were not the same thing as "like" or "dislike." Even though he was not good at competing with others in gymnastics, in his mind that did not mean he didn't like it. I really appreciated his schoolteacher who created an atmosphere in which he could think like this. She made the class believe that even if a student finished last in a race, if the student was running faster than he or she did before, the class should congratulate him or her.

When my son entered junior high he lamented with a sigh, "It took me twice as long today to run a marathon as the other students." But his elder brother, showing the innocent wisdom of youth, said, "That's great! I am proud that you were able to run for such a long time."

Because of my son, I have been continuing to discover new perspectives about myself and others. ✍

I do not want to be a "cute little old lady."
"Kawaii obā-chan" nante, watashi wa iya da
「かわいいおばあちゃん」なんて、私はいやだ

In Japan, the notion *kawaii* (literally, "cute") is ubiquitous. Cute things are found everywhere, from "Hello, Kitty" handbags to six-foot-tall stuffed animals sitting on the couch of a TV talk show. When children are young, *kawaii* can be used for both boys and girls, but the word becomes restricted to females sometime in the early teens. After that, *kawaii* is a term often applied as a compliment to females, especially teenage girls. Young singers and movie stars are rated on their cuteness and often appear in public in their school uniforms or adorable party dresses. But Itoh argues here that being cute is a not a position of power or equality. One of the attractive things about cuteness, which others admire, is that the cute person is always subordinate in her attempt to please others.

While "cuteness" is hardly a robust sociological construct, there is ample anecdotal evidence that Itoh's observations are on the mark. For example, the quintessential *burikko* (cutie-pie) of recent times was Matsuda Seiko. She was a teenage-idol singer and movie star in the late 1980s and early '90s and was a gold mine for her handlers and media production company. When she wanted to forego her cutesy image and become a legitimate artist, she was stonewalled by both fans and producers alike. She finally had to go abroad to the United States and Europe to even make a serious album. For more on the *kawaii* phenomenon see "Why do women have to be cute (*kawaii*)?" in chapter 10.

I often hear comments like, "Someday I want to be a cute little old lady," or "I wish my mother-in-law could be a cute little old lady." One day, however, I met a woman who said clearly, "I *don't* want to be a cute little old lady."

She then she went on to say,

> "Cute little old lady" means that she is someone who goes along with whatever is said. In other words, she does not insist on having her own way; she doesn't criticize anyone; she has no complaints; and she doesn't question others. Even if she feels some of these things, she will ask for a little favor in a cute way or politely refuse at first. This kind of woman is easygoing. In other words, she is like a subordinate who can be easily controlled. Is this our ideal of what a person who has lived well into old age is supposed to be? I, for one, do not want to be such a person. Maybe we behave like that because we often are in a position where someone else is looking after us, and we don't want to be a burden on others. We want to be liked by others, so we behave in this fashion. To me, that is a warped set of values, and I don't want to be that way, and I don't want others to expect that from me.

When I heard her say these words, I was reminded of the comments the novelist Inada Nada (b. 1929) made in the journal *Shisō* [Philosophy] in August 1969. Concerning the worldview of infants, we should try to impart an ideal that says instead of being a "cute person" we should try to be a "beautiful person." Or to put things another way, we should strive for an "aesthetic that has us relate to people equally" rather than an "aesthetic that is just one way."

I have just realized that a "cute" relationship is not necessarily an equal relationship. The "cute" person is the subordinate person. Thus, the typical stages of the life course assigned to Japanese females—from "cute girl" to "cute woman" to "cute little old lady"—form a pattern that definitely needs to be reconsidered. ᖇ

*H*ow can we say it is honorable to be killed that way?
Anna korosare kata o shite, nani ga mēyo-deshō
あんな殺され方をして、何が名誉でしょう

Here once again Itoh criticizes not only the Japanese militarism of the past, but also the idea of an honorable death in war. Once more she uses a female voice, this time of the famous and outspoken World

War II–era actress Tamura Akiko (1905–1983), who also throughout the 1950s worked with the world-famous Japanese director Kinoshita Keisuke. Though never explicitly stated outright, there is an underlying feeling in each of Itoh's several essays that are critical of the war that women—albeit, a brave few—were the voices of reason in a system bent on conquest and the desire to establish an empire.

After I read a book about the prewar actress Tamura Akiko (1905–1983), who was famous in the "New School" of acting in Japan, I could not forget the description of the death of her husband during World War II. Her husband, Tomoda Kyōsuke, was also an actor, and his death was reported in the newspapers with flowery phrases like, "The last great pathos of the New School man . . . ," or "Sleep peacefully, you heroic soul. The field of battle was your greatest stage."

In this book, the author Uchimura Naoya (1909–1989) said, "Until his death in war, he was but an unknown actor who played only in small theaters. However, once he died he became a great actor. He became famous not because of his acting, but because of his death."

On top of that, in the newspapers Akiko herself became "the wife of the honored martyr" or "the wife of the God of the Army." She was furious. She told the newspaper reporters,

> Tomoda was an actor so I think that if he were to have died onstage, that would have been an honorable thing, and he would have wanted that. However, this old man was killed in a completely different place doing a completely different thing. How can we think such a death could be honorable?

And she also said, "Please do not ever write 'Akiko said she is very proud of how her husband died.' Please write, 'I feel his death was very pitiful, and I don't know what more I can say except that I am very, very sorry it happened.'" Uchimura Naoya also wrote, "Even though people were sympathetic about what she said, and sympathetic about those who died in the war, people were not able to say such things at that time."

I think it was really important to note that regardless of the feelings of the times, Akiko did not succumb to social pressure. Even during World War II, she showed her anger. Even now I think we are not always able to show our true feelings without feeling social pressure. In other words, I do not think this is a problem of the past. ❧

If you want, you can call me a traitor. I don't care.
Onozomi naraba watashi o baikokudo to yonde kudasattemo kekkō-desu
お望みならば私を売国奴と呼んでくださってもけっこう
です

Japan invaded and conquered the Chinese province of Manchuria
in 1931, establishing the puppet state of Manchukuo, which lasted
until the end of World War II. Not every Japanese person, however,
supported their government in this incursion, even though dissent
carried dire consequences during this time. In this essay Itoh offers
another indirect feminist critique of nationalism, war, and blind
public obedience. She cautions that a public carelessly following
government edicts, no matter how apparently benign, is a recipe for
a possible disaster, even today in a demilitarized Japan. For more on
Japanese militarism and World War II see "The abundant seeds of
grass that don't know national boundaries are cast upon the ground"
in chapter 10.

Recently, "self-discipline" [*jishuku*] has become the social buzzword of the
day in Japan. I am terrified about the sneaky way "self-discipline" is used to
control people. As this notion spread across the nation, various events have
had to be postponed or canceled. I wonder if such actions resulted from the
true feelings of the people, thinking their own ideas? Did everybody really
agree to this?

When I look back, it seems to me that the majority of those events that
were postponed or canceled were not really part of the national discussion.
People were worried about how others might see them, so they just followed
along with what they thought was public opinion, without really giving it any
consideration. Furthermore, those above us—the powers that be—are portray-
ing this national focus on self-discipline as if it were a "spontaneous" action
of "the people's will," upon which there is "total agreement." But I wonder if,
without us knowing, we individuals start actually thinking this way?

In my whole life, I have never felt such suspicion of the word *self-discipline*
until recently. During World War II many people were asked to cooperate with
the government, and many went along with what they thought was public
sentiment.

However, there was a woman back then who refused to blindly go along
with the government. Hasegawa Teru (1912–1947) was a proponent of the
Esperanto international language movement and was twenty-five years old

when she spoke out against the Japanese invasion of Manchuria in the 1930s. She participated in anti-Japanese protests in China and was called a traitor by the Japanese government.

In spite of public and private pressure she never renounced her beliefs, saying:

> If you wish, you can call me a traitor. I am not afraid of being called that. Rather I feel shame for myself to be part of the same people who have invaded another country, creating hell and misery for people who have committed no crime.

As a woman, I am proud of Hasegawa Teru, and hope myself that I could follow my convictions as gallantly as she did. ॐ

*W*hy do women have to be cute (*kawaii*)?
Onna ga, dōshite kawaiku nakuccha ikenain-dai?
女が、どうして可愛くなくちゃいけないんだい？

Here, as in a previous essay, Itoh criticizes the notion that women have to be *kawaii* (cute). She cleverly does so by enlisting one of the quintessential male symbols of Japan, the famous "Tora-san" character. She uses one of the *Otoko wa tsurai yo* (It's Tough to Be a Man, You Know!) movies to make a point about visions of femininity in modern Japan. The Tora-san comedy films are perennially popular in Japan and have been the longest-running film series in the world. They are about an itinerant traveling salesman, Tora-san, who has many adventures on the road, but always loses the girl in the end. Since the 1970s, forty-eight Tora-san films have been made (the last in 1995). The famous star Atsumi Kiyoshi (b. 1928) died in 1996, ending the series. These films are still widely watched on video and television, and probably every Japanese at least knows about them—though admittedly they are not for most young persons' taste these days. Nonetheless, Tora-san is as much an institution in Japan as, say, John Wayne or James Bond are in the United States.

And speaking of 007, Asaoka Ruriko (b. 1940)—the woman who played Lily in the dialogue below—actually gained some international recognition when she was one of the James Bond girls in the film *You Only Live Twice*. For more on the *kawaii* phenomenon see "I do not want to be a cute little old lady" in chapter 10.

Here is part of a conversation found in one of the very popular "Tora-san" films directed by Yamada Yōjirō (b. 1931):

Man:	I am . . . I am a loser. I am a man who cannot make even just one woman happy.
Lily:	That's a very conceited thing to say.
Man:	Why?
Lily:	To "make a woman happy?" . . . that's none of your business. Do you think a woman's happiness depends on a man? Don't make me laugh.
Tora-san:	But . . . it's often said that a woman's happiness depends on a man, isn't it?
Lily:	Really? I've never heard of that before. I have never thought like that. If you men think like that, it is arrogant of you.
Tora-san:	Well . . . you just aren't a cute [*kawaii*] woman, are you?
Lily:	Why does a woman have to be cute [*kawaii*], Tora-san? It is because you think like that, that you always suffer from unrequited love.

This dialogue was from the film *Torajirō aiai-gasa* [Tora-san's Umbrella of Love], produced in 1975. By the way, I just remembered that 1975 was the International Year of the Woman in Japan. In the above dialogue, Lily is a singer on the nightclub circuit. She is played by the actress Asaoka Ruriko, who brought a lively energy to the role.

In this dialogue, I really like the line "I've never heard of that before." Usually Japanese men like Tora-san believe that a woman's happiness is in their hands, and claims like "I will do whatever it takes to make you happy" as marriage proposals are heard everywhere in the Japanese media, even in serious TV dramas. And yet, in reply to such a promise Lily says here, "Really? I've never heard of that before" and adds, "If you men think like that, it is arrogant of you." How delightfully she puts it! ∾

*W*hatever I have is all mine.
Watashi ga motte irumono wa, subete watashi jishin-desu
私 が も っ て い る も の は 、 す べ て 私 自 信 で す

While this might not be a cultural universal, in both Japan and the United States women are often seen as sex objects. Social scientists on both sides of the Pacific argue about whether this is an instinctual male trait or an innate failing of men holding warped cultural values. Regardless, the problem for women, then, is how to act knowing that half of the time they are being judged on their appearance rather than their accomplishments or character. Itoh suggests that the best way might be to emulate America's first Playmate, Marilyn Monroe. With poise and wit she kept her dignity when others about her were losing theirs. As a role model, women could do much worse.

When Marilyn Monroe was alive she was labeled "a dumb blonde"—a woman who was sexy but stupid—and was thought to always be involved in some sort of sex scandal. However, when I read her Japanese biography, *Marilyn Monroe* (Tokyo: Iwanai Shinsho, 1987), I was very happy to find that although she was emotionally hurt by such labels, she never regarded herself as cheap. She was really intelligent and had a firm personality.

There is a very famous story told about Marilyn Monroe: during an interview she was once asked the provocatively loaded question "What do you wear when you are in bed?" She answered "Chanel No. 5," avoiding being baited by giving the name of a perfume. With her quick wit, she twisted this pointless, risqué question around to her own advantage.

The title of this essay I have written here—"Whatever I have is all mine"—was also her answer to another odd question. Someone once asked her, "Are your breasts real or fake?" What an impolite interviewer and what a stupid question! Her answer, however—"Whatever I have is all mine"— showed poise and intelligence.

Kamei Shunsuke (b. 1932), an American culture specialist and author of the biography I mentioned before, claims that Marilyn Monroe was "not the kind of intelligent woman who was smug or full of herself." (However, if I were the author, I would have written that this is actually how most men appear to women!) Her intelligence was of the social kind, he claims: giving attention to every question she was asked and answering with wit and composure.

The following words really capture Marilyn Monroe's character: "I want to not only be proud of my firm breasts, but I want to be a person who can also be proud of my firm personality." This, I think, is a desirable balance of the soul and the flesh. ❧

I hope the days of the unknown future will be beautiful!
Hatsu goyomi shiranu tsukihi no utsukushiku
初暦知らぬ月日の美しく

The custom in Japan is to send greeting cards on New Year's Day rather than at Christmas. Most of the time these cards are based on that year's symbolic animal taken from the *jūni-shi*, the twelve signs of the East Asian zodiac. Most readers are probably familiar with this repeating calendrical cycle from going to Chinese restaurants. Each year is represented by of one of twelve animals: *ne* (子, rat), *ushi* (丑, ox), *tora* (寅, tiger), *u* (卯, rabbit), *tastu* (辰, dragon), *mi* (巳, snake), *uma* (午, horse), *hitsuji* (未, sheep), *saru* (申, monkey), *tori* (酉, rooster), *inu* (戌, dog), and *i* (亥, boar).

These signs are from the ancient Chinese book, the *I Ching* (The Book of Changes), and were brought to Japan together with Buddhism in the sixth century CE. Though no longer used for predictions as in ancient times, every Japanese person knows the supposed characteristics of the animal of the year they were born, just as most Westerners know their own horoscope sign. For example, someone born in the Year of the Dragon is energetic but high-strung and gregarious, monkeys are talented but aloof, and so on.

Often New Year's cards are prepackaged, store-bought, and perfunctory, but equally often people will try and make them special and unique, to reflect individual thoughts and feelings. Here we see how Itoh went about making her own selection one year.

Kabuki and Noh are traditional Japanese theatrical arts and share numerous plays and themes. Both are noted for their elaborate costuming, which reflects subtle traits of the wearer's character. The mention of Kiyohime's clothes refers to a famous legend about a woman who turns into a big snake when she is rejected by the man she loves. This legend has been made into both Noh and Kabuki plays and is well known to most Japanese.

Yoshiya Nobuko (1896–1973), a writer Itoh mentions here, was a novelist known for her sensitive portrayals of the problems of Japanese women both before and after World War II. She began writing popular stories at an early age, before the 1920s, and continued well into the 1960s. Much of her fiction is about the relationships women have with each other, but she also was a literary critic who focused on Japanese women writers. In addition, she is known for her histories of the women of the Tokugawa and Heike families.

We should mention, too, that the phrase "Best wishes for the New Year" literally means "*Congratulations* on the New Year" in Japanese. For more about New Year's and New Year's cards see "I don't like New Year's" in chapter 1 and "Each individual's words gave me strength" in chapter 11.

I used the phrase "I hope the days of the unknown future will be beautiful!"— from a poem by the writer Yoshiya Nobuko—for my New Year's cards for last year. And since it was the Year of the Snake, I drew isosceles triangles on the cards, symbolizing snake scales, an image from the clothes of Kiyohime found in Kabuki and Noh dramas.

Although I enjoy deciding on the design of New Year's cards every year—depicting the end of winter and the start of the new season—many times I have difficulty choosing the right words for them. This is because if we unconditionally say something like "Best wishes for the New Year," we have to remember that the world is actually not always so good. Thus, I do not feel like sounding so innocent or detached from reality.

Because of my thinking this way, the phrase from the poem, "I hope the days of the unknown future will be beautiful!" seems most appropriate to me. That is, at least we can hope that the unknown days will be bright. This fits my feeling.

On top of that, there is another reason why I was attracted to this poem. I have heard that the author, Yoshiya Nobuko, was not a traditional Japanese woman, just waiting for her husband and basing her happiness completely on her marriage. She valued friendship among women and devoted her life to her writing career. Such life-values are probably the reason I was attracted to her, as much as the beauty of her words.

The phrase "I hope the days of the unknown future will be beautiful!" also reminds me of days that we might say are not so beautiful. Some of these days are filled with regrets. There have been times—shall we say—when I have stepped in the mud puddle without any thought of whom I might splash. If possible I would like to make amends, even if just a little. This poem leads me to think this way.

This poem, though I send it to others, was something I was really sending to myself. After thinking back over the last year, the reason I chose this phrase for my cards was not only to introduce my friends to this idea, but I also wanted to remind myself of this attitude. ✎

*Y*ou should protect your own sensibilities.
Jibun no kanjusei kurai jibun de mamore
自分の感受性くらい自分で守れ

If we were to put things in Western terms, this piece is about Itoh's thoughts on the difference between knowledge and wisdom. However, it is actually a bit more subtle than that: Itoh is speaking of *kanjusei*. Here we translate *kanjusei* as "sensibility," but it really means the process whereby you take in information, feel it, interpret it, and make your own informed opinion. As a starting point she begins with a poem written by Ibaragi Noriko (b. 1926), a noted female tanka poet known for her pleasant style using imagery expressed in plain, everyday language.

A poem by Ibaragi Noriko, "Your Own Sensibilities," starts with the following words:

ぱさぱさに乾いてゆく心を	*Pasa pasa ni kawaite yuku kokoro o*
ひとのせいにはするな	*Hito no sei ni wa suru na*
みずから水やりを怠っておいて	*Mizu-kara mizu yari o okotatte oite*

"The mind is getting very dry, but
Do not blame this on someone else.
You yourself have forgotten to give it water."

So many people think that getting "knowledge" and "information" is the same thing as "understanding." But just "knowing" is not the same thing as "understanding." People who believe that they are the same just try and simply know more and more.

If we do not digest ideas on our own, there will be many things we will never understand. But many people just want to collect information. These people always ask others to teach them things, and they probably believe that if things are explained to them, they will understand them. They just want to accumulate more knowledge, and they want to memorize "right answers."

But if they believe that having a lot of information is the same thing as "wisdom," they are quite mistaken. These people may feel shame or be afraid of their ignorance, but they aren't ashamed of—and don't feel the danger of—their lack of sensibility. I believe that it is worse for a person to be dull or insensitive than merely ignorant.

Ibaragi Noriko finishes the poem in the following way:

自分の感受性くらい	*Jibun no kanjusei gurai*
自分で守れ	*Jibun de mamore*
ばかものよ	*Bakamono yo*

"You should protect your own sensibilities yourself, stupid!" ∾

*T*he abundant seeds of grass that don't know national boundaries are cast upon the ground.
Kokkyō o shiranu kusa no mi kobore ai
国境を知らぬ草の実こぼれ合い

In this piece, Itoh asks some profound philosophical questions, not the least of which is what are decent persons to do when their government or those around them are behaving immorally? As an exemplar she uses the case of Inoue Nobuko (1869–1958) who was an outspoken critic of Japanese nationalism in the 1930s, as well as being a poet and editor. She was the wife of Inoue Kenkabō, the giant of modern senryū poetry and editor of the *Yomiuri* newspaper's poetry column. (He was also the teacher of Yoshikawa Eiji [1892–1962], the best-selling author of many historical swashbuckling novels, and helped him get his start.) Inoue Nobuko started the first association of women senryū poets and was a pacifist ever since the start of the Russo-Japanese War in 1904. In 1937 she was arrested for her antimilitarist activities.

A senryū poem is a variation on the classic tanka pattern of versification in Japanese. The poems are usually satirical or express some social criticism and are free of some of the rigors and limitations of the tanka form. For more on senryū poems see "I have a pet monkey who knows how to tie a necktie very well" in chapter 3 and "Far away, far away, cherry blossoms are falling" and "The winter chrysanthemum is not pleasant" in chapter 14.

We might also explain something about the famous Japanese cheer, "Banzai!" Its Sino-Japanese characters (万歳) literally mean "ten thousand years." Because of World War II movies, most Americans think the cheer is some sort of battle cry or veneration of the Japanese emperor. Its history is a bit more complicated. Philologists tell us that this set of characters first appeared in the *Shoku nihongi* (the continuation of the *Nihon shoki*, one of the Shinto "Bibles" and legendary histories of Japan) around 800 CE. We don't exactly know how these characters were pronounced—likely as "banzei"—but they were supposedly uttered by Emperor Kanmu as a prayer for rain and a good harvest. The clouds burst, and the rest, as they say, is history. With the restoration of the Meiji emperor, and the rise of nationalism in the 1890s, this cheer took on a patriotic panache, meaning that the Japanese Empire would last ten thousand years. For example, Itagaki Taisuke (1837–1919), one of the important founders of the new Meiji state, yelled out "Banzai!" during an attempted assassination. (He added that freedom would go on even if he died. He lived.) During the American occupation after World War II, its use was discouraged. Today, the word carries no special connotations about the emperor. It is used simply as a cheer for special occasions, such as to convey congratulations or at farewell banquets. Following the British custom of "three cheers," ever since Meiji times is it customary to say *banzai* three times.

"The abundant seeds of grass that don't know national boundaries are cast upon the ground."

This line from Inoue Nobuko's *senryū* poem is the one that made her famous. People who do not know this poem and read it for the first time might think it was written recently. This phrase makes me think of today's international affairs. However, this poem was written during Japan's war against China (1937–1945). In other words, it was written during an atmosphere of Japanese nationalism and imperialism. Furthermore, she also wrote the following two poems in 1937, that the same year:

万蔵の声は　　　　*Banzai no koe wa*
涙の捨てどころ　　*namida no sute dokoro*

"The call of '*Banzai!*' is drowned in a pool of tears."

That is, when people are yelling "*Banzai!*"—a traditional cheer often given for the emperor—they are really crying.

戦死する敵にも　　*Senshi suru teki nimo*
親も子もあろう　　*oya mo komo arō*

"I suppose our enemies who were killed in the war also have parents and children."

How could she write these poems in such an oppressive climate promoted by the government? I just think she is great.

Inoue not only bravely vocalized her opinion as a poet but also as a poetry journal editor. She published the following poems written by Tsuru Akira—who died in prison at the age of twenty-nine as a political prisoner—in her journal without any hesitation:

手と足をもいだ　　*Te to ashi o moida*
丸太にしてかへし　*maruta ni shite kaeshi*

"After being turned into stumps without arms and legs, the government returns our sons and husbands to us."

タマ除けに　　　　*Tama yokeni*
産めよふやせよ　　*ume-yo fuyase-yo*
勲章やらう　　　　*kunshō yarō*

"We will give you a medal if you give us more babies—so there are more of us to hide behind when the shooting starts."

That is, the government will reward mothers for giving the country their national treasure: children to be cannon fodder.

仇に着す　　　*Kataki ni kisu*
縮緬織って　　*chirimen otte*
散るいのち　　*chiru inochi*

"I'm losing my life by weaving a silk crepe for our enemies to wear."

半島の生まれで　*Hantō no umare de*
つぶし値の　　　*tsubushi ne no*
生き埋めとなる　*ikiume to naru*

"Because we were born on the [Korean] Peninsula [and are not real Japanese], you might as well take our scrap lives and bury us alive."

That is, these Korean slaves who were brought over to Japan to work in the factories feel they will be worked to death.

These are not daring or bold poems; nor are they courageous. Actually, they are the opposite. The eyes of Tsuru Akira saw the depth of sentiment of human emotion. He wrote these poems as an ordinary citizen who felt a deep sympathy and understanding for the nameless soldiers, or their wives and mothers; the female silk workers; the Korean laborers brought to Japan to work in the factories.

I can say the same thing about Inoue's work. Her phrases are constructed with the full warmth of humanity. I am very interested in how the dignity and intelligence of the masses are expressed in these *senryū* poems.

Reading Inoue's poems now, I cannot help but feel how much they might overlap with the lives of women today. Here was a woman who was neither blindly swept along by the wake of social movements nor who strongly resisted the rising storm of fascism. Without straining, she lived as an ordinary person, living a daily life. ∾

A person whom we can ask for advice is nice.
A person who can be asked for advice is nice.
A person who can ask for advice is nice.

"Sō dan dekiru hito" tte, ii to omō
「相談できる人」って、いいと思う

We have given the title of this essay three translations because the Japanese phrase *sō dan dekiru hito* (marked in the original Japanese in brackets 「」 above) is ambiguous. It can mean three slightly different things, which is the point of discussion of this story. From the first-person perspective, the phrase can mean (1) "A person that I can *get advice from* is nice"; (2) "A person who is *able to give me advice* is nice"; or (3) "A person who is *able to accept advice* from others is nice."

Someone at our community center said, "A person whom we can ask for advice is nice."

All the people who were standing around agreed with her opinion, and we all started talking about this idea. However, somehow people were not all talking about the same thing. When I tried to make sure of the meaning it turned out that some thought we were saying that a person whom we can ask advice from—someone we can count on to talk about our problems with—is nice.

Others understood the phrase as meaning, "It is nice to be a person who can help others who have problems." Yet, the person who started the whole discussion in the first place said these were both wrong. According to her, the phrase meant that it was nice to be a person who is able to talk about problems first with others before making a decision, instead of making it by themselves.

To be able to make decisions for ourselves is very important. But it is not the same thing as deciding things selfishly in one's own way. When we are participating in group work and civic activities, we often enter into situations where I am reminded of this. There are many examples.

For instance, someone might just quit, because he or she had their own private reasons for doing so without explaining what these private reasons are. Or some people might think they are the ones who have to take responsibility, so therefore do things without consulting others; there is no doubt that these decisions were made responsibly in good faith.

Other people believe they are not in a position of important social responsibility, so they shouldn't bother anybody by asking for advice. And some people think they are the group leaders, and therefore they must make the decisions.

However, when we are working as a group, we have to know which things we have to decide for ourselves, and which things we have to ask others for advice about. If we do not know when we have to decide for ourselves and when we have to consult with others, our decisions will always end up being selfish, regardless of how well intended we are. Otherwise we cannot build up trust with others in the group.

In other words, "A person whom we can ask for advice" would really be "a person who can trust others in the group." ∾

*I*t is good that I have a dress that makes my accessory look nice.
Akusesarī ga hikitatsu fuku o motteite yokatta
アクセサリーがひきたつ服をもっていてよかった

Americans often are amused by what they feel are the large numbers of souvenirs Japanese people bring back from trips. While this is a stereotype, of course, it *is* true that many Japanese do fret over things like souvenirs and mementos because these supply a kind of social cement in Japan. Even the exchange of little things forms a bond between the parties involved. Thus, gift exchanges (*zōtō*) can be rather complicated affairs in Japan, as seen in this vignette.

There are at least two periods for formal gift exchanges: (1) (*O-*)*saibo* (or *seibo*) gifts are given at the end of the old year. Also around this time *o-nenga* gifts are presented during the first visit to someone at the start of the New Year. (Sometimes these are combined; if someone has already given an end-of-the-year gift to a person or family, just a small towel will suffice at the New Year's first visit.) (2) At midsummer (*O-*)*chūgen* gifts are presented, usually at the time of the Buddhist *O-bon* festivals (when the deceased ancestors are thought to return home). On both of these formal occasions, exchanges never take place between family members. To a large extent exchanges mark social hierarchy as *seibo* and *chūgen* gifts are given to superiors by inferiors, or by people who owe a social obligation to someone. Thus, for example, one's calligraphy teacher or someone who arranged for one's marriage would receive *seibo* and *chūgen* gifts.

There are many other informal gift-giving occasions, too, and in this story Itoh did not want her friend to feel especially obligated by what she considers a small gift. We see that her friend's use of informal language told Itoh that all is well.

Is there any such word like *letter millionaire* in the Japanese language? Although I do not have much property in my life, I think I am a real "letter millionaire" as I keep getting many good letters from many people. These are my treasures.

I think that I am blessed to have so many good people who send me such wonderful letters. My friend Keiko, who used to live in my town, is one of them. After she moved far away, she sent me letters from time to time. Without fail, she always sent me a simple but nice letter.

One day at a department store, I saw a silk handkerchief made in Thailand to put in a jacket pocket as a decoration. I was attracted by the beautiful material and color, so I bought it. But later I felt that it was too good for me to use, so after that I kept it without using it. One day I thought of Keiko, and when I was sending her a letter I enclosed the handkerchief with it. Later, I received her reply.

"I think the color of the handkerchief is called vermilion. When I put it in my breast pocket, I feel that it is so good that I have a velvet dress that makes the handkerchief look better."

I was so happy and relieved that her reply was very light and had a cheerful touch. I didn't want my present to obligate her. I was thinking that if she felt obligated because of my present, which I bought on impulse—and she replied using formal words of appreciation—I would not know what to do.

Her words were a tasteful choice, saying that she was glad she had a dress that made the accessory look better, instead of saying the accessory made a dress look better. Although I gave a present to her I felt that I received a pleasant lesson in return: the gift of her good sense. For a while I was carrying her letter with me wherever I went. ❧

My father knows only the words, "fall in love."
Chichi wa "horeru" to iu kotoba shika shiranai-no-desu
父は「惚れる」という言葉しか知らないのです

There are many different words for *love* or *to fall in love* in Japanese, none of which have an exact equivalent in English. For example, the most common word for *to love* (*suki*) also means "to like." Actually, until relatively recently a Japanese man would not even think to directly tell a woman that he loved her. The dictionary definition of the word used in the title (*horeru*) indeed means "to fall in love," but *horeru* is a term that carries many sexual and erotic overtones. It has connotations of someone being overwhelmed by desire or attraction, losing one's head in the heat of passion. It is mostly used by men, or women in the world of bars and the entertainment industry. A more neutral word is *ai-shite-iru*, "to love or have affection for." The use of the word *horeru* is the point of this piece.

Later in this essay, Itoh tells us that the wife of Uemura Naomi, a famous adventurer, explorer, and mountain climber, referred to him as a macho guy. The term used for "macho guy" here is *yakuza no otoko*, literally "a guy who acts like a gangster." She is not really accusing her husband of being a thug but is instead saying that he is an adrenaline junkie who sometimes puts himself before his family, going off and having adventures, and . . . well, what are you going to do! The physicality of *gangster* when referring to her husband accentuates the carnal passion Uemura's wife has for him (feelings all carried by *horeru*).

Uemura Naomi (1941–1984), by the way, scaled Mount Everest and the highest peaks on four other continents and usually climbed alone. He also reached the North Pole by dogsled. He died in 1984 trying to make a solo ascent of Mount McKinley.

Itoh also mentions novelist Serizawa Kōjirō (1897–1993) in this piece. He studied at the University of Paris in the 1920s, and this formed the basis of much of his later writing. He was known as a leading exponent of Japanese "proletarian" literature. His book *Pari ni shisu* (Death in Paris) was published in 1942.

When I was in junior high school I read *Death in Paris* by Serizawa Kōjirō, which was one of my mother's favorite books.

At that time, the words of the heroine Mariko stuck in my mind: "My father knows only the words, 'fall in love.'" These words were part of the letter Mariko was sending her boyfriend to explain why her vulgar father would not allow them to marry:

> I guess the people of my father's generation feel falling in love [*horeru*] with someone is a licentious thing. My father knows only the words, "fall in love" [*horeru*]. He does not know that "to love" [*ai-suru*] is the desperate effort of people to liven each other's spirits to make a complete person, one with whom we can share our fate together.

When I read this passage, I was impressed by the noble spirit promoted by love (*reiai*), and I came to have a childlike admiration of love.

However, later on, I wondered when I began to think that this "fall in love" (*horeru*) was not a vulgar term, but rather an attractive word. I started feeling that I would admire a woman who can strongly say, "I love (*horeru* or *horete-iru*) this man, whatever people think about him."

An example is what the wife of mountaineer Uemura Naomi said about him in a newspaper interview: "To me, he is just a guy trying to act macho."

She was not especially proud to be the wife of a famous man who was setting new world records and was seen as a hero by his country.

Very impressive to me was reading about her attitude:"I love this man not because he is famous or society places a value on what he does; I just love him." ∾

*W*hen men are around it is happy and cheerful.
Soba ni otoko ga iru to iu nowa, ureshī hanayagi-dearu
そばに男がいるというのは、うれしい華やぎである

How can romance last in a marriage? Does familiarity breed contempt? Do wives really love their husbands, or do they stay together for numerous other reasons—economics, family, convenience? Itoh addresses these questions in this vignette.

The *Kagerō nikki* (Kagero Diary), which Itoh refers to, is a very famous work of medieval Japanese literature. As mentioned in "Women don't need their own names, do they?" in chapter 4, it was the journal of Udaishō Michitsuna no haha, who was unhappily married to her husband, Fujiwara Kaneie. The Fujiwara family was the noble house that ruled Japan during this period—the years 954 to 974 CE. Diaries kept by women at this time—in vernacular Japanese rather than in Chinese, which was the province of literate males—are some of the most poignant writings in classical Japanese. For more information on Michitsuna no haha (literally "the mother of Michitsuna"), see the discussion in "Women don't need their own names, do they?" in chapter 4.

Later in the essay, we jump to modern times. The word for prostitute she uses here is *pan-pan*, a slang term that probably is better translated as "streetwalker." This term was especially used for professional women who were involved with American soldiers during the postwar occupation (1945–1951).

Itoh begins her essay with a quote from the book *Iutara nan'ya kedo* (I Know I Shouldn't Say This, But . . .) by novelist Tanabe Seiko (b. 1928), published by Chikuma Shobō, Tokyo, in 1973. For more on Tanabe Seiko see "A 'Ms. Ditz' cannot remain a 'bachelorette'" in chapter 10.

"When men are around it is happy and cheerful (even if they look like Frankenstein)." This sentence is from the book *I Know I Shouldn't Say This, But . . .* by novelist Tanabe Seiko.

Don't you think these are the words of a real adult woman? Some women say that "When a couple is filled with peace, it is just because the wife's desires are at a low level." I don't dislike these kinds of strong attitudes. But I think I like more the kind of woman who can feel that "being around men" is "happy and cheerful."

I recall that Tanabe also wrote the following, which also struck me: "Kaneie was a very attractive man whom even his own wife was in love with." This Kaneie was Fujiwara Kaneie, the husband of the author of the *Kagerō nikki* (Kagero Diary). His wife was Udaishō Michitsuna no haha.

Rarely is a husband loved by his wife, and there is not much we can do about that. But at least a wife should not just rely on the social identity and life security of having a husband and be proud of it. Doing so leads to some odd consequences. For example, the women's studies scholar Morosawa Yōko [b. 1925] says in her history of postwar women in Japan (*Onna no sengoshi*, 1971), "Just as wives are ranked by their husbands' social status, so are prostitutes also ranked by their clients."

Whether a wife or not, we should not be judged by "the men around us" (husbands, boyfriends, fathers, etc.). Instead, I think every woman should have the capacity to naturally say, "When men are around it is happy and cheerful." ∾

I would like to age subjectively.
Shutaiteki ni toshi o torō to omō
主体的に年をとろうと思う

In this essay Itoh suggests that "subjective aging" might be as important as chronological aging in the human life course. Just as a child's development and road to maturity are more than mere physical growth, so do we continuously progress through life as both individuals and social beings.

I was feeling a little down the other day thinking about getting older. I thought that if we would gain wisdom as we got older, that would be fine. But, in fact, that is usually not the case. While I was having these thoughts, a woman I knew said, "From now on, I would like to age subjectively."

This person was Ms. M, a young mother. She was attending a workshop on child care held at our community center and learned that a child does not naturally grow into a human being just by getting physically older. Before he or she can develop as a human being the child has to receive external stimuli and subjectively digest them. Only then can he or she finally grow. She believes that this lesson applies not only to child development, but also to self-improvement for adults like herself. Ms. M started to live her life this way, consciously fostering this subjectivity in her life. She described her life philosophy as one in which we are not carried away by the things in everyday life, but one in which we digest what we experience.

Since then, she no longer just dismisses the casual talk of greetings or the off-the-cuff opinions of people. She replies to people with consideration and reflection and might even change her opinion after she gives some thought to what she has heard. When she hears her friends' opinions, she checks their value and sees if she can implement them into her own life. That is how she learns: through associating and trying to grow with people.

The wonderful part is that among the members of her group at the community center, all can build their humanity together, just as if they were sharing communal property. They expressed it this way: "Through changes fostered in discussions about child care, the other aspects of daily life have also become fun."

Now they are a shining light for people around them. ✤

· 11 ·

How Society Should Be

*S*he is a person who lets people "wait without frustration."
Ii matase kata o suru hito-nē
いい待たせ方をする人ねぇ

In this essay, Itoh talks about the power of communication and consideration. Every organization needs teamwork, but Japanese sociologists and anthropologists often tout—along with Western sociologists and anthropologists specializing in Japan—that consensus and cooperation are valued more highly in Japan than, say, the United States. For example, before business meetings oftentimes participants partake in *nemawashi*, behind-the-scenes negotiations that make the actual gathering more of a formality than a decision-making activity. In everyday life, such practices are also values, as Itoh shows here.

When we do things with other people, if we don't keep them informed about what is going on, getting anything done is very hard. Timing is everything, and when we keep each other informed of our progress, things get done more quickly and smoothly, and everyone feels good. This mutual trust creates the spirit of teamwork. However, if some people do not inform us at all about what they are doing, communication becomes strained. In the worst case, projects can even collapse if this happens too often. Just giving us one word can ease our minds.

The other day, this happened: we were supposed to have a meeting of the heads of several group-activity units at our local community center to discuss some important items. Suddenly the weather turned bad. We were worried about whether the members could make it or not, since some of the members had little children or were pregnant. If we couldn't get enough people to show up we would have to postpone the meeting.

While we were discussing the possibilities, someone called us up. According to her, she and the other members were already arranging ways to get to the community center themselves. For example, she said would stop by and pick up Mrs. A; Mrs. B would be driving herself; Ms. C was not going to be able to make it but had lined up a replacement, and so on. She informed us precisely one by one about who would eventually be coming and who could not make it.

At the end of the call she said, "I called because I thought that you folks who were over there waiting might be worried about those of us who were coming." In short, to her credit, she was letting us "wait without frustration" or worry.

Although she was not a group organizer at the community center, she did this out of her own thoughtfulness, and her actions helped unite and support the group. She did this without being asked. I believe that if each person could contribute in this way, all our projects would be a success. I believe that the real value of working together in organized activities such as these is the spirit of cooperation fostered between people. That day everybody felt very warm and said their activities should foster the spirit of cooperation. ✎

The public is us [because the public opinion is our voice].
Seken-tte watashi-tachi no koto dakara
世間って私たちのことだから

Here Itoh examines the power of social pressure, especially social pressure as expressed in language—not just what we might call "conventional wisdom" or the vox populi, but also gossip and just plain talking behind someone else's back. But as one of her friends explains, sometimes there is no difference.

An elementary-school child whom I know well had an accident the other day and broke a bone. I called his mother to pay my respects and see how the child was doing. The mother said she was very lucky that the accident happened on a Sunday. I wondered what she meant by that. Was it because, being Sunday, she could take her child to see the doctor immediately? Or was it that because it was Sunday, the child would not be feeling lonely being home alone?

But what my friend said was, "If today was a weekday, everyone would say, 'Because the mother was out working she wasn't able to watch her child and that's why he got hurt.'"

I also heard a similar kind of story from another friend of mine: "My father-in-law was sick in bed for a very long time. At the end, I was by his bedside, constantly looking after him, and had gotten almost no sleep or rest. I did not have any more strength left to attend his funeral. But people criticized me harshly, saying, 'What kind of daughter-in-law is she, who is lying around in a bed instead of attending her father-in-law's funeral!'"

And I heard another lament from another friend—one who has been divorced. She said painfully, "One time at the office I was just giving my professional opinion about a business matter. However, behind my back people said things like, 'No wonder her husband had an affair and they got divorced! Who could live with such a woman with such a strong character?'"

I said, "How unreasonable, cruel, and painful public opinion is." When I mentioned this, another woman who was listening said,

> Right now I don't participate in any citizens' campaigns or contribute to what is often called public opinion. But in my daily life, when I meet a person who says something is only one way—even though there can be multiple interpretations—I have decided from now on to always simply say, "Well, that might not necessarily be the only way to look at it." This is because the public is us; public opinion is our voice. That is, in daily life what people are saying is what becomes the public opinion. I would like to start changing the public, at least the public around me. ✍

If I become a person who becomes bedridden, I'd rather die.
Netakiri ni narukurai-nara shinda hō ga mashi
寝たきりになるくらいなら死んだほうがまし

Some might argue—quite stereotypically!—that the Japanese are some of the most apologetic people in the world. Even some language textbooks for foreigners say that words like *sumimasen* (I am sorry; excuse me) can be generic sociolinguistic terms, applicable to almost any situation, from receiving a gift to saying good-bye. Yet, the Japanese also say that if all it took was an apology, there would be no need for the police. In this essay Itoh talks about how we can inadvertently cause pain and hurt even though we do not mean to be malicious. Once words are said, we excuse ourselves by taking them back. In English, we might say we cannot un-ring a bell.

Recently I read in the newspaper the following words of a woman who has been looking after one of her elderly parents for a long time:

There are some people, even though they are healthy now, who say, "If I become a person who becomes bedridden, I'd rather die." These people might think, someplace in the back of their minds, that people who are bedridden are unneeded, and they are not worthy of life.

When I read this, I was shocked because I, too, have also said that if I were bedridden I would probably rather die. Maybe unconsciously I was viewing the lives of people who are bedridden as not valuable.

In our daily lives there are many things we say that we really do not mean to say but turn out to be horrible, even if we don't want them to be. As a result, we can hurt people. Often we are also hurt in the same way. Because people who say these kinds of things are not malicious, the pain they give is deep, and this pain cannot be taken away.

And this doesn't just apply to individual personal relationships. For example, we might think that our efforts are contributing to the improvement of the social status of women, but it might turn out, after all, that we are just contributing to making a society where only economics come first, and we destroy our humanity. And when we conscientiously follow these social roles given to us, we can become people who destroy democracy without our realizing it.

The actions of goodwill can turn out to accelerate going to war. What we thought was responsibility turned out to be dominance; what we thought was consideration turned out to be humiliation; what we thought was kindness turned out to be cruelty, robbing others of independence and pride.

Sometimes we can't just say, "I did not mean that." At least we have to remember that we can't be excused by just saying such a thing, and we must always keep these lessons or warnings in our minds. ❧

> *A* medical doctor is a person who cannot understand anything without doing an examination first.
> *O-isha-san-tte iu no wa, kensa o shinakute wa nanimo wakaranai hito nano-yo*
> お医者さんっていうのは、検査をしなくては何もわからない人なのよ

Doctor-patient relationships are some of the most delicate in the world, and Japan is no exception. Some of the same complaints about bedside manner, which Itoh reflects on here, could probably apply to hospitals anywhere.

Japanese medical knowledge and technology are among the best in the world. However, in this essay, we see that in Japan, doctors and hospitals are socially and culturally a little different than in the West. First, physicians in Japan are thought to be almost omniscient, are highly respected, and are almost never questioned. Second opinions, while not unheard of, are rare, and malpractice lawsuits have been nonexistent until recent times.

In Japan, depending on the hospital or the condition of the patient, many patients have a *tsukisoi-nin* (patient attendant) to look after them. If a family member cannot do so, a patient attendant is hired to do many of the jobs that nurses do in the United States, such as feeding or bathing the patient, or assisting them with washroom activities. Though they are not licensed nurses, and this is not a very glamorous job, the pay is adequate.

We should perhaps comment about a remark made by the patient attendant in this story. Itoh claimed, "She tried to understand the patient without examination." What she is probably getting at here is some aspects of *kampō*—traditional (Chinese-based) medical philosophy brought to Japan in the seventh century and still sometimes practiced today. As opposed to the Western germ-theory model of disease that emphasizes treatment of symptoms, *kampō* is more preventative and believes if the body is strengthened, it will cure itself. Herbal and mineral medicines are used, with formulas based on a patient's individual needs. These needs are determined by diagnosing the patient's condition—or nature of malaise—based on observing his or her various subjective expressions and objective manifestations. Detailed questions about a patient's emotional state and physical sensations are the first line of attack by a *kampō* practitioner, as opposed to blood tests or other modern medical diagnostics.

When I went to see a doctor a while ago, I did not think my health was so bad. Thus, I was really confused when I was put into the hospital immediately. I got very depressed just hearing the name of the disease. I always wanted to just be able to lie around in bed all day, but when I was forced to, I could not wait to get out of bed as soon as possible.

Since I couldn't see much of what was going on beyond my bed, I naturally started paying more attention to various sounds and voices. Once I became sick, I started hearing voices I could not hear before.

"A medical doctor is a person who cannot not understand anything without doing an examination first." These were the words of a patient attendant who was looking after the person next to me.

She was a person who was trying hard to understand the condition of her patients. She wanted to listen to what her patients were saying—their requests and needs—rather than relying on a physical examination. In other words, she tried to understand the patient without examination—more than that, I think, she tried to understand *beyond* the words.

I also overheard what a student nurse was told when she was learning how to change bedsheets by an experienced nurse who was instructing her that day: "Before you do anything, you have to explain what you are going to do to a patient. Even small things. If you start doing something without telling them, they will get worried. And besides, it is just not polite . . ."

While I was listening to this I remembered the words of my friend who is working at a day-care center. "These days there are many mothers who just suddenly turn their babies over to change their diapers without saying anything to them," she deplored.

When I heard this, I recalled what the nursing instructor said: "Besides, it is just not polite . . ." I felt these comments were nice. Even with a baby, I think, we have to respect basic human dignity. The nursing instructor also said, "Don't address your patients with some catch-all title like *O-bā-chan* [Grandma], but call them by their names, like 'Mrs. Nakamura.'"

While I was listening to these nurses' conversation, I felt that the basic attitude of being a nurse is the same basic attitude we need in all human relations. ✍

*W*e should not use titles on the rooms of nursing homes.
Sama mo dono mo tsuite wa ike-nai
様も殿も付いてはいけない

Japanese people attach suffixes like *-san* ("Mr." or "Mrs.") or *-sama* (a more polite form of *-san*) to last names when addressing each other. (See "Because I cannot see the faces of my audience . . ." in chapter 6 for another such kind of title.) However, one never uses these suffixes for oneself (unlike in the United States or Britain where someone might say, for example, "I am Mrs. John Smith" or "I am Mr. John Doe").

Japanese houses traditionally have the name of the family that lives there written on a nameplate, much like an address number in the West. But because it is one's own house, of course, no title like *-san* is put on this nameplate. This is not the case in hospitals or other institutions, where a title is used out of politeness to the temporary guest. The point of Itoh's vignette below is that when a title suffix is attached to a name on a door in a nursing home, it sounds like that room is not really the resident's but remains under the prerogative of the institution.

In this vein, Itoh recalls a poem by Ishigaki Rin (b. 1920), a Tokyo poet active since the 1960s. Ishigaki is known for her working-class sensibilities and women's sensitivities. Her book *Hyōsatsu nado* (Nameplates, Etc.)—from which the poem in this essay was taken—won the H-Shi Prize in 1969.

There are some people who are working on a new way to run a nursing home, trying to create a place that is comfortable for the elderly as well as maintaining their dignity. These people are staff members of an assisted-living nursing home opening in a newly developing area in Yokohama this fall. When I visited them—even during the construction of the building—they were continuously discussing small details, like what kind of name tags to use on the doors of the rooms of the residents. They wanted to be sure they were operating on correct principles.

They also kindly asked me for my opinion about making a better nursing home. I told them that I thought that each room's nameplate on the door should just have the person's last name written on it, just as houses have. There should not be a title like "Mr." or "Mrs." I told them that the best thing to do was to have the new residents bring their own nameplates from their previous homes, if they wanted. Even though the nursing home would probably still have to make a lot of nameplates themselves, the policy should be that the residents should still be able to decide what they want to put on the outside of their doors. These nameplates, I said, were not only for the sake of the staff, but were also reflections of the nursing home residents' identities.

When I mentioned this to the staff, I was reminded of a famous poem called "Hyōsatsu" (House Nameplate) by the poet Ishigaki Rin:

自分の住むところには自分で表札を かけるにかぎる。	*Jibun no sumu tokoro niwa jibun de hyōsatsu o kakeru ni kagiru*
自分の寝泊まりする場所は他人がか けてくれる表札にはいつもろくな ことはない。	*Jibun no ne-tomari suru basho wa tanin ga kakete kureru hyōsatsu niwa itsumo rokunakoto wa nai*
病院へ入院したら病室の名札には石 垣りん様と様がついた。	*Byōin e nyūin shitara byōshisu no nafuda niwa Ishigaki Rin-sam to sama ga tsuita*
様も殿も付いてはいけない。	*Tono mo sama mo tsuite wa ihenai*

"It is the best thing for me that I can put my
nameplate myself on the place
where I live.

When others put a nameplate over the place
where I sleep, things always turn
out badly.
When I was hospitalized a staff member put
'Ms. Rin Ishigaki' on my nameplate
on the door.
I don't want to go into a place where there
are titles on the door . . ."

I think if we wish not to institutionalize the elderly but to truly create new homes for them, nursing homes should not be places "where there are titles on the door."

I read the poem again after a long time. It also says later, "Even in the place for one's soul there should not be a nameplate put by there by someone else." ∾

I wish I could always say the right thing in the right way.
Chōdoyoi hodo no koe de arimasu yō-ni
ちょうどよいほどの声でありますように

In this essay Itoh turns once again to one of her favorite topics—the power of words and how we are often unaware of this power, or use it carelessly. Rare, indeed, is a person who knows how to say just the right thing, in the right way, at the right time. Oddly, sometimes we can be too cheerful for the sick person, or too lively for someone who is depressed.

I was hospitalized for a while. At that time my lingering condition made it too painful for me to even talk, so I was quite depressed. I really felt sorry for the people who came all the way to see me at the hospital, as it was hard for me to visit with anyone except very close relatives.

At this time, too, I was receiving postcards from time to time from a friend of mine. Each postcard had an appropriate image and had just a few words on the back telling me about my friend's simple, everyday life written in a calm, matter-of-fact style. During this period, she had been involved in a number of radical social and political movements. Since I knew her social activism kept her quite busy, I was very appreciative of her consideration in thinking about me.

However, when I think back to why I was so appreciative of her postcards, I realize it was not just because she was so busy that I was touched. Rather, it was because of her deep and warm understanding of how sick people feel that I had such warm feelings.

I realized this clearly when I received another nice letter from another friend. In her letter she wrote, "I do not say, 'Please recover soon,' but instead say, 'Take your time to get well.'" I was touched by the warm kindness of these thoughts.

Another person wrote,

When I am depressed, I often feel more down by hearing other people's lively words rather than being cheered up by them. Thus, I hope my words are not too lively for you. I am writing hoping that I have said just the right thing—that my words have just the right amount of liveliness to make you feel better.

I really think these people know how to greet sick people and are really sincerely warm and considerate persons. ∾

The woman who lies here by herself prays for peace.
Onna hitori iki, koko ni heiwa o negau
女ひとり生き、ここに平和を希う

In this essay, Itoh returns to a theme that she addressed previously—the connections between the feminist and antifascist movements before and during World War II. As she shows, these have had lasting repercussions.

In the Japanese version of the title here, the phrase "prays for peace" can mean a desire for the deceased to *rest* in peace, or it can imply an antiwar sentiment. See "We can't stand by and let women's sincere good intentions be exploited anymore" in chapter 7 for more about the feminist Ichikawa Fusae (1893–1981).

The word *ie* means "family," "house," or "household" but implies more than this. The notion *ie* carries is also of the traditional Japanese patrilineal extended family. In Japanese tradition even today a woman is interred at her husband's gravesite at her husband's family temple. For more about the *ie* system, see "It would have been better if I had liked my mother-in-law" in chapter 5.

In the garden of Jōjakkō Temple in the Sagano area of Kyoto there is a memorial monument made of smooth natural stone. This plaque is called the Women's Stone Letters. On it are carved the words of a poem written by the feminist activist Ichikawa Fusae: "The woman who lies here by herself prays for peace."

Because Japan lost so many young men during World War II, quite a few women were not able to find marriage partners and had no choice but to remain single. Thus, many women in that generation were forced into lives quite different from the traditional Japanese woman's way of life. Because they were unmarried, they faced social discrimination from society. Because they were unmarried, they faced problems with their relatives. They often had to support their families or take over as the head of the family, but at the same time, because they were single, their families never really accepted them as normal. Quite a few such women were not even allowed to lie in the family gravesite, where they might sleep peacefully after they died.

I heard that many of these poor women therefore got together before death and arranged to make common graves for themselves at this temple, and that is why there is this stone monument at Jōjakkō Temple.

These women, then, were the victims of marriage discrimination as well as the victims of the war. And yet, I want to make clear that these were empowered women who not only were critics of the war, they were pioneers of women's rights and independence. They learned how to live beyond the *ie* and discovered new ways to be members of society.

After I found out about this women's memorial, I try to visit it as often as possible whenever I go to Kyoto. I stand in front of the stone and read the poem lightly out loud. However, I sometimes change the word *koko ni* (here) in the poem to *tomo ni* (together). Thus, for me, the poem says,

女ひとり生き、共に平和を希う
Onna hitori iki, tomo ni heiwa o negau
The women who lie here by themselves
    together pray for peace (as do I)

I think the word *together* is more appropriate for these comrades who experienced bitter hardship and loneness in life but are now sleeping together peacefully. That is why I would like to change the poem. Also, I think my version not only fits the intent of the memorial stone but also expresses the desire of later generations to wish for peace for all of these women who experienced hardship and loneliness. ✿

*L*ife exists between person and person.
Seimei wa, hito to hito to no aida ni aru
生命は、人と人との間にある

In this essay, Itoh once again addresses a recurring theme in this book: how language mediates and creates social order. In essence, Itoh argues that meaning is not ontologically existent, but only "emerges" through negotiation in the context of social life and interaction—though she might not appreciate using this arcane language of social psychology, cognitive science, or philosophy.

Maruoka Hideko (1903–1990), whom Itoh mentions here, was a rural social activist sociologist. She was particularly concerned with problems of women in Japanese farming villages and was one of the first researchers to write on the subject. Later she became involved in nuclear disarmament, establishing agricultural cooperatives, and educational reform.

One day the commentator and critic Maruoka Hideko asked me, "What do you think? Where does the source of life energy come from?" Seeing my shock and hesitant mumbling as I touched my heart with confusion, she calmly and slowly said, "I wonder if it is in our body or if it is also something that exists between people?"

She asked this as if she were making sure for herself. But this type of thinking about the connection between people was a revelation to me. After I found out that she developed this idea from a physicist's explanation, I was even more impressed, and her idea was embedded deeply in my mind.

When we study life as a material phenomenon, we trace things from the cell, to the molecule, and to the atom (which itself is composed of protons, neutrons, and electrons). And an object is created by the motion between all these parts. After hearing this explanation of an "object," Maruoka thought, "If this is so, life does not exist in an individual solid thing but exists as a phenomenon of invisible nuclear movements."

Maruoka left many wise sayings in this world. The following are just a few examples:

Children watch how their mothers participate in history.

That is, children learn by watching how their parents live in our society—how they create history at every moment.

Labor is deeply related to one's spirit, and is also a basic component of a person's way of life.

One's hometown is not a place, but is sum of all the paths he or she has walked down until yesterday.

However, for me the best of her sayings is "Life exists between person and person." ∾

*ℱ*ortunately my mouth and spirit are still healthy.
Saiwai, watashi wa, kuchi to kokoro ga genki-desu kara
幸い、私は、口と心が元気ですから

In this vignette, Itoh speaks of the inspiration given by her friend Toyoda Masako (b. 1922), an author of note who wrote several important works before the Second World War. The Essayist Club Award, which she won in 1986, is given to three books each year for major contributions to nonfiction. *Hana no wakare: Tamura Akiko to watashi* (The Parting of Flowers: Tamura Akiko and I, Tokyo: Mirai-sha, 1985) received the thirty-fourth award. (For more on Tamura Akiko see "How can we say it is honorable to be killed that way?" in chapter 10.) A book of hers based on her mother's life, *O-Yuki* (Tokyo: Mokkei-sha Press, 1991), introduced her writings to a new generation of readers.

Takamine Hideko (b. 1924), whom Itoh also mentions, was a very well-known actress of the 1950s and 1960s. She made the film *The Spelling Class* when she was only fourteen years old, and this role skyrocketed her to instant fame.

On New Year's Eve a while back, when she was living by herself, my friend, the writer Toyoda Masako, suddenly suffered a stroke while taking a bath. No one found her for two days and nights. By the time they found her and took her to the hospital, she had almost frozen to death. Although miraculously she somehow escaped death, the left side of her body remains paralyzed. Since then, she has been living in a hospital.

Toyoda was called a genius because of her early works written before the Second World War. One of her most famous books was *The Spelling Class*, which became a best seller and was made into a movie starring Takamine Hideko. In 1986 Toyoda received the Essayist Club Award for *The Parting of Flowers: Akiko Tamura and I*. She has recently gained public attention again due to the reprinting of *O-Yuki*, a book based on her mother's life.

People have been discussing her very much these days, and when I talk to young people about her, they often recall her name, saying, "Oh, yes, *that* Toyoda . . . !"

In a letter I received from her while she was receiving rehabilitation in the hospital, she said, "Fortunately my mouth and spirit are still healthy." When I read her letter, I was reminded of a letter written to me by another friend of mine, which I had received earlier. This other friend of mine developed spinal tuberculosis when she was a teenager. She talked about this period in her letter.

> The household that has an ill person tends to become depressed. If the sick person—who is causing the family to be depressed—was crying, everybody became much more depressed. So I tried to be cheerful. Later I remembered that my mother said to me, "Because you were cheerful, you saved us," and I was happy to hear that.

She wrote this letter to me when I was sick and had become depressed myself. Her words made me think about life. And now this time, together with Toyoda's letter, the importance of the message of her words has become much more clear to me.

"Fortunately my mouth and spirit are healthy." I wonder if Toyoda is using this phrase to encourage those around her? ∾

The future really is the power of imagination.
Sōzōryoku towa, yagate kanō ni naru mono no koto-da
想像力とは、やがて可能になるもののことだ

In this piece Itoh reflects on what makes a just society: Immediate pleasure or longer-term happiness? Accepting current conditions and making the best of things or holding out for a perfect world? She is inspired here by the writings of Marguerite Duras (1914–1996) and Eva Forest (1928–2007). Duras was a well-known author in both French and English, and Forest was a psychologist and feminist who was jailed for several years during the Franco regime in Spain (which lasted from 1939 to 1975).

A newspaper column about the French novelist Marguerite Duras a while back started out like this:

> Duras was a member of the Communist Party. She told people that "My soul is communist." However, she also said that the world would never adopt communism. This is because "People are not interested in happiness. They are interested in pleasure . . . people cannot stand happiness based on perfect equality."

While she was talking about the impossibility of communism, I felt that I saw the despair and hopelessness of this age in her words. Nonetheless, she added, "However, my dream of a communist society is still with me."

Often when we try to consider some principle or ideology and try to see if it is worthwhile or not, some people from the beginning try to dismiss the idea by saying, "This won't work in reality" and take measures to defeat it right from the start.

I often find this kind of thing. Each time when this happens, I think, "Confronting reality is not the same thing as approving the current situation, and ideology is different from fantasy."

But I don't know how to explain this to people and I feel frustrated. Thus, when I heard about Duras's way to approach ideology, and to try and make a dream a reality, it opened up my eyes, and I felt we were kindred spirits.

I then remembered the words from a book called *The Diary of Eva Forest: Notes from a Spanish Prison* [Tokyo: Jiji Tsūshin-sha Press, 1972]: "The future really is the power of imagination."

When I read the words of the two women, Marguerite Duras and Eva Forest, I feel encouraged, like seeing the light at the end of a tunnel in which I am traveling together with them. ∾

*E*ach individual's words gave me strength.
Hitori no kata no hitokoto no hagemashi ga donna ni yūki o ataete kureta koto-deshō
一人の方のひと言の励ましがどんなに勇気を与えてくれたことでしょう

As mentioned earlier, *O-shōgatsu*, or New Year's Day, is the most important holiday in Japan. Special foods are prepared, and in many families money is given to children (*o-toshi-dama*). At this time, people also customarily send out *nengajō* or "New Year's postcards." These are somewhat akin to Christmas cards in the United States and Europe, but there are three noticeable differences: (1) cards are based on that year's animal of the East Asian calendar—horse, ox, etc.; (2) these cards are often government-issued postcards with lottery numbers on them, for a prize drawing held later; and (3) there are many more of them (as some families send out several hundred).

The post office keeps these cards until January 1 and delivers them all around the same time. Thus, it is rather exciting each year to see who sent cards to whom. For more on New Year's in Japan see "I don't like New Year's" in chapter 1 and "I hope the days of the unknown future will be beautiful!" in chapter 10. For a more detailed discussion of the East Asian calendar and the animals of the Asian zodiac see "I hope the days of the unknown future will be beautiful!" in chapter 10.

Once I became an adult, New Year's Day was not so much worth waiting for anymore. But that said, I still look forward to receiving New Year's cards every year. Also, it is fun for me to select what I think are the five best cards I received and show them to my family. What kind of cards am I going to receive this year? What kind of words, or news, am I going to hear? With the impressions I get from my cards, I believe I can get a sense for how the coming year is going to be.

The best New Year's card of a few years ago was the one that I received from Ms. S. She was a staff member at the community center, but the year before she was suddenly transferred to a different department and sent to a new location. After she received the notice of the transfer, we other colleagues asked her supervisor to immediately reconsider this decision, and other people in the community also vocalized their disapproval. However, in the end, she had to relocate. In her New Year's card the following year she wrote, awe inspiringly and clearly, that "This transfer was an order that went against the citizens' will."

She went on to say,

I also showed my determination. And the community loyally put all their power against this transfer and expressed their disapproval. In front of all this institutional power, each individual's words gave me strength. At the same time, I felt that I saw the abandonment of individual dignity by those who were forcing an unjust and unreasonable thing upon others. But this experience showed me that what an individual person can accomplish is bigger than what I thought. . . . I would like this year to have a great experience.

I was very impressed by these words about how much strength and power an individual has, and these words have stayed in my mind.

Two years later she was sent back to our community center, and everyone was very happy. Because she was sent back, those words that she wrote in her New Year's card became very important and unforgettable for me. ∾

*T*his is a town that keeps the worst of the country and has lost the best of the country.
Inaka no warusa wa nokoshite, yosa o nakushita inakamachi-nano
田舎の悪さは残して、よさを失くした田舎町なの

In this essay, Itoh and her friends lament the changes taking place locally all over Japan as the result of globalization and internationalization. As seen here, not everything is as it appears.

What passes for modern can actually be conservative; liberal actions can turn out to be repressive; and real problems can be ignored or covered over in a progressive facade.

As we have seen in numerous other selections, English loanwords abound in contemporary Japanese, and we find a special one here in the description of the town: *hai-kara* (high-collar). This is a made-in-Japan loanword and was popular around the time of the First World War, when Japan was still in the process of Westernizing. A person who wore the high, starched, stiff collars of British men's suits of the period was thought to be progressive, modern, and fashionable. The word came to be applied to other things besides people and dress. We have translated it here as "chic," and the feeling is that this town has a kind of 1920s nostalgia or flavor. For more on English in Japanese, see "Even though she is a healthy adult, only a wife gets categorized as a dependent" in chapter 3, "It's become a case of 'the weak fish eat the weaker fish,' hasn't it?" in chapter 4, "They can't stand each other unless they change their surroundings from time to time" in chapter 5, and "I wonder when a home became a thing that can be bought and sold" in chapter 12.

Later on Itoh's friend talks about *katakana*. This is a special writing system in Japan. Besides the famous characters borrowed from China fifteen hundred years ago, written Japanese also has two phonetic syllabaries. A syllabary is like an alphabet except that a symbol stands for a syllable of sounds instead of a single sound. A majority of the languages in Asia use this type of orthography. One of the syllabaries in Japanese is used mostly for foreign names or loanwords. This is the *katakana* being referred to here. For example, the English loanword *hai-kara* mentioned in the previous paragraph would be written as ハイ•カラ in *katakana*. The thousands of loanwords used in Japanese—like *feminisuto fōram* (feminist forum) mentioned later in the main text—are written in this way.

Itoh's friend briefly mentions the problem of Koreans in Japanese society, which is discussed in several of Itoh's essays: see "That woman is like an obstinate, grumpy old man" in chapter 3, "We can't conduct a conversation equally when we only use women's language" in chapter 6, and "The most important thing about being a human being is to learn about the world by ourselves" and "I think it is so good that I am not a Japanese" in chapter 13 for more on this subject.

Several of my friends and I went to visit our friend who had moved to the countryside. When we got off the train, we saw lots of nice fashionable shops around the station. The sidewalks were inlaid with painted tiles, and there were nice statues here and there. Along the sidewalks were old-fashioned gas street-lights. The houses were standing all in a row, each one in the current style.

One of us said, "This is a chic little town, isn't it?" Our friend who lives here answered bitterly, "Indeed it is, but the level of culture is low. It's a town of ostentatious decoration." She added:

> I have started seeing the old connections and local conservatism that con-trol city hall and lie underneath the ostentatiousness of this town. And yet, the natives follow the current trends and pretend they have a cosmopolitan atmosphere. Even though it is pleasant out here in the countryside, this is a town that keeps the worst of the country and has lost the best of the country.
>
> For instance, the members of the local village board and the staff mem-bers of the administration all have connections to the representatives of the national Diet from this city.
>
> There have also been discussions that married women keep their maiden names after they are married. I at first thought that this was a criticism of the traditional family system. It turns out it is not. They say, "In case a fam-ily has only a daughter and she marries and takes her husband's last name, the name of their ancestors—which was passed down from generation to generation—would perish, and that is a sad thing. Thus, we can maintain our ancestors' love by having women keep their last names."
>
> This is a case of appearing liberal but really being conservative. There are others. For example, they even have apparently progressive workshops with names like *feminisuto fōram* (feminist forum) or other things written in *katakana*. Again, they think they are at the cutting edge of new modern views, but they are still conservative.
>
> The current fad of internationalization is taking over the town, and local people often teach foreign students how to wear kimonos or eat sushi. They hold events for their own self-satisfaction, but they do not pay any attention to more important issues, like equal rights for the Japanese-Korean residents who have been living in this area for a long time.

She mentioned many things like this. If what my friend says is true, this problem is not one just of this town. It is a problem of my town as well and is probably a problem throughout all of Japan. That is what we all thought. ∽

• *12* •

Married Life

*T*he only thing I ever did with my husband was arrange for my
father-in-law's funeral.
Otto to chikara o awasete yatta koto-tte gifu no o-sōshiki dake
夫と力を合わせてやったことって義父のお葬式だけ

Here Itoh discusses the perennial problem of how husbands and
wives can live together harmoniously. What is love, and what is the
meaning and import of marriage? While these questions are asked
everywhere in the world, the responses we see here might strike
Western readers as being especially Japanese.

Though cremation is almost universal in Japan, funerals are
complex and expensive ceremonies, and most follow Buddhist ritual.
There is a viewing in the home along with an all-night wake. Guests
must be accommodated, refreshments served, a banquet and banquet
hall arranged for, speeches written and made, and gift exchanges
monitored. Needless to say, planning is critical and requires the smooth
cooperation of the whole family—hence the title of this piece.

One of the women in the essay talks about her life in Manchuria
during the Second World War. Japan tried to colonize the Manchurian
part of China with agricultural settlers in the 1930s and 1940s. Eventually, more than three hundred thousand Japanese emigrated to Manchukuo, the state created under Japanese auspices in the years 1931–1945.
Most Japanese were expelled after the war's end. For more on this see "If
you want, you can call me a traitor. I don't care" in chapter 10.

A woman of almost seventy once casually told me,

My husband and I like watching baseball games on TV. But these days, I
sometimes wonder if I will be able to watch baseball on TV alone without

167

crying when my husband passes away. When I think of our time remaining, every minute together is precious.

Upon hearing her say this, a woman in her fifties said with a sigh,

I envy couples like you. With my now-retired husband spending all day lying around underfoot—with neither of us saying much—I get rather depressed and gloomy. I do not like myself when I resent my husband being home all day long. When I hear something like the love you have for each other, I am very envious.

The old woman modestly replied,

No, I don't think we are particularly close to each other. It is just that we had to stick together as we went through some difficult times. We got married during World War II and came back after living abroad in Manchuria. And after the hardships of the war, there was illness and economic problems.

Some of the women in their thirties and forties started talking with some uncertainty. One said, "After hearing a story like that all I can say is—fortunately or unfortunately—we have never as a couple had to work together like that in our lives."

One of the women said, as if she had discovered this for the first time, "When I think about it, during the whole twelve years we have been married, the only thing I ever did with my husband was arrange for my father-in-law's funeral. That was the only time I felt like he was my partner." Everyone looked around at each other, and there was a long pause.

I wonder if the lifestyle of young couples these days makes it hard to understand one of life's everyday obvious lessons: when a couple goes through difficult times together, the relationship is strengthened.

Although I would like to say that it is normal for couples to be naturally devoted to each other, in fact, it looks like very hard work. ໑

It is just that "my domestic life comes with me."
"Katei-seikatsu" ga idō shiteiru dake nan-desu-mono
「家庭生活」が移動しているだけなんですもの

In this essay Itoh addresses a concern that probably many women have in both Japan and the United States: how to separate life outside the home from life inside the home, the individual from the family, the public from the private. Itoh argues that even career women often bring a "housewives'" attitude to the job. Full-time housewives—who often have few options in Japan of working outside the home if they have children—are burdened even more so with a domestic mindset, 24/7. It is the long-term effects of this on the psyche that Itoh discusses here.

Women who have small children tend to have narrow worlds, spending most of their time in the house all day long. Even if they go out, it is only around the neighborhood. For them to want to go out once in a while is therefore very natural. It seems to me that this is the reason why we see the trains and highways crowded with family travelers during the holiday season or why there are so many people in family restaurants. The destination is not important; they just want to go out.

When I said this at the community center, a young housewife replied, "But even if I go out there is no difference because 'my domestic life comes with me.'" I agree with her completely. Although the stage may change, the cast and the roles we play are no different. Our relationships do not change just because we are someplace else.

The phrase "my domestic life comes with me" really strikes a nerve because it applies not just to women who have little children, but to all women.

For example, even women who work outside the home bring the attitude of "housewife" to their jobs. They often have no hesitation about referring to their husbands as "Papa," and I think this is an instance of "my domestic life comes with me." There are lots of women I meet whose sole topic of conversation is the family, and who can only say "My husband . . ." or "My son . . ." After thinking about this, I see this "domestic life comes with me" pattern everywhere I look.

When I was talking about this to someone she said, "When it comes to the point that you can only talk about your family, that's the first sign of senility." ✵

*W*hy did you get involved with *that* kind of woman?
Dōshite anna onna ni
どうしてあんな女に

In the essay here, Itoh broaches a very sensitive topic in probably most cultures: how should a wife act when she finds out her husband is having an affair? She discusses this problem through the work of Yoshiyuki Junnosuke (1923–1994), a best-selling novelist with a reputation himself for sexual promiscuity, both in his books and in real life. He won the Noma Literary Prize in 1978 and the Akutagawa

Prize in 1954 (see "A 'Ms. Ditz' cannot remain a 'bachelorette'" in chapter 10 for more on the Akutagawa Prize). Itoh recalls here her early reading of his book *Yami no naka no shukusai* (Festival in the Dark). We see, however, that perspectives change as we travel through the life course.

"Of all the women you could have chosen, couldn't you have picked a better one? Why did you pick such a slut?!?"

This was how the novelist Yoshiyuki Junnosuke described the wife's feeling in his book *Festival in the Dark*. When I first read this novel a long time ago when I was an impressionable young girl who could be easily swayed, I felt sympathy for the wife. That Yoshiyuki Junnosuke based the "other woman" in this novel on his real-life lover, an actress whom I didn't like, was commonly known. In reality, she might not have been such a bad person, but in those days I could not see her as anything but a shallow, phony flirt trying to get by on her looks. Therefore, I could not possibly understand why Yoshiyuki Junnosuke could be involved with her, and I guess it was very natural that I would think the character's wife in the novel would feel the same way.

However, when I think about it now, any wife would feel betrayed and ask, "How could you become involved with a woman like that?" no matter what kind of person the "other woman" really was. For a wife, such an affair is unreasonable, and thus, she would make an unreasonable judgment.

The novel continues,

"I did not have just an affair," said the husband.
"Then what was it?" the wife asked.
"I fell in love with her!" he replied.

He was not having an affair! "What?" By putting down her husband's lover, she barely manages to keep a semblance of her pride, which was totally smashed by the actions of her husband. As Yoshiyuki describes it in the novel, she became faint the moment she heard these words. "Her eyes lost their focus and all life went out of them, looking like glass beads."

When I talked about this novel to a friend of mine she said, "I just realized that when I read this book before, I read it through the eyes of the lover. But I when I look at it now, I see things from the point of view of the wife." She continued, smiling, "I wonder if this is because in real life now I am the wife." ∾

*W*hat is a family? When we become ill, we find out very
soon.
Kazoku towa nan-da rōka yande mite, hakkiri suru
家族とは何だろうか　病んでみて、はっきりする

In this essay Itoh asks some very important, though not really obvious, questions: What is a family? What is our responsibility to our aging parents? What is our responsibility to our aging in-laws? As a starting point, she quotes from the novelist Nagahata Michiko (b. 1930), an author known for her sensitive portrayals of women and family life, from her book *Onna kankaku de ikiru* (To Live with a Woman's Sense, Tokyo: Shinhyōron, 1986). Nagahata argues, and Itoh concurs, that the answers to these questions become clarified in times of crisis or stress.

As we have mentioned several times in these introductions, the Japanese population is quickly aging. In 2003 over 19 percent of the population was over the age of sixty-five (compared to 13 percent in the United States). There are now sixty times more people over one hundred years old than there were just thirty years ago. For the seventh year in a row, in 2003 the number of people over age sixty-five exceeded the number of people fourteen or younger. While nursing homes are not unknown in Japan, there are certainly fewer of them than in the United States. Until recent times, the parents would live with their children. Though lessening to some extent, this trend is seen even today. In 2003, for example, more than 36 percent of all households in Japan contained "elderly persons" over age sixty-five living there. However, half of these were households where the elderly were living with younger family members (*Japan Almanac* 2003, 33–34; *Japan Almanac* 2005, 37–38; *New York Times 2003 Almanac*, 274–76). For more on the aging Japanese population see "I do not like my age no matter how old I am" in chapter 3 and "I am getting to know how to get along with my illness" and "I already passed the age when I should have died" in chapter 13.

What is a family? When we become ill, we find out very soon. Families are the companions and comrades with whom we go through a crisis. . . . I guess because they have gone through various crises together, they have strong ties that bind them that outsiders may not see.

This is a quote from the book *To Live with a Woman's Sense* by Nagahata Michiko. When I read this book, I surely can understand that this family she is talking about is strongly bound together. However, sometimes it is clear that once we become sick we may find that things are not necessarily like this family.

The following discussion came up in an interview that was conducted among the residents of a nursing home. In this interview there was a question asking people the reasons why they were living in a nursing home.

One woman answered, "I was not able to look after my family any longer." I had instead expected her to say, "My family was not able to look after me." In other words, because she was "not able to look after" her family, she was not able to stay in her home. What a shame!

When family members become sick or old, some of these family "ties that bind" that "outsiders may not see" do indeed become stronger. But there are also quite a few cases where we find—whether we want to or not—that these ties are not so strong. For example, one woman told us, "My husband forced me to take care of his elderly parents while he would continue to escape to work. Since that time, I felt our relationship became quite strained."

Nagahata also wrote that

> I lived with his old parents, looked after them, and faced their deaths. At that time, I wondered, deep in my heart, if my generation would find that the next generation would look after us someday when we become old and feeble, without making us feel like we are a burden. ❧

*B*ut you love that kind of man, right?
Demo, sō iu otoko ga suki nan desho
でも、そういう男が好きなんでしょ

Probably in all cultures married people typically complain about their spouses. We doubt that either gender has a monopoly on this. Rarely, however, does an outsider bluntly call us on this, reminding us that we actually married that person, after all. The repercussions of this can be surprising, as seen in Itoh's vignette here.

Some friends and I heard the following diatribe from one of our other girl-friends the other day:

> There are many women who talk about their husbands quite a lot even when we women are chattering among ourselves. Indeed, there are very few women who do not speak about their husbands at all. Why do they talk about their husbands, I wonder? Is it because their husbands are such an important part of their lives, or is it because they have nothing else to talk about? Regardless, most of these times I find that these kinds of conversations are not interesting at all. I think it would be cute if the reason they talk about their husbands all the time was because they respected them so much

or loved them so much that they could not stop telling everyone else about them. However, most of the time it is nothing like that. They just talk about their husbands, period. I do not feel any close connection to such women.

The above rant was said by a single woman who is always harshly critical of married people. We married women who were listening felt a little abashed and a little guilty. She then added more:

I especially don't like a woman who grumbles about how difficult her husband is and claims he does not understand her at all. Hearing a continuing lament like this about a husband's excuses, some outside women might say, "What a narrow-minded and immature man he is." But from a wife's point of view, when he gives such excuses to her, he always looks like he is trying to give her difficult and unfathomable logic. Then I think, too, "If he says such a stupid thing, and keeps going on and on, just ignore it." However, the wife is nervously trying to read her husband's mood. As women ourselves, after all, this makes us frustrated. Therefore, these days I say to women who complain about their husbands, "You are living with that kind of man, aren't you? So, you must love him, don't you?"

After hearing her observation, we all looked at each other's faces. Someone said softly with a sigh, "Do we really love our husbands, then?" All of us smiled sheepishly, understanding exactly what she meant. ❧

I wonder when a home became a thing that can be bought and sold.

Itsunoma ni katei ga kau mono ni nattan darō-ne
いつのまに家庭が買うものになったんだろうね

This story centers around several important English loanwords in Japanese, *mansion* (*manshon*) and *my home* (*mai hōmu*). Both are concerned with the meaning of the domicile in today's Japan and the difficulties of acquiring housing in a very crowded country. First, the borrowed term *manshon* does not mean a country villa but is a condominium or apartment. Second, the notion of *mai hōmu* is rather subtle and quite complex and has no exact counterpart in English. Because housing is expensive and is at such a premium, the goal of owning "my own home" has become an end in itself for many people. This devotion to the physical house—as opposed to the idea of the home—is what Itoh is talking about in this piece. For more on the use of English loanwords in Japanese see "Even though she is a healthy adult, only a wife gets categorized as a dependent" in chapter 3, "It's become a case of 'the weak fish eat the weaker fish,' hasn't it?"

in chapter 4, "They can't stand each other unless they change their surroundings from time to time" in chapter 5, and "This is a town that keeps the worst of the country and has lost the best of the country" in chapter 11.

A person who went to visit a young couple who had moved into a new expensive apartment *mansion* in my neighborhood told me with surprise, "The life of that couple is right out of an advertisement in a real estate magazine. I even thought the baby who was sleeping in the crib was a doll."

It seems to me that many others these days have had similar kinds of experiences and share similar opinions, as I found out when I was talking with some friends recently.

"I agree with you. The houses of today's young couples are just too fashionable, and even if they have small children, they don't feel like home," said one friend of mine.

"The color of the furniture is always a well-coordinated monotone, and on the floor there are decorations of large seashells or large glass balls, and things like that . . ." said another.

"It looks like they are living in a showroom, doesn't it?" added yet another.

"I wonder if their home is becoming a showplace rather than a place to live?" queried still one more person.

The talk went on and on. During the conversation, somebody asked, as if she had suddenly realized it, "Don't you think there is something wrong with the word *my home*?" I see headlines in the newspaper all the time saying things like "The Dream of *My Home* Is Beyond Hope for Ordinary People." Sometimes I overhear people greeting each other with words like "I finally got my own *my home*." Of course this *my home* is a house or building—a piece of real estate rather than a "home."

One person said, "There is something wrong these days when the word *my home* is now taking on that meaning."

"When you mentioned it, it is really true, isn't it?" agreed another.

"I wonder if it could be because people are mistaking the meaning of the word. Doesn't the creation of 'home' start with the buying a of 'house'?"

Yes, it is very ironic that the meaning of *my home* has become "house," a building.

"I wonder when a home became a thing that can be bought and sold?" ∾

· 13 ·

Social Issues

ℐ am getting to know how to get along with my illness.
Byōki to umaku tsukiau kotsu ga wakatte kita-no
病気とうまくつき合うこつがわかってきたの

As we mentioned a few essays ago, Japan is one of the most long-lived societies in the world, and coping with the problems of old age is a concern of both individuals and communities. Itoh gives us some of her thoughts on aging and acceptance in the following essay.

She begins with a reference to the famous Japanese economist Uchida Yoshihiko (1913–1989). He is most noted for his theoretical tome *Sakuhin toshite no shakai kagaku* (The Work of Social Science, Tokyo: Iwanami Shoten, 1981), a book that received the famous Osaragi Jirō Award in 1981. The Osaragi Jirō Award was established in 1974 by the *Asahi* newspaper and is named in honor of novelist Osaragi Jirō (1898–1973). It is given each year for the book that best explores the human spirit in history or contemporary culture.

Ōtake Hitoko (b. 1914), whom we are introduced to later, is the author of a famous autobiography about growing up with the socialist activist Kutsumi Fusako, *Mother and I: Days with Kutsumi Fusako* (Tokyo: Tsukiji Press, 1984).

For more on the aging Japanese population see "I do not like my age no matter how old I am" in chapter 3, "What is a family? When we become ill, we find out very soon" in chapter 12, and "I already passed the age when I should have died!" in chapter 13.

The noted economist Uchida Yoshihiko passed away in March 1989. Mr. Uchida said he was having a good relationship with his illness; he did not resist it, but yet did not become its slave. In fact, he had been ill for about fifteen years

175

before he passed away. During his struggle with his disease, he wrote some of his best works, including the award-winning *The Work of Social Science*.

When I heard his words, "I am getting to know how to get along with my illness," I thought, "What a wonderful attitude." At the same time, I remembered a similar kind of life philosophy held by Ōtake Hitoko, and I felt warm inside.

Since Ms. Ōtake and I live in the same town, we see each other off and on. Each time we meet she never fails to tell me something memorable, even in our most casual conversations.

For example, a while back she mentioned she was feeling dizzy. So when I saw her the other day, I asked how she was feeling. She answered, "I have learned how to get along with Ms. Dizziness, so I don't feel such a big load anymore." That sounded very much like her. I thought what a wonderful attitude she has.

I always believed that dealing with a major disease was either a heroic superhuman fight, or something a patient suffered all alone. Either way, I was not sure I would be able to handle it if I had one. In one sense, the attitude of "getting along with" a disease could be much more difficult than being in a "fight" against it or being a "patient" because of it. However, I could understand how this concept could make us feel we could do it. Regardless, the way we cope with disease reflects not only our own individual personality, it also represents our philosophy of life, as well as how we associate with the people in our lives. ✍

The most important thing about being a human being is to learn about the world by ourselves.

Ningen to shite daiji na koto wa jibun de manabu mono
人間として大事なことは自分で学ぶもの

A perennial problem in post–World War II Japan and Germany is war guilt. The postwar generations have to address the fact that their relatives might have participated—however unwittingly or unwilling—in a terrible tragedy. The World War II generation no doubt has lingering second thoughts about their own role and behavior. In this essay, Itoh recalls the first time the women in her community center—mostly women who were alive during the Second World War—heard about some war crimes committed by the Japanese armed forces. In particular, thousands of Korean women were forced into service as "comfort women" for Japanese troops in East and Southeast Asia. For more about these "comfort women" see

"That woman is like an obstinate, grumpy old man" in chapter 3, "We can't conduct a conversation equally when we only use women's language" in chapter 6, "This is a town that keeps the worst of the country and has lost the best of the country" in chapter 11, and "I think it is so good that I am not a Japanese" in chapter 13.

Every year at our community center in Kunitachi we offer a workshop on women's issues. The theme of this year's lecture in the "History" category was "Gender and Labor."

In this lecture we learned not only about female inequality in the labor force but also about sexual slavery during Japan's modernization period. The lecturer, Yūko Suzuki, presented lots of historical facts and documents about this issue. We could hardly face some of these facts without shame. For example, one disgusting incident was the existence of "comfort women" during World War II and the way the military treated these women while officially sanctioning the practice.

Many of the participants were shocked and surprised, some saying, "I didn't know about this." Some women became angry at the Japanese military and cried over the miserable conditions these Korean women were forced into as "comfort women."

This part of the workshop was painfully shocking enough. But I think the thing that made the biggest impact was the opinions of two Korean women who were attending the lecture. The first one said,

> If things happened slightly later, I might have been forced to become a comfort woman. If things were only a little different, so could some of you or your relatives. I kept thinking this while listening to the lecture.

The second Korean woman then said,

> To tell the truth, today I was disgusted when I heard you Japanese women crying and showing surprise. Some of you said, "I did not know this. I never learned this at school." Even in Korea, in our standard school curriculum we do not learn such things.
>
> But in Korea, everybody knows we don't get everything at school and that we have to seek out things for ourselves—the facts we need know as human beings (*ningen toshite shitte oka nakute wa naranai daiji na koto wa*). ๛

*T*just attend events because they have day care.
Takuji tsuki no ibento o watari aruite ita
託児つきのイベントを渡り歩いていた

In 1995 the famous surrealist writer Murakami Ryū (b. 1952) wrote a novel called *Koin rokkā baibiizu* (Tokyo: Kodansha, 1984; translated as *Coin Locker Babies*, Tokyo: Kodansha, 1995) about children abandoned by their mothers inside coin lockers at the Yokohama railway station. Presumably this story was based on a real incident of a mother giving birth in the station toilet and then abandoning the child in the coin locker. Here, however, we see Itoh speaking of coin lockers of a different kind (though perhaps not as different as we might at first think). The coin locker she is talking about here is "short-term" day care offered by various places while mothers shop, hear a lecture, or attend some kind of activity or event.

In a society that generally still offers more recognition to stay-at-home moms than career women, being confined to the house all day can be a stifling experience, both psychologically and physically. As Japanese homes and apartments are usually very small, and buildings very close together, in most cities there are many tiny neighborhood parks every few blocks. These consist of some trees, a few benches, and a swing set or two. As Itoh notes here, these are often meeting places for local mothers with babies or small children.

But regardless of the number of these cute little playgrounds, the real social problem, Itoh says, is providing proper day care. This would not only take the burden off the growing female workforce, it would also offer real child-rearing support for mothers. What is really needed, ultimately, is a healthy environment for children.

A person once told me,

> The reason why I want to attend some event, is not because they have something I really want to see or do; it's because they have day care. But I found that even if I went around one time to a bunch of different events, it did not change my life all that much, and in the end I still was raising my child by myself.

Another mother said that because she spends her days only with her children she feels alone and suffocated. In order to escape, she goes out—going from one small neighborhood park to another, where at least she can talk to other mothers. She said, "We are child-care refugees."

I heard that there are many cases where mothers send even their one- and two-year-olds to elite preschools—not to get early academic preparation, but simply to get a break from taking care of their children sometimes.

The mass media has even coined a new word for these mothers confined at home raising children: *misshitsu ikuji* (literally, "child care in a closed room").

I wonder if these parks and schools are simply opportunities for these young mothers to escape from their closed rooms.

However, these young child-care refugees or elite preschool mothers are not looking at the real essential problem of women, which is that women are forced to be in their homes and raise their children by themselves. Instead, it seems to me that they are just trying to get through the child-rearing years by taking occasional breathers, whenever they can find air, like when they go to the park.

To see women in such a psychological state that they will go anyplace as long as it says, "We offer day care," is almost painful. Because I understand how painful this situation is, I am worried about this current trend of offering "coin locker"—or short-term—child care. There seem to be three types of problems:

(1) Some places offer child care but do so only to make money and do not have the best interests of the mother or child in mind.
(2) Some places that offer child care *are* well intended and sympathetic to mothers. But focusing on the place and not the underlying institution makes the social problem invisible.
(3) Some places that offer child care do so believing in the common myth that until a child reaches the age of three, mothers should look after their children. The care they offer will give a mother a break, but this also hides the essential problem. Actually it spreads the problem even further by causing people to focus on peripheral issues.

What we really need is not only some temporary breaks or breathing space, but people who will share child care together on a daily basis, people with relationships to support each other, and institutional support. I don't think we need a place of coin lockers for child care for the parents' convenience. But we do need a place where we can provide a healthy environment for children, where they can grow. And everyone in the community should have access to such a place. This is what we need, isn't it? ∽

> *I*f it is a love affair, it is an offense against a wife, but if it is prostitution, it is an offense against all women.
> *Uwaki nara tsuma ga okoreba ii keredo, baishun dakara onna ga okoru-noyo*
> 浮気なら妻が怒ればいいけれど、 買春 だから女が怒るのよ

Itoh here examines how men and women view prostitution differently and the possible reasons for this difference. Prostitution was legal in

Japan until after the Second World War, when the 1956 Prostitution Prevention Law was enacted. However, there has been a long tradition in Japan of rich and powerful men having mistresses or girlfriends, who often receive substantial financial support. Thus, it is not always clear who is a "kept woman," a mistress, a prostitute, just a friend, or even a wife. Itoh foregrounds these issues here.

We should also note the interesting way *baishun* (prostitution) is written in Japanese. The word is a compound of two Sino-Japanese characters: 売 and 春. The first character (*bai*) means "to sell" and the second character (*shun*) means the season "spring." However, in the first position of this compound, another character can sometimes be used instead: 買. This character is also pronounced *bai* but means "to buy." So, depending on your perspective, *baishun* can be written as the *selling* of a body or the *buying* of a body. Since the mid-1970s, this second way of writing *baishun* was popularized, and both forms are acceptable now. Here, as Itoh is focusing on the men's act of buying women, she uses this second form, writing 買春.

There was a miserable prime minister a while back who had to resign because of a scandal with a woman. He tried to hide his secret affair by giving her money, but rather than staying quiet, she publicized their relationship. At that time, the consensus was that he was just stupid. But there were some differences in the views of women and men.

Men believed, "Why couldn't he just keep this under wraps? How could he be so careless to let this get publicized?" They looked at this scandal and seemed to say, "Sure he was dumb to let this get out, but the public should not concern itself with private things that are not political or policy issues."

Women claimed, "If it is just a love affair, his wife has the right to be furious at him. But since money was involved, this is prostitution, which is a human rights issue. That's what infuriates us women."

When women explained the situation like this—putting it in terms of a love affair versus prostitution—most men more or less got the point. I, too, thought this reasoning was correct. However, recently I was surprised to learn that this was not actually a case of prostitution at all.

Legally in Japan, prostitution is not only a sexual relationship involving money. There has to also be an element of anonymity or "specificity" involved for it to be a real case of prostitution. That is, if the people are not strangers, it is not prostitution, regardless of whether a man has multiple partners. "What? Really?" I felt when I learned this. I could not believe it.

But the female lawyer who told me this explained,

> Some people said to me that when the law was drafted making prostitution illegal, an action was considered prostitution whenever there was money involved, regardless of whether or not the people knew each other. But when they tried to pass it, the majority of the male politicians opposed it, so they put in the "specificity clause."

When I heard this, I was amazed, but then I somehow thought, "Hmm . . . indeed." ∽

> *I*t is a mother's love that makes her want to not draw attention to her child in a crowd.
> *Sono ko o ta no hito ni kizukare-mai to suru haha no kokoro zukai-desu*
> その子を他の人に気づかれまいとする母の心づかいです

In Japan most children with disabilities go to a special school called *yōgo-gakkō* (literally, "school for protective care"). This type of school enrolls both mentally and physically challenged children. Also, children who do not require intensive care and can attend regular public school, but need some special assistance, take special classes called *yōgo-gakkyū* or *tokushu-gakkyū* (literally, "class for protective care"). Recently, there have been claims from the parents of children who attend *yōgo-gakkyū* that their children are stigmatized—and sometimes bullied—at regular school, and they have advocated changing the education system for challenged children. These are the issues that Itoh discusses in this essay.

Itoh also mentions the American writer Pearl Buck (1892–1973). She was the daughter of Chinese missionaries, and she won the Pulitzer Prize in 1932 and the Nobel Prize for Literature in 1938. She was most well known for her novels about life in China.

On the bus I use from time to time, I occasionally run into children who are coming home from a school for handicapped children [*yōgo-gakkō*]. Regardless of curious people staring at the children, the volunteer-chaperon mothers try to act naturally and do not avoid eye contact. They act very normally to both their children and the people who are looking at them. I am touched to these mothers' attitude.

There is a passage that Pearl Buck wrote in *The Child Who Never Grew* (1950) about own her experiences with her daughter's mental retardation: "I very easily notice children like my daughter in any crowd. At first the children come to my attention, and then I notice their mothers who are smiling at their children and joyously talking to them. The reason they are talking to them normally as if they were having a good time is that it is a mother's love that makes her want to not draw attention to her child in a crowd."

Before, when I read this book the first time, I was fully convinced of the correctness of her view: to "not draw attention to her child." I think that I felt it was part of a mother's love to protect her child from curious public eyes.

However, now I see things differently. I see a mother's loving attitude in the people I sometimes run into on the bus, who do not avoid people's stares. Their attitude is very accepting of their children, and they want them to make their place in society by just being who they are. I feel their strong maternal love toward their children, and I think this is a healthy attitude.

After I came to feel this way, I understood the deep lonely feelings Pearl Buck had. I do not think that we should let any mother feel such loneliness. ∽

> *I* think it is so good that I am not a Japanese.
> *Watashi wa jibun ga nihonjin de nakute yokatta to omoimasu-yo*
> 私は自分が日本人でなくてよかったと思いますよ

This piece is concerned with several very controversial issues in Japan today. The first is the question of war guilt and responsibility. No one from the Japanese government has given an official, formal apology yet for the cause of the war or any subsequent war crimes, and this is still a significant problem for Japanese foreign relations in East and Southeast Asia.

The second is the place of Koreans in Japanese society. From 1910 to 1945, Korea was a de facto colony of Japan, and as many as two million Koreans came—or were brought—to Japan for work. Many stayed in Japan after World War II ended either because they had established lives and families there, or the postwar situation in a divided Korea was thought to be not much better than life in Japan.

There are now about three-quarters of a million people of Korean ancestry living in Japan, some fourth generation. Still, because Japan defines citizenship by blood rather than by place of birth, these people are technically foreign aliens and face numerous legal and social barriers. (The woman Itoh is talking to in this piece, however, is not one of these people but is a true Korean national.)

There is still some discrimination against Japanese-Koreans, even though many now have little cultural, ethnic, or linguistic allegiance to Korea. When we hear about girls being attacked for wearing *chima choguri*—traditional Korean costumes still sometimes worn by Japanese-Koreans at ethnic festivals or at Korean schools—we know we are hearing about some of this lingering prejudice.

The most conspicuous and controversial problem surrounding Koreans, however, has been the revelation that at least one hundred thousand "comfort women" were forced into prostitution by the Japanese military during the Second World War. Japan has not yet completely come to terms with this, either. And, as seen here, this topic is frequently discussed in the popular media. For more on Koreans in Japan and "comfort women" see "That woman is like an obstinate, grumpy old man" in chapter 3, "We can't conduct a conversation equally when we only use women's language" in chapter 6, "This is a town that keeps the worst of the country and has lost the best of the country" in chapter 11, and "The most important thing about being a human being is to learn about the world by ourselves" in chapter 13.

Two violent incidents involving Japanese-Koreans still fester, and both created firestorms in Japan at the time they occurred. The first is the case of Lee Jin Woo. Ōta Yoshie, a high school student in Tokyo, was raped and murdered on August 20, 1958. Lee Jin Woo, an eighteen-year-old Japanese-Korean, was accused of the crime, and he indeed confessed. He also confessed that he raped and murdered Tanaka Setsuko (aged twenty-three) previously.

However, the circumstances surrounding the investigation and the confession were controversial, and many suspected Lee Jin Woo was framed. The Japanese-Korean community became entangled in debate with nationalist Japanese who were prejudiced against Koreans. Some prominent Japanese, like the author and Communist activist Ōoka Shōhei, took Lee's side, saying that because of the tremendous discrimination Koreans face in Japan, he should be given leniency. Nevertheless, he was executed in 1962. The controversy still lingers. In 1999 the novelist Nozaki Rokusuke wrote a book called *I Jin'u nōto: Shikei ni sareta zainichi Chōsenjin* (Notes Written by Lee Jin Woo: A Korean in Japan Who Was Put to Death) in which he argues that the police set Lee Jin Woo up because he was Korean.

The second was the case of Kim Hui No. His story is couched in ambiguity, and still much is conjecture. Kim Hui No—a thirty-nine-year-old second-generation Korean born in Japan, who spoke no Korean—in 1968 killed with a rifle two gangster loan sharks who came to collect money from him. He then took a woman and three young children hostage at an inn in Shizuoka Prefecture. Again, some argued that his Korean-ness precipitated his circumstances, and his sentence should be lighter. He was sentenced to life imprisonment.

In 1999—at the age of seventy—he somehow vanished when he was conditionally released, and he ended up in South Korea, where he was welcomed as a national hero who fought ethnic discrimination in Japan. (However, the following year he supposedly was also arrested in South Korea when he tried to murder a woman's husband.)

Girls who were wearing *chima choguri* were attacked. What an awful thing. When I heard this news, I felt an ache in my heart, and at the same time I remembered the following incident.

One day when I was talking with a Korean woman who was now living in Japan, she said,

> Today, Japanese are asked about the issue of "comfort women" during World War II, but I doubt this makes Japanese people confront their past. But Japanese do not reconsider their own history regardless of how many chances they have. For example, look at the case of Lee Jin Woo or the case of Kim Hui No. Japanese saw these things but did not change their attitude. They have accumulated many such incidents up to now. I really think that it is hard to be Japanese. I think it is so good that I am not a Japanese.

She genuinely trembled when she said that, "If I were a Japanese ..." From her words I realized how we Japanese have been seen abroad. Since then, whenever I hear about the issue of "comfort women," I always recall her words, "But Japanese do not reconsider their own history regardless of how many chances they have."

These words spread out in my mind like clouds growing in the sky. While I was thinking about these issues I ran across the following comments by Lee Mi Rang as well:

> I think that when Japanese choose to give us pity, instead of accepting responsibility for war crimes, it allows them to keep their pride. Not only that, it allows them to feel superior to us. (*Sengo hoshō nyūsu* [News about Postwar Compensation] No. 11)

When I read this, I felt that my guts were ripped apart. But at the same time, I thought her point made us clearly see that we Japanese are physically standing right now at a fork in the road of history. The road we choose to take will show what kind of people we want to be. ⌘

*V*olunteer activities, in other words, are underpaid part-time jobs.

Borantia-tte, yasui arubaito no koto nano-yo
ボランティアって、安いアルバイトのことなのよ

What is the value of community service? How much should everyone contribute? What is the role of women in all this? Itoh addresses these issues in her essay.

As mentioned earlier, there are many part-time workers in Japan, and many of them are volunteers. These are often housewives or retired men, and they do jobs from manning the city bicycle parking lots by the commuter train stations to working in schools and community centers. These volunteers are usually given some small compensation for expenses or transportation. For more on part-timers see "Even though she is a healthy adult, only a wife gets categorized as a dependent" in chapter 3.

There is a group of volunteers who babysit children while their mothers attend workshops at our community center. The community center civil service staff member who supervises these volunteers complained about them.

According to her, since they are asked to "Just help us out whenever you have some spare time that doesn't conflict with your daily schedule," she cannot say anything to those volunteers when they cancel or want to return home early without advance notice. She added, "Because we feel bad for them working for absolutely nothing, we provide them with a little compensation."

"We feel bad for them working for nothing." I think this points out the public attitude toward volunteer activities. In other words, the word *volunteer* is just a substitute for *unpaid worker*.

But after considering this, one person said, "Doesn't 'volunteer activities' mean no payment for these jobs?" The supervisor replied, "No, not in our case. Therefore we call them 'paid volunteers.'" They seemed to be talking at cross-purposes, focusing on completely different issues.

When I talked about this with the others later, one friend mischievously explained to me, trying to calm me down, "In government work, volunteer activities are underpaid part-time jobs! Didn't you know that?"

Under the name of "volunteer," women's goodwill or good intentions to work are often used by the government bureaucracy to save money or to try and at least have some women on the job. Also, among women, there is a tendency to think that volunteering is easier than having a real job or that they can take a volunteer job if they are in between regular jobs.

Today, volunteerism is getting a lot of public attention and is becoming an accepted part of public policy. But I am really worried that people are warping the notion of volunteerism and are also decreasing the quality of women's participation in society. ❧

*T*already passed the age when I should have died!
Mō ikite ite wa ikenai toshi nan-desu-yo
もう生きていてはいけない年なんですよ

Japan has one of the highest life expectancies of any country in the world: more than eighty-five years for women and more than seventy-eight years for men in 2003. However, the population structure is also skewing due to a later age of marriage and smaller families. The average hypothetical nuclear family in Japan has only 1.29 children (much less than the 2.1 children per family required to maintain a population at its current level). This is causing a serious "graying" of the population. For example, in 2003 the number of people sixty-five and older increased by 683,000, while the number of people fourteen or younger *decreased* by 197,000. The social consequences of these new demographics will no doubt be extraordinary, as Itoh discusses here.

Keirō no hi (Respect for the Aged Day) is September 15 and has been a national holiday since 1966. On this day people honor the elderly and wish them a long life and good health. It is the eighth of the dozen national holidays in Japan. For more on the aging population see "I do not like my age no matter how old I am" in chapter 3, "What is a family? When we become ill, we find out very soon" in chapter 12, and "I am getting to know how to get along with my illness" in chapter 13.

I've heard that life expectancy for women in Japan is now almost eighty-five years old. But why do they publicize this number so loudly? One older woman I know told me that whenever she hears about life expectancy she feels that people are telling her, "You are not supposed live beyond a certain age."

Another person said that when she asked a young-looking elderly person, "How old are you?" the elderly person answered, "I already passed the age when I should have died! I've exceeded the life-expectancy age." She felt she had asked something she should not have asked.

The public makes a great fanfare about life expectancy: "It is going to cost a lot to take care of the increasing number of elderly people we will have in the future."

Doesn't anyone find this kind of attitude among our politicians despicable? Everybody, including the mass media, gives the same kind of argument, as if the source of all evil in society is longevity. It seems to me no wonder that the elderly feel badly about living so long—as if the elderly were officially and publicly branded as leeches or burdens.

The current rise in life expectancy is due to improvements in medical science and, most importantly, living in a time of no war. To say that peace provides longevity is no exaggeration. Instead of thinking about the value of longevity, people just nonchalantly push the elderly along, saying what a bother they are. Hypocritically, we celebrate a Respect for the Aged Day in this kind of social climate.

People have to be guaranteed the right to live in human dignity until the last moment. The basic measure of a country's wealth and degree of social advancement is how the elderly are treated. I firmly believe that it is unfair that people only look at aging as an urgent political problem that needs to be solved, rather than as a basic human issue. Moreover, the political solution to the problem of an aging society that is often proposed—that we should encourage increasing the birth rate—is a terrible one. Given this kind of social environment, I wouldn't be surprised if children didn't want to be born. ∾

• *14* •

Nature and Beauty

$\mathcal{O}$utside I wear clothes that suit my figure, but at home I wear
   clothes that I like.
Soto dewa niau fuku, uchi dewa sukina fuku o kiru
外 で は 似合 う 服、内 で は 好 き な 服 を 着 る

In this essay, Itoh examines an ordinary and mundane daily task
each woman faces: What am I going to wear today? Again, Itoh
claims, this is not as simple as it looks. Not only do we have to
find something that fits and we can move around in, we must also
taken into consideration how we appear to others. To just wear
what we want, says Itoh, is both self-indulgent and even stupid. As
clothes express our feelings and personality, likewise they express
our membership and participation in society. Whether we like it
or not, there are social rules and conventions about clothes, and
every member of a culture knows at least the rudiments of them,
even if they are not fashion designers. To put things in an American
vernacular, the person who wears a tuxedo to class or jeans to the
prom does so at his or her own peril. The attitudes that people have
when they see us reflect back to us. Others may feel comfortable—
or *uncomfortable*—about what *we* wear. Thus, Itoh says, we have
a social duty to factor in others when we open the closet or the
drawer in the morning.

   As an aside, we should note that colorful clothes are really the
prerogative of the young in Japan. The Japanese salaryman is known
worldwide for wearing conservative suits, for example. On a daring
day he might wear brown instead of the compulsory dark blue or
black. If an older person is seen wearing something too bright, they
might be ridiculed for "dressing like an American!"

A person I know who is famous for being a fashion plate said to me, "Outside I wear clothes that suit my figure, but at home I wear clothes that I like."

The clothes that suit us are not necessarily the clothes we like. Likewise, the clothes that we like may not necessarily suit us. Your favorite clothes may not always go with your face or body shape, but you may still like them; or perhaps they just fit your mood at the time. I think this person's words signify how she uses her public sphere and her private sphere.

There are some people who say they don't care what others think about them—about what they wear—as long as they themselves like the clothes they are wearing. While it seems silly to be bound by the opinions of others or to be slaves to tradition, we cannot be completely free of other people's scrutiny. This is because our clothes represent our personalities, and the attitudes of those who see us reflect back to us.

I sometimes think that a woman whose makeup is always perfect and who always makes sure her clothes are just right is really overemphasizing her looks and is overeager to be accepted and fit in with society's expectations. That, I think, is pitiful. Imagine seeing two different people wearing unconventional clothes. One style might appear "happy" to us, leaving a favorable impression; the other might make us feel that the person is insisting that "I am out of the ordinary, and I am different from others."

To say that a person has good taste or not is not so easy, but the person who can wear clothes that make not only themselves, but also others, feel comfortable probably can understand themselves, and others, very well. I like my clothes because they are comfortable, and I wear them anytime, anywhere, but I think this really reflects my selfish and lazy lifestyle. ∾

*F*ar away, far away, cherry blossoms are falling.
Haruka haruka ni sakura chiru
はるかはるかにさくら散る

As most Westerners have heard, cherry blossoms are very important in Japanese culture. They are valued for their delicate, fragile, and transient beauty, and metaphors of falling cherry blossoms abound in Japanese prose and poetry of all eras. Itoh discusses some of these feelings here. We should note, too, that because of Japan's geography—running fifteen hundred miles from north to south—cherry blossoms bloom at different times, depending on their location. In spring—usually sometime in April on the main island of Honshu—cherry-viewing parties are found in almost every park during the two weeks when the trees are in bloom.

Also, in Japan, there are school admissions ceremonies every year in April when the new class of students arrives.

In this essay Itoh quotes a famous cherry blossom poem by the Buddhist priest Saigyō (1118–1190). Saigyō is one of Japan's most revered classical poets. The idea of February as a cherry blossom month in this poem might strike the Western reader as a little unusual unless he or she remembers that this is literally "Second Month" in the Japanese lunar calendar used in medieval Japan. The Japanese New Year (in First Month) extended from around the middle of January to the middle of February. There were also "leap" months put in to balance the days out with the solar annual calendar. In addition, Saigyō might be making a joke or a metaphor in this poem. Buddha's "death day"—when he detached himself from the sentient world—is February 15. The pronunciation of this date is close to "Second Month" given in the poem, so Saigyō might be making a pun between falling cherry blossoms and Buddha's withdrawal from life.

Later Itoh quotes a poem by Yosano Akiko, a radical and feminist poet of the early part of the twentieth century. The Gion District that she talks about is a very lively entertainment district in Kyoto. Kiyomizu is a beautiful and famous temple on a cliff. For more on the poet Yosano Akiko (1878–1942) see "Being the perpetrator is very hard" in chapter 6.

Itoh ends this piece with a *senryū* poem by Tokizane Shinko (b. 1929). A *senryū* poem is a satirical or humorous version of the classic tanka poetic form. Tokizane has been one of the influential *senryū* poets of the twentieth century, known for her bold and liberating phrasing. For example, she makes her poem here even more memorable by using the word *aikō*. This is actually a combination of two Sino-Japanese characters created by Tokizane herself. It might mean a bird's call or the sound of a kiss or lovers' embrace. For more on *senryū* poetry see "I have a pet monkey who knows how to tie a necktie very well" in chapter 3, "The abundant seeds of grass that don't know national boundaries are cast upon the ground" in chapter 10, and "The winter chrysanthemum is not pleasant" in chapter 14.

Without thinking, I once said to my friend, "I cannot imagine a school admission ceremony without cherry blossoms." This person, who is from the southern part of Japan, said, "That is a pretty Tokyo-centric idea."

When she sees pictures of her school admission ceremony when she was a child, she feels a little strange because they have drawings of cherry blossoms. For her, because they are in the south, school admission ceremonies take place after the cherry blossoms are gone. She is right about being a little offended. Every Japanese certainly knows that cherry blossom season does not arrive in the same place at the same time. Every year during cherry blossom season, I tell myself that I would like to make a trip and follow the cherry blossoms as they bloom all over Japan.

Because cherry blossoms are such a symbol of the Japanese spirit, it is very hard to simply say "I like cherry blossoms" if someone asks you to choose your favorite flower. But nonetheless, I do like cherry blossoms the best. During cherry blossom season, I am so cheerful that I cannot focus on anything else. During the day I imagine cherry blossoms blooming all over the world, creating a phantasm of beauty, and during the night I feel that the falling of willowy cherry blossoms has a supernatural power, creating voluptuous illusions of heroic grace in the wind.

Here is one of my favorite poems about cherry blossoms:

> ねがはくは花の下にて春死なむその如月の望月のころ
> *Negawaku wa hana no shita nite haru shinamu sono kisaragi no*
>   *mochizuki no koro*
> I really do hope I will die under the cherry blossoms
> in the full moon in February
>
> —Saigyō

When I read the following poem by Yosano Akiko I feel a full abundance of happiness, and I am as light-headed as if I were falling in love:

> 清水へ祇園をよぎる桜月夜こよひ逢ふひとみなうつくしき
> *Kiyomizu e gion o yogiru sakurazuki-yo koyoi au hito mina*
>   *utsukushiki*
> Tonight as I head to Kiyomizu going
> through the Gion district,
> viewing the moon through the blooming cherry blossoms,
> makes everyone on the street look so beautiful
>
> —Yosano Akiko

The *senryū* poems that adult women like me really like are the ones about beautiful cherry blossoms. Therefore, the following poem by Tokizane Shinko really strikes my heart:

> 愛咬やはるかはるかにさくら散る
> *Aikō ya haruka haruka ni sakura chiru*
> The sound of *aikō* means
> already the cherry blossoms are falling down ❧

*T*here is no such thing as a plant called "weed."
Zassō to iu na no hana wa nain-da kedo
雑草という名の草はないんだけど

Once more we see Itoh tackling a very subtle scientific issue in a rather straightforward way. She speaks of one of her flower-loving friends, who reminds us that there really is not a plant called a "weed." At first glance, the underlying moral seems to be that we should not make hasty value judgments. Just as "One man's revolutionary is another man's freedom fighter," so someone's weed could be another's beautiful blossom.

But there is more. "Weeds" are actually cultural rather than biological categories. Different species of growing things exist, of course. For the most part, there is little confusion and overlap, and both botanists and nature know the difference. But higher-order classifications—whether scientific, such as *deciduous*, or everyday, such as *tree, flower*, or *weed*—are social conventions and, thus, culturally constructed.

Cognitive scientists tell us that these so-called generic terms are actually rather tricky. When asked to think of a "bird," what first comes to mind: a best example like a robin, an oddball like an ostrich, or a some kind of imaginary catchall having all the ideal properties of birdness (even though such a perfect bird may not really exist)? Even though she doesn't use the language of psychology or cognitive science, the point, Itoh claims, is that we often get confused in our thinking about these general categories, believing them to be real when in actuality they are just social constructions. In other words—though Itoh would not want to make the statement this way—"weed" is not even a scientific category but a "folk" category instead.

I have a friend who is very fond of living among wildflowers. She is a great artist and likes to sketch the plants around her. This year I used her sketch of a wild rose briar patch as the design for my New Year's card. In her sketchbooks, she draws the everyday wildflowers she finds all around her. For example, for February she has *ōbata-netsuke bana*, and for March she has drawn *hime-odoriko-sō* (a kind of nettle), and so on. In her sketches, we can see the unique characteristics and beauty of each flower, which we otherwise would not notice if we just thought of them as grass or weeds.

When she speaks of plants (*kusa-bana*), she simply talks about them as if they were her old friends from childhood whom she is introducing to us. She is not showing off her extensive knowledge of botany, nor is she being overly warped or enthusiastic, saying, "I am protecting these *poor* plants." Her attitude toward plants is just natural and warm. I see her character displayed in this attitude.

She once told me matter-of-factly, "There is no such thing as a plant called 'weed.'" Her words reminded me of myself after I had my first child. One day a man greeted me on the street saying, "How is your 'baby' these days?"

For him this was just a natural greeting, a common, not-discourteous, expression used in casual encounters. However, at that time I thought, "My god, a 'baby'? My child is not just a 'baby.' He has an individual character; he has a name, J." I didn't say this, but I really felt this way. The words of the typical parochial parent almost came out of my mouth.

That everybody knows there is no actual plant called "weed" is a fact. But my friend says those who think in such general terms should be careful. She contended that such plants should not be denigrated. Her simple affection for each plant still lingers in my mind. ∾

*O*h, . . . I am still beautiful!
Ara, watashi, ima datte, kirei-desu-wayo
あら、私、今だって、きれいですわよ

Probably in every culture, women are sensitive to the notion of beauty. Also, most women are probably concerned about the fading of beauty as aging takes place. The woman who says "I am still beautiful" in old age, of course, knows her skin no longer shines as in her youth. She is claiming that her beauty now resides within her inner spirit, personality, and manners. This attitude, Itoh claims, actually *does* make her beautiful.

In English we say that "Clothes make the man," but as Itoh again reminds us, they make the woman, too. For more on Japanese kimonos see "I already passed the age when I should have died!" in chapter 13; for more on dress as an expression of personality, see "Outside I wear clothes that suit my figure, but at home I wear clothes that I like" in chapter 14.

These words were said to me by a woman who will turn seventy years old this year. She has a very fresh and keen critical eye toward conventional power and conservative authority. Her free and unique fashion sense represents her individuality.

One day I ran into her when she was wearing a very elegant formal kimono. I had a hard time imagining her in such attire after always seeing her in her usual casual clothes. Although I had always thought she was a beautiful person with a great fashion sense, when I gazed upon her in her graceful and elegant kimono, I was astonished.

I said with admiration, "Oh, you look wonderful!" I continued saying, "I can just imagine how beautiful you were when you were young," which, of course, I should not have said. Her response to this was quite interesting. She said with a mischievous grin, "Oh, . . . I am still beautiful!"

Since then I have come to like her more and more. If in this situation she had returned with the usual humble answer, that would not have been much fun. Not only would it not have been much fun, but my impoliteness could have come out more clearly (and could have been embarrassing).

More importantly, there was a reason for her to dress up. She was going to attend a ceremony of a male friend whom she had known for a long time who was receiving a medal from the government. Her old friend lived somewhat apart from the world and cared little for social position or honors. "Although I usually do not care for such official accolades, his case is meaningful, and I wanted to honor him as much as I can."

Her dressing up, then, was not an excuse for her to show off but was to show her respect for her friend through the formal clothes she wore when she attended his ceremony. I thought that exactly showed her character.

Since then, whenever I hear the words *beautiful* or *fashionable* I think of her in the formal kimono. Of course, I never say that to her in person . . . ∿

$\mathcal{T}$he winter chrysanthemum is not pleasant.
Kangiku no nintai to iu kitanarashi
寒菊の忍耐という汚らし

Fittingly, we end Itoh's collection of essays with a piece on winter and chrysanthemums. However, the following story is not just about flowers but is as much about politics.

The chrysanthemum (*kiku*) appears on the crest of the Japanese imperial family, and since the Heian period (794–1185) it has been the flower of the emperor's court. This symbol appears on Japanese passports and other official documents. In post–World War II Japan, there has been much discussion about the meaning of the imperial system, with liberals being rather critical of the system and conservatives and nationalists typically being staunch supporters. For more about the role of the emperor in Japan today see "Please discriminate against women" in chapter 4.

Later in the essay Itoh again quotes from one her favorite poets, Tokizane Shinko (b. 1929). For more about Tokizane Shinko see "Far away, far away, the cherry blossoms are falling" in chapter 14. For more on *senryū* poetry see "I have a pet monkey who knows how to tie a necktie very well" in chapter 3, "The abundant seeds of grass that don't know national boundaries are cast upon the ground" in chapter 10, and "Far away, far away, cherry blossoms are falling" in chapter 14.

Itoh ends with a reference to Akutagawa Ryūnosuke's *Shuju no kotoba* (The Words of the Dwarf, Tokyo: Iwanami-bunko, 1932).

Akutagawa Ryūnosuke (1892–1927) was one of Japan's most famous novelists of the early twentieth century. He is known for his psychological, antinaturalist stories; two of them became the basis of the movie *Rashōmon*, one of the most admired Japanese films in world cinema. In 1935 a prize was created in his honor. This is still the most widely sought-after literary prize in Japan. For more the Akutagawa Prize see "A 'Ms. Ditz' cannot remain a 'bachelorette'" in chapter 10 and "Why did you get involved with *that* kind of woman?" in chapter 12.

When I said, "I am not so fond of winter chrysanthemums," I was surprised that many of my friends agreed. One, however, said, "I think so, too. I am especially unhappy about the chrysanthemum emblem we have on our passports. It isn't right to force this 'emperor worship' on us, is it?"

The reason I said I do not like chrysanthemums is because they don't die so quickly, and even as a cut flower they stay around for a long time, so I am not attracted by them.

But after hearing these reasons, my anti-imperial radical friend looked at me as if to say "That's it?" Then she said, "You like flowers like cherry blossoms that bloom quickly and die quickly. Your character is very right-wing."

This time she had a rather aggressive attitude toward me. And since I responded back, we two surprised each other, and the others around us laughed. As they laughed, we started laughing, too. While I was laughing, I thought of the poem of the *senryū* poet Tokizane Shinko:

寒菊の忍耐という汚らし
Kan-giku no nintai to iu kitana-rashi
The winter chrysanthemum is not pleasant.

When I heard this poem the first time, I was very impressed how greatly this represented of my feelings of "patience" and "passiveness."

When I was at the height of my impertinent and snobbish period in junior high school, I also read the phrase "Passiveness is the romantic way of saying meanness" in Ryūnosuke Akutagawa's *The Words of the Dwarf*. When I read this, I thought, "Wow, that's really true."

Furthermore, I also remembered another favorite passage in the same book: "The most dangerous philosophy is the philosophy that tries to practice the obvious." But if I would have mentioned this to my radical friend, she no doubt would have called me a "right-winger" again, so I said nothing. ✍

A Conclusion?

Nobuko Adachi and James Stanlaw

$\mathcal{W}$hat will be the place of Japanese women in the twenty-first century? What will the role of housewife become? The one thing that can be said with confidence is that things will probably change in wildly unpredictable ways. That said, however, there will probably be at least some strains of continuity from the past that reverberate for many years to come. Let's begin by going back a few decades to an affair that captured the nation's attention—and is *still* discussed.

WORKING HOUSEWIVES AND DAY CARE

When Itoh Masako first began her series of essays in the *Shufu no tomo* women's magazine in the late 1980s, Japan was in the midst of its miracle financial "bubble" of postwar recovery and becoming the world's second-largest economy. But for several years Japanese society focused on the so-called *Agnes Ronsō*, or the Agnes (Chan) Controversy. Agnes Chan was one of the more beloved of the ubiquitous pop "idol" singers who—still—dominate the Japanese mass media. Her being born in Hong Kong, and her accent, probably added a bit of exotic appeal to her stage persona. The controversy began when, right after giving birth to her first child, she opted to continue her career and bring her baby to work. Not only was this unusual, but she could find no adequate day care at work.

Agnes became very vocal in her criticism of a society that makes a mother stay at home by default. According to her, in Hong Kong women commonly kept their jobs even after childbirth. But in order for this to happen, child-care facilities at work—as found in Hong Kong and the West—were necessary. The recently passed Gender Equality Employment Act of 1985 said that women should have not just the legal right, but also the practical ability, to be both mothers and career women. But this was hardly the norm.

Agnes was harshly attacked for these views from a number of directions. However, conservative men or traditional women were not her harshest critics. She was criticized most severely by successful professional women, in particular by two famous female writers, Hayashi Mariko and Nakano Midori. These debates and insults were traded back and forth in magazines, newspaper columns, and television shows, literally, for years.

The basic position of the elite professionals was that one had to make a choice—albeit a tough one—between career or family. Bringing children to work was impossible because both the mothers and their coworkers would be distracted. Yet giving one's children to a substitute family like day care—no matter how temporary—was said to be selfish, irresponsible, and antimaternal and would have dire psychological effects on both parent and child. They made this tough choice—sacrificing having a family for the sake of career—and were not especially sympathetic to women who believed they could have it all.

Later, noted academic feminists like Ueno Chizuko joined the fray, pointing out that this was an opportunity to raise social awareness of how male-dominated institutions stifle women's opportunities and options. They thought this was a chance to move the debate to a discussion of gender roles where men and women could share equally in the public and domestic spheres.

Again, professional women remained unconvinced. *They*, after all, were successful in this male-dominated world. If you truly believe in equality, you should expect no special privileges or accommodations. To ask for them would be to admit the natural, inherent inferiority of women.

Interestingly, men were generally more sympathetic to Agnes Chan than most women, at least in spirit. Many men saw the issue as a personal one: here was a cute foreign singer who needed help. Unlike the new upstart and pushy career women who were often opinionated and unfeminine, this was a woman who was really trying to do her duty and be the quintessential traditional "good wife and wise mother" long spoken of, and admired, in Japan since the beginning of time. She wanted to be with her child as much as possible—to breastfeed her and so on—without making her husband stay at home or hiring a costly nurse. "What's the problem?" they asked. However, while men may have offered a pat on the back and a sympathetic ear, no company day-care centers were ever actually built.

Discussions of the so-called Agnes Controversy have continued off and on in Japan for the past twenty years. Now, it is indeed true that day-care centers at work in the United States are still not necessarily widely available (even though this was claimed to be the case by Agnes Chan and her supporters). While some lip service may have been given to finding better day care for Japanese women, nonetheless day-care centers at work in Japan continue to be extremely rare.

The explanation for this is that many Japanese women still do not keep their jobs after marriage or childbirth. And one simple reason is the Japanese commute. Unlike Agnes Chan who goes to work with her babysitter by private car and driver, most Japanese have to ride crowded public trains—usually for about an hour one way—to get to work. Bringing children along to a job-sponsored day-care center would likely not be much of a relief.

The second reason is more subtle, but apparently equally motivating. There seems to persist in Japan the idea that a woman should *not* work after marriage. As the sociologist Ono Hiroshi claims (Ono 2003, 1), traditionally "for a man, having a non-working wife symbolized status insofar as he could afford to support his wife and family. Viewed another way, a successful marriage was one in which the wife did not work, or *did not have to work*" (emphasis in the original). His survey data not only support these claims, he also found that husbands' earnings were generally higher if their wives (1) were currently not working, (2) had never worked, and (3) had no intention to ever work. Such data clearly show that the richer a husband is, the less likely it is for his wife to work. And in a consumer society that is conscious of the finer points of conspicuous consumption and its symbols, there are pressures on a wife not to work even if her income is needed. Regardless, the most important fact is that the norm in Japan is now for a woman to remain at home while the children are young. She will likely venture out into the workforce later as the children grow older.

There is another obstacle working Japanese women face: the Japanese economy. The Gender Equality Employment Act of 1985 has improved working conditions for women, and its effects are now clearly visible. For example, the percentage of female corporate department heads rose from 1.0 percent in 1980 to 3.1 percent in 2003; section chiefs from 1.3 percent to 4.6 percent; and chief clerks from 3.1 percent to 9.4 percent (*Japan Almanac* 2005, 210). But for the majority of women, employment conditions and opportunities are probably getting worse, despite some recovery in the Japanese economy after the prolonged stagnation.[1] Most important, perhaps, *seiki* (regular) workers are being replaced by *hi-seiki* (nonregular, part-time, or temporary) workers. More than a third of the workforce is now of the latter variety. Many women who do seek work are being employed as *hi-seiki* workers.

VIEWS—AND WORDS—FOR HOUSEWIVES

The mass media—television shows, newspapers, nonfiction books, and novels—are certainly not perfect one-to-one correspondents to real life. But there is no doubt that culture, society, and the media are somehow inexorably—though not necessarily causally—related. Thus, even a fleeting glance at some of the representations of Japanese women can be worthwhile, if nothing else, to see some of the names or labels or "folk categories" people use.

Barbara Sato (2003) argues that there were three main tropes in discussions of womanhood in Japan between the two World Wars. The first was the "modern girl" (*mo-ga*), the Japanese equivalent of the American flapper, who largely defined herself by hairstyle, dress, and addiction to all things Western, especially popular culture. The professional working woman (*shokugyō fujin*) also made her appearance at this time, taking important steps toward having a career and personal freedom. Finally, the last image was of the "self-motivated housewife." She formed the basis of the new fledging middle class and largely educated herself through the new women's magazines appearing in the 1920s. (*Shufu no tomo*, or "The Housewife's Friend"—the magazine where these essays by Itoh Masako were first published—began to be published at this time as well).

Each of these three views of Japanese women has twenty-first-century counterparts. While the '20s *mo-ga* (modern girl) has disappeared, she has been replaced by any number of young *ko-garu* (literally, "little girls" or "imps," decked out in teased colored hair and microscopic skirts) (Miller and Bardsley 2005) who rattle the chains of the establishment in various ways, from outlandish dress to adopting the mannerisms and vernacular of male speech. The career woman is now ever-present in Japan, and the West takes great delight in charting her progress—mostly as a measure of Japan's social advancement and modernization. And like her earlier interwar cousins, she still often will leave her job after marriage and childbirth. Lastly, the housewife—*shufu*—is still around, too, in various forms old and new.

As some of these essays have shown, many married women consider themselves to be *sengyō shufu*, or "full-time housewives." They see themselves primarily as homemakers and captains of the domestic sphere. And as has been noted in the literature, Japanese housewives often have a great deal of control over the household, from the supervision of the children's educational success through college to handling the family income.

Lately, however, we are seeing the rise of the *karisuma shufu*, or "charisma-housewife." *Karisuma* is an English loanword meaning someone—generally a woman—who is especially talented in her realm of expertise. The Japanese charisma-housewife puts American Martha Stewart wannabes to shame. She can create the most delicious of meals, with the artist's flair for detail and color. She can prepare an *o-bentō*—the Japanese school lunchbox carried by every kindergartener—that is the envy of the class. Her table settings are immaculate, her attire—even the most casual—exquisite, and her manners always appropriate. She is more of a professional household "manager" than a house "wife."

There are numerous charisma-housewives in the Japanese popular media today. Perhaps the most famous is Kurihara Harumi, who has even brought her domestic gospel to the United States in her book *Harumi's Japanese Cooking*. Other homemaking specialists include Kondō Noriko on budget planning and finances and Arimoto Yoko on Italian cuisine. But this is not just a media creation or passing phenomenon; there are indeed many Japanese women who aspire to reach various levels of domestic sainthood, regardless of public fame or fortune.

But are all Japanese housewives domestic goddesses? Not according to the mass media. For example, a popular television program in 2004 was *Oni-yome nikki*, the story of a henpecked husband whose daily chronicles of his wife's antics are the subject of the show. This title might literally translate as "The Demon-Bride Diary," but as the characters have been married for some ten years, this is slightly misleading. *Oni* are ogres or demons of Japanese lore, and the audience—if not the husband—certainly sees the wife as such. *Nikki*—diaries or journals—have a long literary history in Japan and are considered a genre unto themselves. Thus this term suggests the whole glory of medieval Japanese literature to the viewer (such as some of the works by Lady Murasaki and Sei Shonagon, as discussed in Itoh's essays).

Interestingly, this TV program is based on fact (at least as portrayed by the husband). The incidents depicted in the show came from stories he posted on 2-Channel, one of Japan's most famous and visited Internet bulletin boards. Every day the poor husband uploaded his latest trials and tribulations, attracting a wide readership—so much so that eventually the show became a hit "reality" TV series.[2]

But though such depictions are impossible to measure, this demon-house-wife is probably mild compared to most wives portrayed on contemporary American TV sitcoms or soap operas. Yes, she is opinionated, stubborn, strong willed, and a little loud and shrewish, but we suspect that most American viewers would really not get the joke. Much of her behavior might be perceived as common sense, or justifiable, if similar situations were portrayed on American sitcoms. But it is her exceptionalism that makes her an interesting character to Japanese. Most Japanese women probably think, "At least I am not as bad as that!" while most Japanese men celebrate, "At least I am not married to her!"

At the opposite pole from the Japanese charisma-housewives are the *katazuke-rarenai onna-tachi*, or "women who can't clean up." Just as America has *Extreme Makeover* in which a team will come and remodel a family's home, on this Fuji Television series a team of sanitation engineers will come and clean a compulsively dirty woman's house, while the rest of us are able to watch. A book by the same name appeared in 2005, documenting some of the more outlandish cases: garbage (bagged and not) piled to the ceiling, mountains of *manga* comic books hiding long-forgotten furniture, and so on. If many of these women suffer from serious psychological problems such as obsession-compulsion or adult attention deficit disorder, what is striking is the fact that men are never shown in comparable situations.

And what of women who choose not to be housewives at all? The expectation used to be that a woman would get married by her early twenties and have children soon thereafter. A woman who did not accomplish this goal was said to be a *make-inu*, or "loser dog." But marriage and fertility rates in Japan have dropped drastically since the 1990s. In 2003 the rate of marriages was 5.9 per thousand persons in Japan, compared to more than 7.8 in the United States.[3] The total fertility rate in Japan—the average number of children per woman—was 1.29 compared to 2.01 in the United States (*Japan Almanac* 2005, 20–21). These days we are seeing best-selling books like Sakai Junko's 2004 *Make-inu no tōboe* (The Loser Dog Howls) arguing for the joys of the single life: the (loser) dog howling at the moon, to phrase it in American terms.

SUMMING UP OR WINDING DOWN?

A team of a thousand sociologists and anthropologists would be needed to summarize—even incompletely—the conditions of Japanese women today (to say nothing of what their future might be). Even then, such a position paper would likely be self-contradictory, tentative, or—at times—simply wrong or instantly obsolete. Nevertheless, if challenged to provide broad generalizations, we might risk the following: many Japanese women today still yearn for some sort of domestic role, however demanding—and changing—this might be.

Child care and education are still thought to be primarily the mother's responsibility. Ideally, the mother should stay at home and raise the children. For many women, and perhaps even in Japanese society in general, work outside the home is still primarily the male domain. For example, in a catchy ad for beer some time ago, the famous actor Mifune Toshiro simply stated, "*Otoko wa shigoto da*" ("A man is his work"). Such sentiments are not as often expressed toward women, even now.

But that said, how might we explain such phenomena as the drastically declining birthrate and the decision by many women to delay marriage or avoid it altogether? After all, not everyone can be an elite professional or an entertainer like Agnes Chan. Most working women in Japan—as in the United States, for that matter—have a "job," not a "career." Thus, the decision for many to forgo the social advantages and economic benefits of marriage is one that still needs to be addressed.[4]

And then we come across comments such as the following made by family therapist Ikeuchi Hiromi in 2006 in the widely read *Shūkan posuto* (The Weekly Post):

> We've gone past the age of equality of the sexes and instead now feel like a time when women have started to become excessive in their demands. They get into the belief that their husbands aren't looking after them enough, are filled with discontent, then race off and have affairs, demand divorces, rack up debts and declare bankruptcy. I kind of feel like we're in an era when women have lost control of their desires and no longer know how to be patient.[5]

He was discussing why a supposedly increasing number of bored, or cash-strapped, Japanese housewives are taking to appearing in amateur porn movies on adult video websites. Still, to know how even to begin to respond to something like this is hard.

When we were at a Japan seminar in the United States recently, someone brought up the question of why Japanese women have been taking so long to become liberated, socially and economically. Some anthropologists answered that it could be that Japanese culture has firmly indoctrinated its women. But then why did women in the West overcome these social and cultural biases? There was no good answer. Some said it was just a matter of time, assuming that women's liberation was a historical inevitability. Others asked how long? Some said that the physical-geographic features of the workplace of Japan—long commutes for most jobs, implying the need for someone to be at home to take care of the children and the family—were natural impediments to any social changes in the immediate future.

If you find such comments frustrating, take consolation that we do, too. Finding the key questions, and asking them in the right way, is extremely difficult, and even professional social scientists struggle hard. The twenty-first century has arrived, and Japan is one of the most economically advanced nations in the world. Many scholars argue that Japanese women need to reform society according to their own needs, regardless of what the West is doing. Others say that Japanese women should more actively join the international struggle for universal women's rights. Regardless, we hardly ever hear what that mythical creature, the "average" Japanese woman, feels about these issues. We have tried to present some of these voices. But we hope this book will help others see Japanese women as individuals, as well as part of the greater ebb and flow of local and worldwide forces. We have learned many things from Itoh Masako and her friends, and we are wiser for these encounters. We hope our translations and comments have conveyed some of the flavor of the changing worlds of Japanese women and men.

NOTES

1. The Japanese economy has only made moderate improvements over the −1.2 percent growth rate in 2001. As a result, companies are having to forgo many of the special perks traditionally given to workers, such as lifetime employment.

2. This was similar to the adventures of the *Densha Otoko*—the "Train Man"—a comic book–obsessed geek who saves a beautiful girl from being accosted by a drunk on a commuter train. However, he has no idea how to pursue her romantically, so he seeks advice from friends on an Internet "site for loser single-males." Amazingly, he gets the girl, and these public posts also became a hit TV show and best-selling book.

3. We should note that most industrial societies besides the United States are seeing declining birthrates. Nonetheless, Europe's or East Asia's decline still pales beside anything found in Japan.

4. The usual explanations, we suspect—an old-fashioned patriarchal society, widespread sexism in employment, institutionalized governmental discrimination, a lack of feminist consciousness among Japanese women—all are lacking in certain

ways (though we acknowledge their truth and efficacy and by no means dismiss them).

5. See a summary in English in the *Mainichi Daily News*, July 8, 2006, at mdn. mainichi-msn.co.jp/waiwai/archive/news/2006/03/20060331p2g00m0dm017000c .html.

References

Akutagawa, Ryūnosuke. 1932. *Shuju no kotoba* [The Words of the Dwarf]. Tokyo: Iwanami-bunko.

Allison, Anne. 1994. *Nightwork: Sexuality, Pleasure, and Corporate Masculinity in a Tokyo Hostess Club*. Chicago: University of Chicago Press.

Beauvoir, Simone de. 1968. *La femme rompue*. Paris: Gallimard.

———. 1969. *The Woman Destroyed*. Trans. Patrick O'Brien. New York: Putnam.

Birnbaum, Phyllis. 1999. *Modern Girls, Shining Stars, the Skies of Tokyo: Five Japanese Women*. New York: Columbia University Press.

Buckley, Sandra. 1997. *Broken Silence: Voices of Japanese Feminism*. Berkeley: University of California Press.

Condon, Jane. 1985. *A Half Step Behind: Japanese Women of the '80s*. New York: Dodd, Mead.

Doi, Takeo. 1973. *The Anatomy of Dependence*. Trans. John Bester. Tokyo: Kodansha.

Downer, Lesley. 2003. *Madame Sadayakko: The Geisha Who Bewitched the West*. New York: Gotham.

Forest, Eva. 1972. *The Diary of Eva Forest: Notes from a Spanish Prison*. Tokyo: Jiji Tsūshin-sha Press.

Golden, Arthur. 2005. *Memoirs of a Geisha*. New York: Vintage.

Hiragana Times, ed. 2000. *Japan: A Paradise for Picking Up Women*. Tokyo: Hai-Tai Books (Yohan).

Imamura, Anne, ed. 1996. *Re-Imagining Japanese Women*. Berkeley: University of California Press.

Inoue, Miyako. 2006. *Vicarious Language: Gender and Linguistic Modernity in Japan*. Berkeley: University of California Press.

Ishii, Momoko. 1967. *Non-chan kumo ni noru* [Non-chan Climbs upon a Cloud]. Tokyo: Fukuinkan-shoten.

———. 1987. *The Tongue-Cut Sparrow*. Trans. Katherine Paterson. New York: Lodestar.

Iwasaki, Mineko. 2003a. *Geisha of Gion*. New York: Simon and Schuster.

———. 2003b. *Geisha: A Life*. New York: Washington Square Press.

Japan Almanac. 2003. Ed. Ouchi Yozo. Tokyo: Asahi Shimbun.

——. 2005. Ed. Ouchi Yozo. Tokyo: Asahi Shimbun.

Kamei, Shunsuke. 1987. *Marilyn Monroe.* Tokyo: Iwanai Shinsho.

Kawano, Yūko. 1984. *Hayari* [In Vogue]. Tokyo: Tanka-Shimbunsha.

Kawazu, Chiyo. 1984. "Convivo." *Kagetsūshin,* Vol. 2, p. 3.

Kelsky, Karen. 2001. *Women on the Verge: Japanese Women, Western Dreams.* Durham, N.C.: Duke University Press.

Komashaku, Kimi. 1991. *Murasaki Shikibu no messeēji* [The Message of Lady Murasaki]. Tokyo: Asahi Shimbun.

Kondo, Dorinne. 1990. *Crafting Selves: Power, Gender, and Discourses of Identity in a Japanese Workplace.* Chicago: University of Chicago Press.

Lebra, Joyce, Joy Paulson, and Elizabeth Powers, eds. 1976. *Women in Changing Japan.* Stanford, Calif.: Stanford University Press.

Lippit, Noriko Mizuta, and Kyoko Iriye Selden, eds. 1991. *Japanese Women Writers: Twentieth Century Short Fiction.* Armonk, N.Y.: M. E. Sharpe.

Long, John Luther. 1903. *Madame Butterfly.* New York: Grosset and Dunlap.

Loti, Pierre. 1985 [1888]. *Madame Chrysanthème.* London: Kegan Paul.

Michitsuna no haha. 1964. *The Gossamer Years; The Diary of a Noblewoman of Heian, Japan.* Trans. Edward Seidensticker. Tokyo; Rutland, Vt.: C. E. Tuttle.

Miller, Laura, and Jan Bardsley, eds. 2005. *Bad Girls of Japan.* New York: Palgrave Macmillan.

Murakami, Ryū. 1984. *Koin rokkā baibiizu.* Tokyo: Kodansha.

——. 1995. *Coin Locker Babies.* Trans. Stephen Snyder. Tokyo: Kodansha.

Murata, Eiichi. 1981. *Dono ko mo 100-ten o toru kenri ga aru* [Every Student Has a Right to Achieve a Hundred Percent]. Tokyo: Shufu-to-seikatsu-sha.

Nagahata, Michiko. 1986. *Onna kankaku de ikiru* [To Live with a Woman's Sense]. Tokyo: Shinhyōron.

New York Times 2003 Almanac. 2002. Ed. John Wright et al. New York: Penguin.

Okazaki, Hideko. 1972. *Han-kekkonron* [Anti-Marriage Theory]. Tokyo: Akishobō.

Ono, Hiroshi. 2003. *Re-Examining the Housewife Myth: Husbands' Earnings and Wives' Employment Status in Contemporary Japan.* European Institute of Japanese Studies Working Paper 181. Stockholm: Stockholm School of Economics. Electronic document, www.hhs.se/EIJS/Research/WorkingPapers/WorkingPapers.htm.

Ōtake, Hitoko. 1984. *Mother and I: Days with Kutsumi Fusako.* Tokyo: Tsukiji Press.

Palmore, Erdman. 1975. *The Honorable Elders: A Cross-Cultural Analysis of Aging in Japan.* Durham, N.C.: Duke University Press.

Plath, David. 1975. The Last Confucian Sandwich: Becoming Middle Aged in Japan. *Journal of Asian and African Studies* 10 (1-2): 51–65.

Rosenberger, Nancy. 2001. *Gambling with Virtue: Japanese Women and the Search for Self in a Changing Nation.* Honolulu: University of Hawaii Press.

Sato, Barbara. 2003. *The New Japanese Woman: Modernity, Media, and Women in Interwar Japan.* Asia-Pacific Series. Durham, N.C.: Duke University Press.

Serizawa, Kōjirō. 1942. *Pari ni shisu* [Death in Paris]. Tokyo: Shinchōsha.

Shinkawa, Kazue. 1997. *Watashi o tabane-nai-de* [Please Don't Tie Me Down]. Tokyo: Dōwaya.

Sievers, Sharon. 1983. *Flowers in Salt: The Beginnings of Feminist Consciousness in Modern Japan.* Stanford, Calif.: Stanford University Press.

Smith, Robert, and Ella Wiswell. 1982. *The Women of Suye Mura.* Chicago: University of Chicago Press.

Stanlaw, James. 2004. *Japanese English: Language and the Culture Contact.* Hong Kong: Hong Kong University Press.

Takenishi, Hiroko. 1980. *Ai suru to iu kotoba* [The Words Called "To Love"]. Tokyo: Shinchōsha.

Tanabe, Seiko. 1972. *Mado o akemasu ka?* [Do You Wish to Open the Window?]. Tokyo: Shinchōsha.

———. 1973. *Iutara nan'ya kedo* [I Know I Shouldn't Say This, But . . .]. Tokyo: Chikuma-shobo.

Tanaka, Yukio, ed. 1987. *To Live and to Write: Selections by Japanese Women Writers, 1913–1938.* Seattle, Wash.: Seal Press.

Tanaka, Yukio, and Elizabeth Hanson, eds. 1982. *This Kind of Woman: Ten Stories by Japanese Women Writers, 1960–1976.* New York: Wideview/Perigee Books.

Tanikawa, Shuntarō. 1985. *"N" made aruku* [Walking until Omega]. Tokyo: Sōshi-sha.

Toyoda, Masako. 1985. *Hana no wakare: Tamura Akiko to watashi* [The Parting of Flowers: Tamura Akiko and I]. Tokyo: Mirai-sha.

———. 1991. *O-Yuki.* Tokyo: Mokkei-sha Press.

Tsujimura, Natsuko. 1996. *An Introduction to Japanese Linguistics.* Malden, Mass.: Blackwell.

Uchida, Yoshihiko. 1981. *Sakuhin toshite no shakai kagaku* [The Work of Social Science]. Tokyo: Iwanami Shoten.

Ueda, Makoto, ed. 1986. *The Mother of Dreams and Other Stories: Portrayals of Women in Modern Japanese Fiction.* Tokyo: Kodansha International.

Yamazaki, Tomoko. 1999. *Sandakan Brothel No. 8: An Episode in the History of Lower-Class Japanese Women.* Trans. Karen Colligan-Taylor. Armonk, N.Y.: M. E. Sharpe.

Yoshihara, Mari. 2003. *Embracing the East: White Women and American Orientalism.* Oxford: Oxford University Press.

North America, 2
Nozaki Rokusuke, 183

obā-chan (grandmother), 129, 154. *See also* grandmother
oba-san ("aunt" or "middle-aged woman"), 123–24
o-bentō (school lunchbox), 201
ofukuro no aji ("mother's taste"), 30
Oka Yuriko, 35–36
Okazaki Hideko, 18–19
oku-san (wife), 4, 53, 63, 64. *See also* wives
o-nē-san (elder sister), 123
Oni-yome nikki ("The Demon-Bride Diary"; television show), 201
onna (women), 2, 27, 32, 36, 43–44, 50–51, 59, 61, 95, 104, 112, 133, 147, 157–58, 162, 169, 171, 179, 202. *See also* women
Onna kankaku de ikiru (To Live with a Woman's Sense; Nagahata), 171
Ono Hiroshi, 199
Ōoka Shōhei, 183
Orientalism, 1
o-saibo (gift-giving period), 143
Osaragi Jirō, 175
O-shōgatsu (New Year's Day), 25, 76, 162. *See also* New Year's Day
Ōtake Hitoko, 175–76
Ōta Yoshie, 183
otoko (man), 4, 27–29, 32, 51, 53, 107, 109, 133, 145–46, 172, 203–4. *See also* men
Otoko wa tsurai yo (It's Tough to Be a Man, You Know!), 133
o-toshi-dama (giving money to children on New Year's Day), 162
overtime, 3
Owada Masako, 75
O-Yuki (Toyoda), 160

pain, 9, 20, 24, 28, 36, 83, 86, 103, 151–52, 161, 164, 179
pan-pan ("streetwalker"), 146

Pari ni shisu (Death in Paris; Serizawa), 145
particles, 5–7; sentence-final, 5–7
Parting of Flowers, The (Toyoda), 160
part-time work, 55, 76–77, 184–85, 200; instructors and, 77; workers and, 55, 76, 185
pāto taimu (people who work an extra job outside the home), 55, 76. *See also* part-time work
perpetrators, 20, 92–93, 191
personalities, 18, 39, 41, 56–57, 74, 122, 135, 176, 189, 190, 194
Plath, David, 37
poems, 19–21, 35, 42–43, 92–93, 109, 120–21, 123–24, 136–41, 155–58, 191–92, 196
poetry, 19–20, 92–93, 109, 139–40, 190–91, 195
politeness, 5, 7, 95, 154. *See also* impoliteness
polite speech, 6
preschools, 27, 72, 178–79
professional relationships, 5
pronominal system, 7
pronouns, 5–7, 13, 48, 54, 68–69, 124, 139, 180
prostitution, 63, 179–81, 183
Puccini, Giacomo, 1
Pulitzer Prize, 181
purple, 48–49

reiai (love), 145. *See also* love
relationships, 5, 11, 19, 25, 35, 39, 41, 50, 52, 57–58, 64–68, 74, 82, 85–86, 88–89, 91–92, 97–98, 112, 128, 130, 136, 152, 168–69, 172, 175, 179–80
remains, 154, 160
Respect for the Aged Day (*Keirō no hi*), 186–87
reunion, 50
ritual, 4, 45, 167
Russo-Japanese War (1904–1905), 139

Sagano (Kyoto district), 157

About the Author, Translators, and Editors

Masako Itoh is a Japanese feminist cultural critic and community activist long associated with the Kunitachi Public Community Center in Tokyo.

Nobuko Adachi is an assistant professor in the Department of Sociology and Anthropology at Illinois State University. She received her Ph.D. in anthropology from the University of Toronto in 1997 and was awarded a Rockefeller Residential Postdoctoral Fellowship in 2000. She has been the editor of *Pan-Japan: The International Journal of Japanese Diaspora* since 2000. Her edited volume *Japanese Diasporas: Unsung Pasts, Conflicting Presents, and Uncertain Futures* was published in 2006, with a Japanese edition appearing soon. Adachi has also published numerous articles including "Japonês: A Marker of Social Class or a Key Term in the Discourse of Race?" in *Latin American Perspectives*, "Japanese in Brazil" in *Encyclopedia of Diasporas: Immigrant and Refugee Cultures around the World* from the Human Relations Area Files, "The Negotiation of Speech Style in Japanese Women's Language: Vantage Theory as Cognitive Sociolinguistics" in *Language Science*, and "Japanese Brazilians: The Japanese Language Communities in Brazil" in *Studies in the Linguistic Sciences*.

James Stanlaw received his Ph.D. from the University of Illinois, Urbana-Champaign, where he studied anthropology and linguistics. He is currently professor of anthropology at Illinois State University and has also taught at Illinois Wesleyan University, Columbia University, the University of Illinois, and St. John's University in New York City. Stanlaw is coeditor of *Pan-Japan:*

The International Journal of Japanese Diaspora. He is contributing editor to *Anthropology News* and served on the editorial board of *World Englishes*. Stanlaw has received a number of scholarships and awards, including Fulbright and National Defense Foreign Language fellowships, and support from the Spencer Foundation and the National Science Foundation. His book *Japanese English: Language and Culture Contact* was nominated at the 2005 American Anthropological Association meetings for the Francs K. Hsu Prize as best new book on East Asian anthropology. He has been nominated for teaching awards several times, including the national Mayfield Award for Excellence in Undergraduate Teaching of Anthropology given by the American Anthropological Association. He was chosen as one of Illinois State University's College of Arts and Sciences teachers of the year in 1994.